D1446852

"Charles Silverstein has written a memoir about the great love of his life—an eccentric, androgynous genius whom Charles adored and cared for despite all his flaws and addictions. Most writers idealize their lovers, especially if they've died young, but Silverstein presents his William with all his charm and sexual allure and intellectual brilliance—and all his maddening faults. I wept at the end of this brave, honest book—and I suspect you will too."
—Edmund White, author of *City Boy* and *Sacred Monsters*

"From his Brooklyn childhood to his climactic gay-Scott and Zelda relationship, Silverstein's *For the Ferryman* is a searing, unafraid, and indelible self-portrait of a distinguished and amazing life. Not the coolly calculated look-back we might have expected but instead a roller-coaster ride of emotion recollected in anything but tranquility."
—Felice Picano, author of *True Stories* and *Like People in History*

"When I received a request from Charles to do a blurb for his manuscript, I had no idea what a treat I was in store for. It is a memorial to the twenty-year love affair of Charles and his life-time partner. Charles relentlessly and courageously analyzes the neurotic wounds in both their lives that led to their loving partnership with all its ups and downs, an extraordinary faithful love that persevered to the end. Charles also describes the very painful experiences of the innumerable human losses to the AIDS plague during the 80s and early 90s. I was particularly delighted in his decision to hold the Charles Silverstein Memorial Vacation for a group of his closest friends while he was still alive and could come along. Well done Charles!"
—Reverend Doctor John J. McNeill, author of *Sex as God Intended: Reflections on Human Sexuality*

Other books by Dr. Charles Silverstein

Silverstein, C. (Ed.) (2011). *The Initial Psychotherapy Interview: A Gay Man Seeks Treatment.* Elsevier Insight Publishers.

Silverstein, C. & Picano, F. (2003). *The Joy of Gay Sex: Third edition.* New York: HarperCollins. Translated into German and Polish.

Silverstein, C. & Picano, F. (1992). *The New Joy of Gay Sex.* New York: Harper-Collins. Translated into Hebrew, German and Japanese.

Silverstein, C. (1991). (Ed.). *Gays, Lesbians and Their Therapists: Studies in Psychotherapy.* New York: W.W. Norton.

Silverstein, C. (1981). *Man to Man: Gay Couples in America.* New York: William Morrow. Banned in Great Britain.

Silverstein, C. (1977a). *A Family Matter: A Parents' Guide to Homosexuality.* New York: McGraw-Hill. Translated into Dutch.

Silverstein, C. & White, E. (1977b). *The Joy of Gay Sex.* New York: Crown. Translated into French, Swedish, German and Polish. Banned from importation into Canada, banned or burned in Great Britain and France, banned in many bookstores in the United States.

Professional Awards

2011—Gold Medal for Lifetime Achievement in the Practice of Psychology from the American Psychological Foundation for bringing unbiased psychological treatment to the LGBT community.

2009—Presidential Citation from the American Psychological Association for leadership providing therapeutic services to the gay community.

2005—Distinguished Professional Contribution award from Division 44 (The Society for the Psychological Study of Lesbian, Gay, Bisexual and Transgender Issues) of the American Psychological Association.

2002—Award from the Gay and Lesbian Psychiatrists of New York

For the Ferryman

A Personal History

Charles Silverstein

Chelsea Station Editions
New York

For the Ferryman: A Personal History by Charles Silverstein
Copyright © 2011 by Charles Silverstein
All rights reserved.

No part of this book may be reproduced in any form without written permission from the publisher, except by a reviewer, who may quote brief passages in a review where appropriate credit is given; nor may any part of this book be reproduced, stored in a retrieval system, or transmitted in any form or by any means—electronic, photocopying, recording, or other—without specific written permission from the publisher.

This memoir is the product of the author's recollections and is thus rendered as a subjective accounting of events that occurred in his life.

Cover and book design by Peachboy Distillery & Design
Paper boat art by Johnny Hall, used by permission of the artist.
Cover background art by John Bloor, Shutterstock.

Interior photos and drawing by Michael Leonard used by permission of the artist.

Published as a trade paperback original by Chelsea Station Editions, 362 West 36th Street, Suite 2R, New York, NY 10018
www.chelseastationeditions.com / info@chelseastationeditions.com

ISBN: 978-0-9832851-2-0
Library of Congress Control Number: 2011935707

First U.S. edition, 2011

To Virginia Record

For so many years of friendship.

Charles Silverstein being awarded
a Gold Medal for Lifetime Achievement
in the Practice of Psychology in August 2011
by the American Psychological Foundation.

Photo by Terrance M. Flynn and courtesy of the author.

Table of Contents

The Ferryman of Greek mythology transported the dead across the River Styx from this world to the underworld, called Hades. A gratuity was always expected.

Preface

Isn't it Silly for an Exhibitionist to Complain about Being Exposed?

I always thought that writing one's autobiography represented the stage of life that precedes being taken to the glue factory. I no longer believe that, but I cannot tell if I was wrong then or denying the truth now. I have been working on this book for a few years and along the way many friends asked whether it was to be an autobiography or a memoir. I always got annoyed with them because I never knew (and still don't) the difference between them. This is certainly not an autobiography in the sense of its being a chronological history of my life starting with birth and including a detailed account of family life, education and work history. No, it is not that.

Perhaps this is a memoir since that sounds more limited in scope. But memoir, from the French *le mémoire* sounds effete; I mean the sound of the word itself. It is not quite right. Another problem with memoir is that I have chosen not to write about significant periods of my life so that there are gaps of decades in the work to follow. There are two reasons for this, one literary, the other emotional. From a literary standpoint I have purposely focused my attention upon certain time periods because I have something worthwhile to say about them and ignored everything else, including friends and colleagues who will not be mentioned in these pages and will resent me for their omission. My emotional motivation is different. I do not mind being called a bad writer or even incompetent; what I really fear is being called boring. That would be untenable and my way to deal with this potential problem is to clear away the historical brush and concentrate my attention on just a few issues that are interesting. So I end up with my literary and emotional motivations being congruent. Let us just call this a personal history and be done with it.

I should mention a few events that are not covered in the book. I'll make it brief. As a youngster I decided to become a commercial photographer although the reasons for that decision now escapes me. I therefore attended a New York City high school called the School of Industrial Art (now the School of Art and Design) where I majored in photography. After graduation I began working in the field only to learn that I was an abysmal failure at it but had the good sense to quit and choose another path, although this was not as smooth a road as I make it sound.

I then went to college to become an elementary school teacher. There was a certain irony to this decision because the State University of New York at New Paltz had a female to male ratio of seven to one. My male friends on the block in Brooklyn expressed the greatest envy toward me assuming that with such a preponderance of women over men that I would get laid day and night, when of course I was more interested in the men. But since I was in the closet my sex life there was extremely "dry." The irony became more intense when I learned that I was very popular with women (not so much the men) but here I may be overlooking the more parsimonious explanation that with such an unbalanced ratio, any man could be popular.

For the next six years after graduation from New Paltz I worked as an elementary school teacher in Larchmont, New York. They were wonderful years from a professional point of view. I loved the kids and some of them are still in touch with me after I left teaching in 1965 in order to attend graduate school. I was also a head counselor in a summer children's camp (called Camp Farrington) for years and as with teaching, I found the experience rewarding and working with the kids a pleasure.

The clinical psychology department at the City College of New York was my home from 1965 until they kicked me out in 1968 because I had twice failed the comprehensive examinations. The next year was probably the lowest point in my life and although I could have returned to teaching, my choice was to go through another graduate psychology program. I was accepted into the social psychology department at Rutgers where I completed my Ph.D. in 1974.

My work in gay liberation overlapped my graduate studies at Rutgers because I continued to live in New York City and traveled each day to school. While at Rutgers I founded two gay counseling centers in New York, Identity House and the Institute for Human Identity, and the *Journal of Homosexuality* a scholarly journal that publishes academic papers. It was in 1973 that I made a presentation before the psychiatrists that led to the deletion of homosexuality as a mental disorder.

As a child of my generation, I entered psychoanalysis during my years teaching elementary school, in order to change my sexual orientation from gay to straight. After seven years and lots of money I stopped and finally came out. Some of those experiences are told in the following pages, but I have kept them at a minimum because other writers have done a fine job of explaining the effects of shame upon gay people.

I admit to being embarrassed by publishing an autobiography or memoir (or whatever the Hell this is), because it represents the height of narcissism and all of my professional training regards it as often pathological. It is also boldly exhibitionistic and while I know that exhibitionism is in my character, it is not a trait that I admire. On the other hand, isn't it silly for an exhibitionist to complain about being exposed? I should get over it. I expose myself a great deal in the chapters that follow because I have decided to be faithful and honest in telling these stories. Is there a relationship, gay or straight, of twenty years that has not had its moments of acrimony and trouble? I think perhaps a few, but not many. There are events in my relationship with William in which I acted with great love, and at other times when I feel embarrassed about my behavior. Perhaps writing this book helps to make peace with myself. My work in the radical gay liberation movement is less conflicted even though there were constant conflicts between competing ideologies. But in gay liberation in contrast to personal relationships, we all perceived ourselves as invincible and self-righteously correct; there was never uncertainty that societal and psychiatric discrimination were our enemies.

This book documents two periods. The first is the decade of the 1970s in which radical gay politics determined the gay agenda. Of course it is from the point of view of New York gay politics because I am from there, and the Gay Activist Alliance was my home and training ground. Other cities also made their contributions and I mean no slight to their work in our march toward civil rights. Other books have documented some of these achievements. I have also included a discussion of the theory of radical gay politics, such as the use of symbols and the symbiotic relationship between radical and moderate organizations. Because of the achievements of gay liberation, radical gay politics no longer exists. Its last flame was Act Up fighting for the proper treatment of AIDS patients.

The AIDS epidemic is the second period. I have tried to portray the death and dying of the time as if the reader is witness to the epidemic that led to the deterioration of the gay male community. Gay people generally call it "The Plague," and for good reason. It is not a pleasant story, but we should not forget it. Whereas earlier generations worried about pesky things like syphilis and gonorrhea, in the 1980s and 1990s some gay men had sex with death—or rather, slow death. This brings us to William Bory, my lover for twenty years.

Twenty years we lived together. I remember a radio call in program in which Dr. Charles Socarides and I presented opposing views about the moral and psychological equivalence of homosexuality with heterosexuality. In customary pompous fashion Socarides maintained that gays and lesbians could not establish long-lasting relationships. I announced that I only had one lover and that we had been living together for fifteen years. "And how many wives have you had?" I asked him. He refused to answer, saying that it was a personal question. The answer is three wives! Q.E.D.

I think it was Oscar Wilde (our patron saint) who wrote that we only hurt the people we love. He was right. We are offended by others, but deeply wounded by those who we hold very close emotionally. And lovers are experts in knowing how to hurt one another, sometimes only a sneer or glance away, or more destructively "the silent treatment" can result in turning a lover (or anyone for that matter) into either a plate of Jell-O or a raving, mean lunatic. Other small actions can just as easily express the greatest intimacy. Sappho said it well when she wrote, "We came together like two drops of water." William and I often came together like two drops of water, but we also occasionally warred upon one another, but especially after the diagnosis.

Fictitious names are used in some places in the book. There is no reason to identify them when I have no evidence for the crimes that they have been accused in these pages. I have changed the names of everyone from William's London period for that reason and a few others. Most of them are dead anyway and why should we gratuitously malign the dead even if it is legal to do so?

Charles Silverstein and William Bory

Photo by Michael Leonard. Used by permission of the photographer.

Prologue

With the Dissappearance of the Monasteries The Proliferation of Gay Bars was Inevitable

January 8, 1994. William was a bibliophile and for his memorial I had reserved the Grolier Club in Manhattan, an institution dedicated to book collecting. It is a nineteenth-century Georgian-style building containing a two-story high exhibition hall with floor to ceiling shelves of books. When I had visited there earlier I noticed the layers of dust on the shelves and imagined how William would have loved it there because of, not in spite of the dust. I pictured him sitting on the floor, a tower of books a century or more old tottering beside him, hoarding them from unseen borrowers, grateful that he had them all to himself. He would have forgotten time, meals, even whether it was day or night and left only when they threw him out, unless he decided to steal a few volumes.

A week after his death I received his ashes in a plain, plastic rectangular box. In the next few weeks I resisted every suggestion by friends to spread them. During the day I tried to ignore them as I did his remaining books, tattered clothes and papers. I put the ashes in a bookcase in the living room, William's beret on top. At night I talked to him, not long conversations as some widowers do, rather little comments about people he particularly did or did not like. I was sure that he would especially like my meaner comments and I was not stingy there. Every night before I went to sleep I kissed the box and said, "Good night, I love you." I did not know how long I would continue to kiss his ashes, and following the advice I would have given to a patient mourning the death of his lover, I made no arbitrary rules, knowing that I would continue for as long as I needed.

I created a whirlwind of activity around me during the eight weeks between William's death on November twelfth and the memorial. Close friends and colleagues made plans to meet me for lunch or supper or to go to a movie. I thought of everything, but felt nothing—exactly how I wanted it. I had felt enough during the previous couple of years and I wanted a holiday from emotion, from feelings of love, resentment, rage, and abandonment—the ambivalence that makes up the stew of a long-term relationship.

During the previous twenty years I had repressed much of the past, the days of my childhood and the pain of coming out. I was about to learn about the ghosts that haunt our memories. After the death of one's spouse all the old terrors return, the fears and inadequacies as if one must once again re-experience all the hurts of childhood—but more painfully than before, since one now sees the damage more clearly.

The previous December I had made an attempt to start socializing again by accepting an invitation to an afternoon party thrown by a former supervisee. Our friend Daniel Neudel joined me, I think to watch over me. Good thing too because I slipped on the ice only twenty feet from the building and snapped my left hand like a bar of chocolate. We spent the next five hours in St. Vincent's Emergency Room. ("Go to the Boo Boo room," the nurse directed.) I, therefore, showed up to the memorial with my left arm in a cast surrounded by a metal armature, my hand looking like an accessory to an erector set.

I had helped many other gay men to let go of their dead lovers by identifying the symbolic acts, the little ways we have of keeping a loved one alive. I knew I had to do that for myself as well. The first of these was my anxiety while having lunch or dinner with a friend or colleague. As the meal progressed, I felt the urge to flee. At lunch with Al Sbordone one day, I felt this panic. "I have to go home," I told him. Al was impatient with me. "Why do you want to go home?" For the first time since William's death, I understood this compulsion. I was subconsciously returning home to take care of William. I sat back down and cried and told Al, who had always been a loyal friend how I had no one to care for anymore. I had not yet realized nor wanted to accept that I had to start taking care of myself.

Soon I recognized another way in which I was symbolically keeping

William alive. As I walked from my office to the kitchen, I found myself looking into the living room as I had a thousand times before to check on William. Making these unconscious symbolic acts conscious pained me, but I was glad to free myself of them. I wanted William as my dead lover, not as a ghost.

Hal Kooden, a longtime colleague, advised me about holding a memorial service. His lover, Jim, had died in 1991 after a long siege of the disease and in the end, Jim's body was covered with KS lesions. I had thought the two of them so brave and loving in their relationship, that I dedicated my next book, *Gays, Lesbians and Their Therapists: Studies in Psychotherapy*, to Jim. Hal cautioned me not to hurry into the memorial service; to give myself time in which to plan it.

I worked for over a month on the memorial program. I had wanted it to be a public symbol of my love for William, but one that hid the darker side of our relationship. It was filled with photographs of him, of the two of us, with samples of his poetry, and paintings of him by Michael Leonard and Miles Parker. After his death, I found a few colored pencil drawings of street scenes William had completed over the years. No one, not even I, had seen them before. He must have drawn them at night when I was asleep. I put reproductions of two of them into the book.

Jeffrey Shaw, another old friend, put together a video about William's life to be shown at the memorial. Like most of us in New York, Jeffrey had watched many friends die from AIDS including Ira, his former lover. After Ira's funeral, Jeffrey began to cry but stopped walking. "There's no more milk in my tits," he said, echoing the feelings so many of us who had experienced multiple loses because of the AIDS plague, what my friend David Bergman called, "the culture of morbidity."

Jeffrey scanned hundreds of pictures into his computer including movies of William as a child. Jeffrey had known William during a period when he was obsessed with the Russian ballet dancer Vaslev Nijinsky. Thus the background music was Debussy's "Afternoon of a Faun," and as the music neared completion, Jeffrey projected a photo of William taken at Halloween, 1992, dressed in a home-made faun costume.

Many people spoke: Margaret who represented her family; Danny who never wavered in his loyalty; Virginia who washed his dying body; Albert who greeted hostility with love; Marilyn who spent hours smoking pot with him; Michael Leonard who came from London to say good-bye to one of his favorite models. Keith McDermott read a few of William's poems and a tribute from Ed White then living in Paris. I read his last poem, William's birthday present to me the previous April, composed through a veil of dementia. I also showed a video of William reading his poetry and gave copies of his book of verse to everyone who attended.

Friends accompanied me home afterward, but left soon after. I napped. Awake again, I walked through the apartment noticing our possessions; reminders of a life together. I returned William's ashes to the bookcase, dished with him for a while about the memorial and kissed the box.

I had lots of time to reflect upon our early years together. I especially remembered how William looked when we first met. He was twenty-one years old with a youthful, androgynous face, a slim body and very long legs that allowed him to walk so quickly through the streets that few could keep up with him. His hair came down to his waist, remarkable even in those years of long-haired men. His radiant smile put people at ease, while at the same time his clothes were generally mismatched and the very notion of shopping threw him into a depression. He was still living at home in Queens (which he called "The Terminal Moraine"). The surrounding neighborhood was composed of lower middle class families living in small but adequate homes. Though William had hated growing up there, he had noticed the beauty of the neighborhood boys, all of whom he had avoided from shyness and fear of being teased for being a sissy.

But what was he really like, I mean the inner man? William was a person of many assets and equally strong liabilities. Above all he loved knowledge and his reading material was esoteric and obscure. He had, for instance, memorized the Order of Precedence of the British Empire, the line of succession from the King/Queen downward. He also studied and kept notes on the financial holdings of various churches in England from medieval times to the present. He studied the Kings and Queens of Europe, diagrammed their family trees, noted their sexual proclivities (especially the gay ones), as well as the family histories of important members of the House of Lords. But he was no snob about reading material. One night, for instance, while reading *The Epigrams of Martial* (in Latin)—*Reform School Rape*, lay at his side, one of those filthy porno books with large type meant to pander to gay men's sexual fantasies. "This one," William said pointing to the Martial book, "is for my mind. The other is for my hand."

He had a snob's respect for aristocratic titles (the Lords and Ladies of Britain) and contempt for the newer ones based upon something he considered so flimsy as achievement. He read books on the French Revolution in French, about ancient Greek gods in Greek, on the Spanish Civil War in Spanish—all languages he taught himself by the process of picking up a book and "figuring it out." He had even read some hieroglyphics. "It's obvious," he said to me one night as I watched him pick up a book in modern Greek and slowly figure it out. When he got tipsy during a dinner party, he would sometimes recite Russian poetry punctuating the beautiful lines with great flourishes of his arms, unconcerned that no one else in the room knew what he was singing about. (I think he preferred it that way.)

William's respect for things ancient, preferably dead civilizations was daunting, since I recognized from the beginning that it was in part a reflection of his inner psychological state. He was born Catholic but hated the church for its hypocrisy. He used to say; "Confession is a place where people who commit small sins confess them to people who commit large ones." William could deftly delineate parallels between pagan and Christian holidays, and (often with tears in his eyes) relate the slaughter of one religious group by another, such as the killing of the Cathars in Southern France, the slaughter of Jews by the Crusaders and mutual attempts at extermination between Catholics and Protestants during the Reformation. He expressed a special affection for the Jews (and for Jewish lovers) in large part because of their suffering over the centuries. He was convinced of their inherent intelligence and abilities.

He could never discuss the Holocaust without crying. His attitude toward Hitler and the Third Reich was unique, horrifying some people, but demonstrating an insight few others possessed. He wrote the following in his journal: "One should not condemn too readily Hitler's anti-Semitism, for this was his fatal flaw and our saving grace. Had he instead allied himself with the Jews, the Reich may well have lasted the thousand years he dreamed of."

The only religious service he enjoyed was an occasional mass at a Russian Orthodox Church, and this only because people were required to stand throughout the hours-long service. The painfulness of the ordeal appealed to him.

He enjoyed pain in others—not in a sexual sense—rather like a child watching an adult trip and fall. It was as if he were getting even with the grown-up world for failing him. One summer, for instance, during our visit to Ed White and Chris Cox in Key West, I brought William along, kicking and screaming, on a sea-going glass-bottomed boat. He sat glaring at me for putting him into close proximity with people who possessed two characteristics he hated: they were straight and they were adults. His fury, however, turned to ebullient enthusiasm when the boat hit rough water and the other passengers became nauseated and seasick. William's eyes lit up when the first passenger vomited, wrung his hands in pleasure as two or three more heaved their lunches onto the floor and loudly recited Russian poetry when the deck was transformed into a multicolored rug of vomit. Alone again on shore, William thanked me for providing him his best day yet in Key West.

William's personality was complex and conflicted. Intellectually he was a genius, his breadth of knowledge wider and deeper than that of anyone I had ever met and far above my own. His passion for books was so great that I realized they were his closest and most cherished companions even before me. In contrast to his scholarly side, he was a passionate lover in private, but through his body language advertised a hostile sexuality in public so that when we walked down the street together some people thought that I had picked up a hustler—street trash at that. He had been a sissy as a child and like so many other gay boys, had felt the sting of rejection by society, leaving a wound that had never completely healed. He hated and feared straight people, especially macho, blue-collar men, and shunned them whenever possible. He also hated the police, the legal system, all people in authority.

William's hostility knew no bounds, but here I should tread softly, because hostility toward others is a trait that we shared. Neither of us could think of a sufficient reason to restrain from firing barbed arrows at targets (colleagues for me, everyone else for him) convinced that their stupidity or arrogance was good enough reason to cut them down to size.

The difference between us was that William did so with elegance.

He advertised his rapier wit in the form of epigrams. ("There are only three things in this world that I cannot stand: people, religion and civilization.") When he wanted to insult, he did so with a skill that left potential adversaries in the dust. ("New Jersey: The other side of any river.") He composed epigrams against the church too. His favorite was: "With the disappearance of monasteries, the proliferation of gay bars was inevitable." When briefly employed reviewing gay pornography films, he wrote the following about the release of *Sodom and Gomorrah*, "The book was better."

William was also a grand master at passive-aggressive behavior. After depleting an ice-tray of its ice, he would place it empty back into the freezer; he kept lights on and doors open; he refused to say in what restaurant he wanted to eat but criticized my choice after we had finished eating. But it was when smoking cigarettes that William's art of passive-aggressive behavior was at its zenith. He always had cigarettes but never matches. He would borrow my matches, keep them and when about to light up again, conveniently have lost them. He would ask for my matches again. William made sure that there was never an ashtray nearby and as the ashes on his cigarette grew longer, he would hold it ever closer to the vertical until they were so long that even a whisper would topple them—as all eyes in the room were riveted on them—and him. At the very last moment, he either make it to the nearby plant in which he would dump the ashes (and later the butt) or he would not, in which case they fell to the floor. The cigarette routine often turned me into a raving maniac.

He adamantly refused to compete with other people about anything. This was, however, only the facade of a personality that was deeply competitive and vindictive. The only time his aggression rose to the surface was when he was playing the board game Risk. The object of the game is to win the world, tapping a player's sense of grandiosity. William always expected to win. Anyone who interfered with this expectation was in for a devastating verbal *Blitzkrieg*. For instance, when playing with our friend Alexander, who was winning, William stole the dice and refused to give them back unless Alexander agreed to change the rules in order to make them more favorable to William.

William never forgot anything that anyone said—especially me. The words were stored in his brain, ready to be retrieved at any time and used with devastating accuracy. He believed in Schopenhauer's dictum, "To forgive and forget is to throw away valuable experience."

One summer, because of financial problems, I decided to rent our house in upstate New York. William did not like the idea of allowing strangers into our home and did what he could to sabotage my efforts. I placed an ad in *The New York Times*, and William fielded some of the phone calls. When a caller asked about the exact location of the house, he told them, "It's just up the block from the toxic waste dump." We had the house to ourselves that summer.

"The child is father to the man," it is said and William's early years as the first-born were the foundation for his adult troubles. His childhood was depressing, his family life bleak. He was a model child in school, beloved by all his teachers for both impeccable behavior and academic excellence. Always neatly dressed, his posture perfect, feet on the floor, he never spoke out of turn or got into fights with the other boys. His homework assignments were completed on time, strikingly neat and correct in every detail. He was always the "teacher's pet." Well-trained by his family that children should be seen but not heard, it never dawned on William to tell either parents or teachers that he was bored to death by the dull curriculum taught by equally dull teachers. For years he sat, hands clasped and face smiling, while underneath he seethed with rage, deprived of an adult who might stimulate and challenge his intellect. This sad state of affairs would eventually germinate into a fierce hatred of our educational system.

William knew that he was a "queer" child. Most of his world took place inside his head, imaginary worlds and countries that he would construct, including the monarchs who ruled, the language, religion and its history, the private universe of a boy composed of three parts genius and one part madness. He liked to spin like the Whirling Dervishes, twirling his body around for hours, which in any other child would have caused dizziness and eventual collapse. Not him. He never got dizzy, never fell, and loved the stimulation. If thrilled by something, a joke, an idea, whatever, he never spoke out loud. Instead, he clasped his hands together tightly and rubbed the palms so hard that one expected them to burn. At the same time his face contorted into an open-mouth, frozen smile, soundless and rigid—when combined with the hand-rubbing, this was a bizarre sight. It frightened observers who did not know how to interpret or respond to it, so they ignored it. For at least a year into our relationship, I could not tell if it was a sign of a troubling psychosis.

William admitted to being a bizarre eater. This is not unusual in a child. They often invent eating rituals obeyed with the force of law. One child eats a slice of bread by poking a hole in the center and eating the bread from the inside out, while another starts by eating the crust, and working his way inward. Each thinks the other is mad. Compulsive food rituals are similar to other rituals in childhood, such as never stepping on the pavement street cracks—or always stepping on them. William disliked the fats in meat which had to be cooked so long that every trace of them vanished. Bacon was ready when it was almost black and crumbled in your hands. He much preferred vegetables. (Isn't that audacious in a child?) He also demanded that every food on his plate be placed apart from the others so that they never touched. If the mashed potatoes touched the pork chop, both were contaminated and unacceptable. No matter what the punishment, he would adamantly refuse to eat them. His mother had tried to compromise by buying William his own dish, a Blue Willow ceramic plate with three clearly delineated compartments that separated the foods. He loved that dish and used it for years.

We need to step back one generation to understand William's relationship to his mother. His maternal grandmother had three daughters. After William's mother was born, the first died of Scarlet Fever at the age of six and his grandmother went into a deep depression that lasted for years. She simply sat down in a rocking chair and never got up. The significance of this tragedy is that William's mother had to learn to fend for herself. Although she never expressed resentment for having lost her mother, how could she have felt otherwise? The grandmother awoke from her depression the day William was born and she showered him with love from that moment forward. He became her reason for living and she expressed all the unconditional love toward her first grandchild that is associated with a loving parent. One wonders what William's mother felt observing her mother's love to her son, but never to her. It is the kind of question seldom asked in any family, certainly not in his. Yet he was close to his mother and identified with many of her values. He trusted and confided in her, at least to the extent that he confided in anyone.

William's told me many stories about his alcoholic father who operated on the basis of force majeure. William was required to eat every morsel of food on the plate and to remain at table until it was empty. Every child subjected to similar absurd demands is forced to invent devious ways of escaping the torture. The family dog who sat under the table near William was well fed. The rest of the food eventually ended up rolled into napkins on his lap and later flushed down the toilet. He also developed an uncanny ability to pretend to be eating, when in fact he ate nothing. He would pick up a bit of food on his fork and bring it to his mouth, but just before eating it, start talking (as a distraction), lower the fork to the plate and move the food around. Then he lowered the fork, only to pick it up in a few seconds and start the process all over again. He called this the "Mish-Mash" system of dining. I often saw him use the Mish-Mash system at dinner parties when he did not like the food. Our host or hostess would be charmed by his compliments about the cuisine, oblivious to the fact that he had not eaten a morsel.

William hated his father, not only for his cruelty, but for the fact that he was named for him. William was in fact William, Jr., but never in any document did he include "Jr." as part of his name. I seriously doubt that any of his friends were even aware of it. William told many stories about his father's cruelty. For instance, as a child, William loved to play with his huge block collection and he would build high towers over castles, structures so complicated that they took weeks to complete. They may have been the earliest fantasies of different worlds that he would later improve upon in his minutely drawn walled medieval cities. Then he would take them apart and start again, much like other children. William remembers his younger brother, Gerard, coming home one day carrying a bunch of wooden blocks he had found at a construction site as a present for his older brother. They were the remnants of discarded pieces of wood and they joined the extensive block collection. William appreciated his brother's thoughtfulness. Then one day, his father decided that William was too old for blocks and while William was at school, took them down to the basement and burned them in the furnace.

William was terrified of water. Even in our long relationship, including the many times when we vacationed at beaches, he rarely entered the water. If we were staying at a hotel with a pool and if there were very few people around (preferably none) he might (with much encouragement from me) step into the water up to his knees, no more, and that for only a few minutes. It was as if he had been asked to step into a bath of acid. The etiology of William's fear of water was once again attributed to his father who, when William was six years old, had decided that the best way to teach a child to swim was to throw him into the water. William screamed in terror as he sailed through the air and crashed through the surface. He immediately started to drown, instinctively trying to gulp air, but inhaling mouthfuls of water instead. The elder William finally pulled his terrified son from the pool.

William never forgot these experiences, never softened his hatred toward his father for his insensitivity and cruelty. It was, no doubt, a major contributor toward William's rejection of his home as a place of safety and the reason he put himself in harm's way as a late adolescent. With an unbridgeable emotional chasm between father and son, William, like so many other gay boys would be forced to choose between living without a father or finding a replacement in the gay world.

At twenty-one, William left college for good. "Incompletes" filled his transcript, the result of not completing term papers or cutting classes for the whole semester. He did not formally withdraw, just walked out, an impulsive act that would haunt him for years afterward. Instead of obtaining his degree, he hung out with friends, smoked pot and had sex. It was remarkable to me, someone who fretted desperately over his homosexuality, that William never gave a second thought to it. He knew that he was queer and that was that.

My own early childhood was remarkably different. Because I had suffered repeated bouts of pneumonia, a serious illness in the days before antibiotics, our family doctor had ordered that I be sent to a convalescent home in the country. I was six and a half years old. Overcoming their reservations, my parents acquiesced, despite the fact that "the Home" prohibited parents from contacting their children. No phone calls, visits or letters. Like the other youngsters in that medical prison, I felt abandoned.

Weeks before I had mailed away a dime to buy a "Lone Ranger" ring which had a secret compartment. My mother mailed it to me. The ring gave me instant status with the other boys.

"Put that away right now," said the white-coated matron. When I did not obey, she snatched the ring from me. I begged for it back, but she never returned it and it felt to me as if the ring had died. I was inconsolable.

I was also a bed-wetter and while my mother handled this problem with kindness, it was a serious infraction of the rules in the Home. We offenders were forced to lie the entire morning in our cold pajamas on top of cold, wet sheets as we listened through the dormitory windows to the muffled shouts of the children playing outside.

When I returned home, my mother asked if I had liked it there. "I liked it a lot," I said. "It was fun and everyone was very nice me," I lied. I claimed to have lost the Lone Ranger ring and she rebuked me for it. I know why I lied to her. I was terrified that if I told her the truth, she would send me back. *The Lone Ranger* ring, therefore, came to be a metaphor for my fear of abandonment and it affected all my adult relationships.

My parents were remarkably different from William's. My mother was a member of that generation of Jewish mothers publicly revered in print and privately reviled by their children. Regularly feigning weakness or impending illness, in reality they exerted the power of Mafia Capos, especially against their husbands whom they considered completely incompetent and their children whose lives they micro-managed from dawn to dusk. They would nag day and night and since the only alternative to giving in was to kill them, they usually got their way. In the case of my own mother, she probably did the best she could given that she came from a family of seven children with a father who spent all his money gambling and a mother who pushed all the children into a closet during thunderstorms.

My father was much like the American Jewish father of his day, passive, generally unresponsive to his children (which consisted of my six and one-half year older brother and me) and unable to communicate with his wife. He was very quick to anger and at such moments he would strike out and hit us hard on the head or the face. When punishment was due, he demanded that I stand before him, arms at my side. Then with the speed of an attacking pit viper, he would smack me on the head. If I flinched he hit me again. I always flinched, so he often hit me repeatedly until his rage abated or my mother successfully intervened. Sometimes he used a belt. At other times he took me into the bathroom, pulled down my pants, placed me across his knees and whipped the hell out of my ass.

Much of my family life was played out over the kitchen table. "Why are you so ugly, Charlie?" my father used to say humorously while patting my cheek. I always felt humiliated and the light touch on my cheek felt like a physical threat. I remained silent and felt paralyzed during these attacks. In time I came to believe that I was physically unattractive. He would also tell me that I was stupid and I believed that too.

I only started to know him after his first heart attack when he was forty-eight while I was in high school. After his convalescence he returned to work to the only job he had ever held, driving a newspaper truck at night. He needed a helper to load his truck and asked if I would do it because his doctor forbade him from picking up and throwing the heavy bundles of newspapers. I welcomed the opportunity even though it meant a long trolley car and subway ride to and from the city on Saturday nights.

I was struck by the contrast between my father at home and at work. At home he was sullen, depressed, and hostile toward his children; at work he was fun and affectionate toward me, and even joined in telling dirty jokes with the other men. It dawned on me that all the men were probably like my father when at home. The Jewish fathers were transformed at night into rather decent men when their wives weren't around to humiliate them.

My father became deeply depressed during my freshman year in college. I think he was unable to stop worrying about his damaged heart. Returning from school during some holiday period, I sensed that something was wrong. I walked through the open bathroom door and saw my father standing before the mirror, shaving cream on his face and a safety razor frozen in the air. When he saw me he started to cry, something I had never witnessed before. I walked over to him, unsure of what to say or do. He put his arms around my neck and his head on my shoulders and held me tight. "I love you very much," he said, as the shaving cream slid from his face to mine.

"I love you too, Daddy." I was moved and terrified, wishing that time would stop so that I could feel the warmth of his love forever. The shaving cream on both our faces provided the humor with which to diffuse the intensity of the moment. My father laughed at it, wiped it off my face, turned back toward the mirror and started to shave. We never discussed what had transpired or why. The language of intimacy was foreign in my home.

I was in scout camp a few months later when the call arrived announcing that he had died. Thankfully, my mother asked that the casket be closed. At the grave, relatives whisked us away before the coffin was lowered into the ground, while family members and friends threw shovels of earth upon the coffin. I remained emotionally cold toward my father's death.

Many years later, my mother remarried. After five years, his sister died. After the service, the casket was lowered and the family lined up for the traditional shoveling. I got on line and found myself shoulder to shoulder with this group of people with whom I had nothing in common. When the shovel was finally handed to me, I thought what the fuck am I doing here? But I started to cry as I heard the dirt land on the coffin below me. The person behind me, noticing the redness in my eyes as I handed him the shovel, said, "Gee, I didn't know she meant so much to you."

By the time I came out I was already a jumble of conflicting feelings and unresolved problems. I wanted to be good in order to please my mother, but like my father, felt rage toward her. I still thought I was stupid, ugly, and sexually undesirable. I was searching for my "other half," another man who would make me feel whole, someone whose umbrella of beauty, intelligence and desirability might shield me from my worst fears about myself.

I found all those characteristics in William. He moved in with me on February 1, 1973. He was twenty-three while I was thirty-eight. The dynamics of my relationship to William were patterned after my parents' marriage. I observed how my mother had given into my father's irrational demands so as to curtail his rage. That was the model of communication I learned at home and expressed in my relationship with William whose behavior was also often irrational and who could call up a reservoir of rage at a moment's notice. I was vigilant not to disturb the smoldering volcano inside him. When I was a child, my mother had only to express her pain, physical or psychological, real or imagined, and I would respond by helping her feel better. I copied that pattern with William and did everything I could to make him happy and need me. I gave him the most valuable gifts. These were not expensive clothes or jewelry, which he never cared for, but the most precious gifts of all: love; support in his moments of crisis; reassurance in his times of desperation; and most deadly of all, anticipation of his needs even before he was aware of them. The stubbornness with which I held onto this self-destructive behavior is not hard to understand. Its origin lay in the fear of being alone, the terror of abandonment. A component of it was my belief that being ugly and stupid, I could not be loved by being myself. I had to please someone.

William and I were perfect mirror images of each other's needs. He was looking for a father to take care of him, while I in the role of an idealized father, searched for my "son," myself, to love as a substitute for the father who had abandoned me. In a psychological sense, it was a marriage made in heaven, a perfect union of two gay men in search of their phantom fathers. When I made William happy, I felt vindicated: when I failed, I was sure that I was culpable for his discomfort. And I continued to believe this tortured reasoning until the day he died.

Alone after the memorial I removed a bunch of files from my cabinet and sitting on the living room floor, spread them out around me. There were pictures of me from book tours and others taken at our country house. There were my articles and books, each one corrected by William for grammar and style. Memories flooded back from our days of fighting for gay liberation. We were like Achilles and Patroclus, for two decades, political soul mates side by side battling against homophobic institutions. What a time we'd had embroiled in the political quarrels of gay liberation of the 1970s. My life was like the threads on a loom spinning a new garment. The warp threads (William) held under tension, and the weft threads (gay liberation) passing through on a shuttlecock to give rise to the pattern. Those two strands of my life became integrated and inseparable in the same way as the joining of its vertical and horizontal threads unifies a cloth. We would from then on join with others to fight for the civil rights of gay people.

Charles Silverstein, School of Industrial Art, New York City

Photo courtesy of the author.

One

Don't Squeeze the Pickles

My earliest memory is of crawling on the floor of the living room of our apartment in a six family house in East Flatbush, Brooklyn, calling to my parents "ee da people," by which I meant "We the People," the name of a popular radio program starring Kate Smith. The "da" part is Brooklynese, "d" sounds replacing "t" and "th" as in the sentence "Hay Ma, om goin ta da beartrum." I would later feel ashamed of my Brooklyn speech after a high school teacher called it "the garbage pail of the English language," giving me yet another reason to feel ashamed.

The streets of Brooklyn were my playground, my education, my social group. Much like Elmer Rice's play "Street Scene," our block was a society of its own, a stage filled with characters, adults and children who hardly envisioned a world outside the boundaries of our own borough. We did not even think of ourselves as being part of a larger city; we called Manhattan "New York" or "The City."

On summer nights the buildings were hot and clammy since no one owned an air conditioner in those days. Everyone gathered on the street, in front of or on the stoop ("stup" to us). We children stayed up late until exhaustion guaranteed sleep under a blanket of humid air. Block parties were common during hot weather. The street became a dance floor and a large truck housed the P.A. system and kegs of beer. Released from most grown-up restraints, we children ran wildly around the street as if participating in some primitive bacchanal. If we got too far out of line, some grown-up would temper our wild excess—any adult could do so. The absolute authority of grown-ups was one of the salient characteristics of our block society. All parents supervised all children and had what we kids thought of as life-and-death power over us. Well, not exactly. Mothers took care of children while fathers worked. Fathers delivered family punishment. "Wait 'til your father gets home," was a line spoken by every mother to every child, time and time again.

It was like having multiple mothers with all the assets and liabilities such riches entail. If any of us needed a mother and our own was not available, we simply picked out any other mother who then provided as much nurturance to us as she did for her own children. If my mother were out shopping when I came home for lunch during a school day, a friend's mother fed me. When a child fell ill, all the mothers visited providing encouragement and food—especially chicken soup. I remember coming down with some childhood illness and every Jewish mother, Italian mother and Irish mother walked into our apartment with a large pot of chicken soup (not a bowl, mind you), which I was forced to eat twice a day for the next couple of weeks. It seemed a far greater punishment than the disease. To this day I do not eat chicken soup.

"Will you cross me, please?" we children said to any passing stranger when we wanted to visit a friend or go to the candy store across the street. We dutifully put out our hands and held tight because we were not allowed to cross "da gutta" by ourselves. And we would say "thank you" when we reached the other side. We also needed adults in order to get into the movies for late afternoon shows since children were not allowed without being accompanied by an adult. "Take me in, please," we would say to any sympathetic looking man on the ticket line. (Only men were asked because women always asked where our mothers were and why were we outside without her.) He would take the money, buy the ticket and enter the theater with us, then let us go and sit by ourselves in the adult section, a real treat. Every once in a while we would sit with the man, perhaps wanting his grown-up company and say "thank you" when we left. We were disgustingly polite.

We also went to the movies on Saturday mornings. Our mothers prepared lunches for us containing sandwiches and fruit and we walked in large groups to the theater, ready for four hours of a double feature, cartoons, the coming attractions, movie news and the cliff-hanger serial. But especially we went for the madness. Children were shuttled off into the children's section (usually the narrow section of the orchestra on the right). There were rarely adults in the audience at that time of day, since they had sent the children away precisely to be rid of them. Guarding the tightly packed group was a woman dressed totally in white like a nurse in uniform called the "Matron." The Matron was one of the unsung heroes of the day, one woman standing alone against a sea of unruly children who gave every sign that they came to the movie house with only two goals: to terrorize the poor woman since she obviously represented mother and control, and to watch the films at least occasionally. Needless to say, hundreds of children possessed hundreds of pieces of fruit ("It's healthy," said our mothers), most of which became ammunition, one block against the other, our missiles lobbed indiscriminately in the air.

Sometimes Matron got us quiet, although I cannot remember how she accomplished the feat and silence prevailed for a minute or two. Then the commando attack would begin. Ducking under our seats we started loudly chomping on carrots and celery. "Who's doing that," screamed Matron. "Can I go to the bathroom, Matron?" one kid would ask, intending to distract her and the whole right side of the theater echoed with deafening laughter. Once again, the kids had defeated Matron. If she were particularly resilient (we firmly believed the Matrons were unemployed SS guards) we tried fart sounds. First from the rear of the section, then a response from somewhere up front, followed by a Greek chorus of obscene noises. I have often wondered how poor a woman had to be in those days to put on the white uniform and face that crowd. I would not have wanted to be one of Matron's own children when she returned home Saturday afternoon.

Street games were an important part of Brooklyn kid society and we often played them on our way to and from school. In one game, "Heels," we got discarded rubber heels from the shoemaker on the corner and playing for baseball or war cards, would then "shoot" (toss) the heel, aiming for every third crack on the sidewalk. Good players were as popular as war aces.

After lunch and if we were flush with money, we might stop into a grocery store and search for a good sour pickle in a large pickle barrel near the front of the store. We would dip our arms into the barrel often up to the elbow, in order to search for just the right one. Small ones cost two cents, big ones cost five. Four or five hands dove into the brine, feeling up the pickles and each other's hands at the same time. "Don't squeeze the pickles!" yelled the proprietor, predating by decades the Charmin commercial. Satisfied with our choices we skipped off to school, sucking the juice out of our sour pickles as if it were ambrosia.

We also made scooters on which to ride around the neighborhood, often in packs of boys like a motorcycle gang. Using discarded wooden orange crates we got at the vegetable store we hammered a section of two-by-four to the bottom and two sticks of wood for handle bars on the top, separated the two parts of a worn-out roller skate (they were adjustable in those days), put one half on the front of the two-by-four and the other half on the rear, and voila! A scooter.

Making a hole through a chestnut, we knotted one end of a shoe-lace and threaded the other through the hole to play "chestnuts." Taking turns, one boy would try to crack another boy's chestnut. The receiving chestnut, which had to be stationary, was held at the top of the string. The hitting chestnut was swung through the air and if aimed well, smacked the stationary one square on the side without the strings getting tangled. If neither chestnut had fought before (virgin chestnuts, so to speak) and yours cracked his, you had a "1 killer." The killings added up day after day until the chestnuts dried out with age and cracked.

Getting the chestnuts was itself a problem. All the chestnut trees in my neighborhood grew a few blocks away in Holy Cross Cemetery. For reasons I cannot now fathom, we believed that children were not allowed in the cemetery. We were convinced that if caught, that we would be murdered by the caretaker, a crazy man who walked around carrying an axe ready to chop off the head of any child he caught. We Jewish boys were terrified of the cemetery—we were brainy, not brave. Gathering chestnuts was left to the Italian boys, more heroic or stupid (take your pick) to jump over the cemetery wall at night, avoid the crazy man with the axe, and pick fallen chestnuts off the ground. They then sold them to us.

Our relationship to the Italian boys went beyond paying them for chestnuts, but since most of them went to parochial school, we did not play together often. They ended up in the public schools only when they had been expelled from a Catholic school either for being hopelessly illiterate or for behavior problems. Their expulsion and inability to compete intellectually with the brainy Jewish kids only served to further alienate them from learning. (This is part of the etiology of "the Hood.")

They did, however, have other things going for them. For instance, their mothers knew how to cook. It was a real treat to be invited to supper at an Italian kid's house. Their kitchens were filled with enticing exotic odors, from meats that were not overcooked and tasteless (like they were back home) and great vats of pasta smothered with home-made sauces.

One day we Jewish kids challenged the Italian boys to a "rumble." We were a bunch of namby-pamby Jewish kids, almost all of whom wore glasses. We rarely got into fights, yet wanting to "rumble" with Italian kids, all with whom we liked and who would in any event kick the shit out of us. I cannot remember why we proposed doing anything so stupid. Whatever the reason we met on the corner, the Italians on one side of the street and the Jews on the other. One of the Italian boys shouted "Charge!" and yelling war cries they attacked. We Jewish kids suddenly realized that we did not know how to fight. Nor, for that matter, did we feel any animosity towards the screaming gang almost upon us. (Perhaps we were also thinking of not being invited to supper again.) So we lay down on the street and gave up. The Italian kids jumped over our prostrate bodies and declared victory. No one got hurt or even hit. The victors walked away puzzled about the encounter, while we Jewish kids started playing some game and agreed not to talk to anyone about what had just happened.

The Italian boys fascinated me because they were everything I was not. They were "bad." They did not listen to their teachers and they did not do their homework. They smoked cigarettes in school, if they came to school at all. They hung out in large gangs like a meeting of the Mafia and if challenged in the slightest way became belligerent. Worst of all, they did not listen to their mothers. Their fathers used to kick the shit out of them regularly, which probably explains their own aggressiveness. They had lithe bodies, olive complexions, dark hair, and wore tight pants. They excelled at sports and were unconcerned about physical contact or getting hurt. They removed their shirts in warm weather, then quite unconsciously and publicly started feeling themselves up, rubbing their chests, running a finger or two over their nipples and forever scratching, tugging and rubbing their genitals. They even touched each other, wrestling shirtless or just walking with arms over each other's shoulders. In school they stood away from the urinals with their uncircumcised cocks in plain sight, creating ever-changing trajectories while trying to write their names on the porcelain and talking constantly while pissing to whomever was near. They even looked at you while doing it.

We Jewish kids were so conservative by comparison. While an Italian kid could quickly whip off his polo shirt we had to shed about four layers of clothing before we could even find our skin and then felt profoundly ashamed of it. We stood close to the urinal, lest anyone see our small dicks, then tucked them back inside in a nanosecond. Of course we also knew that when report cards came out the Italian kids would get beaten by their fathers, while we Jewish kids would only suffer guilt for not getting even higher grades.

I admired them secretly from afar, drawn to their unconventionality and independence. By puberty I was well aware that I wanted to touch those lithe bodies and wanted to grab hold of those uncircumcised cocks. In my masturbatory fantasies, I would watch one of them finger a nipple with one hand and rub his crotch with the other. Then I would substitute my hand for his and while he smiled at me, get him off—which of course meant getting myself off.

One day when we were about eleven or twelve, an Italian boy named Peter came over to my house after school to play. He was a pleasant, good-natured kid. The usual games getting boring we started feeling each other up. Fully clothed, we proceeded to get on top of each other and rub our hard-ons together. At that point my mother walked into the apartment. Peter jumped off me instantly both our dicks still at attention. My bedroom had no door. My mother had removed it about a year before cheating me out of even the least semblance of privacy. After our hard-ons went down, Peter went home and we never played our sex game again.

How idyllic this all sounds now. But the picture thus far is incomplete. There were storm clouds on the horizon. My two favorite radio programs while in elementary school were *The Lone Ranger* ("and his faithful companion Tonto") and live broadcasts from the Metropolitan Opera House in which Milton Cross would tell the radio audience the story of the opera they were about to hear.

There were no books on opera in our house, nor had anyone except me expressed an interest in seeing a performance. The literary standard in my home was Reader's Digest, and Kate Smith's rendition of "God Bless America" was considered the zenith of music. Yet somehow I developed an appetite that was fueled on weekends. On Saturday nights I would sneak my radio under the covers and holding it next to my ear, listen to the opera.

I carried my books the wrong way during my preadolescent years. No matter how many books there were boys carried them at their sides. Girls, on the other hand, bent their arms at the elbow and carried them close to their chests. I carried my books like a girl. Of course I instantly switched back to the proper position whenever I caught myself breaking the rules, and glanced around to see if anyone else had noticed. I did not want to be a girl, or even play with them. I did not dress up in my mother's clothes nor did I want to. All my social conditioning reinforced carrying books like a boy, but something drove me robotically to carry them between my arms.

As time went on, my status in the boy group changed related to the maturational change from kid games to what my colleagues call "rehearsal for manhood." From playing "Heels" we moved to punch ball. If I hit the ball at all, it fell feebly to the ground. Tagged out in no time I was jeered at and taunted for my failure. In school we learned how to play basketball and how to block opponents with our bodies while passing the ball to teammates or shooting for the basket ourselves. I liked passing the ball because it felt like a time bomb in my hands. I would throw it to another kid, half hating, half admiring him for his ability to sink a basket, hoping it would explode in his hands.

I remember the day a bunch of us played our first football game. We went to an empty lot after school and one or more kids explained about yards, goals, downs, throwing and catching the ball and how to score points. It all mystified me. In the first place, that thing did not look like a ball; God knows what idiot had designed it. "Here, look, you have to spin it when you throw it," said a friend who after 10 minutes of practice was light years ahead of me. I could not spin it, could not catch it, and did not understand in which direction I was supposed to run. And I didn't give a shit about any of those things anyway. But most of all I did not understand why all the other boys were having fun while I found the whole experience hideous. My friends were marching off into manhood and I felt left back, as retarded as a dummy in school.

Captains took turns choosing teams on the street alternately selecting a player until the roster was complete. As the countdown was in progress, teammates already chosen would consult with one another, searching for the right strategy to force me to be chosen by the other team. This was not a subtle process, mind you. These were after all, the same boys who just a short time before had regaled each other with fart sounds at the movies. When I was finally chosen—last, of course—a cheer went up from the team that did not get me. My own team hung their heads in shame, accepting their fate as if they had just been sentenced to a meal of calf's liver and spinach.

I was forced to play intra-mural softball in Junior High School and there was no choosing up sides, since one class played the other. I vividly remember one game. The night before I had prayed to contract smallpox and be excused. As luck would have it, I remained disgustingly healthy and I kept striking out at bat and playing right field (often called the gay position). We were in the bottom of the ninth inning, with my team at bat, the score three to one in favor of the enemy. Our first two men were tagged out (at least I knew the rules of this game). The next two hit singles. Down two runs, two out, two men on base, and guess who was up to bat next?

Hideous screams arose from my teammates. A few of them pretended to faint. One of my best friends started hitting himself over the head with a bat. (We were Jewish, so we hurt ourselves, not others.) From the field came loud guffaws, the opposing team already celebrating their certain victory. One boy suggested we end the game there and then, an idea seconded by me. My team members ran over to the gym teacher and begged him to allow a switch hitter. Their request denied, they walked away scuffing their heels and unable to look me in the face. How I wished the gym teacher had agreed to their request and sentenced me to death.

The outfield sat down and dropped their gloves (were they called "mitts?") as a sign of contempt. The infield moved in expecting the ball, should I actually hit it, to dribble out to them (or was "dribbling balls" about some other sport?). I batted wildly at the first ball. Strike one. I tried even harder at the second pitch but with my eyes closed (so that I shouldn't get hit by the ball). Strike two.

Two outfielders starting walking off the field. My own team screamed every filthy word in their repertoire at me and their knowledge of profanity was extensive.

The last pitch. It will all be over in a second, I thought. Then I can go home and kill myself. I swung at the ball with as much force as before—and connected. With a loud crack the ball sailed high into the air, over the heads of the dumbfounded (and sitting) outfielders, higher still and over the schoolyard fence. A home run!

No one was more shocked than me. Even our two runners on base stood gaping. "Run, schmuck!" advised my teammates. I started running. "Drop the bat, scumbag," someone screamed. I dropped the bat. "You didn't touch second, you fuckhead," admonished a teammate, holding his head in disbelief. I went back and touched second.

When I finally reached home base and therefore scored the winning run, my whole team greeted me with cheers and lifted me up in celebration. Only a minute before I had been the millstone around their necks and now I was their hero. How fickle are the favors of the crowd! I asked the coach if I could now retire from baseball. No such luck.

It was during my prepubescent years that I learned the meaning of social morality, that there was a wider world outside of my neighborhood in which adults helped or hurt each other. When I was ten (in 1945), my family spent the summer on Miami Beach (now known as South Beach) at a small hotel on Sixth Street across from the ocean. It took us three days to drive there from Brooklyn because there were almost no super highways in those days. Route One wove from state to state the whole length of the Eastern seaboard passing through the black section of each town or city along its way. These slum communities contrasted sharply with the green manicured lawns and plantation homes for which the South is famous. We slowed down as we drove through these ghettos, looking at the people and the environment in which they lived. Though we ourselves lived in a working-class neighborhood we had never seen slums like this. As a family we talked about how sad the people looked and how poor they were.

At various times we passed gangs of prisoners performing tasks around the road. We slowed down to get a look at what was going on, but the guards always shooed us on. They stood straight-backed in brown uniforms with black leather belts, wide-brimmed hats on their heads, each of them armed with a large rifle or shotgun (I didn't know the difference then.) Their faces were mean and angry. I was sure that any one of them would not miss a heartbeat to shoot a prisoner.

It was the first time that I realized that there was a class of men who could kill. I never wondered what crimes the prisoners had committed. I felt sorry for these anonymous men wearing drab prison outfits silently breaking rocks, perhaps wondering about their chances to escape. They were mostly black and looked just like the men we passed going through the ghettos.

My family discussed the road gangs and the mean looks of the guards. I listened intently as my parents talked about how badly "Colored" people, or Negroes were discriminated against. "There should be a law against it," my father said. It was one of his favorite expressions.

World War Two had just come to an end and the racial enemies of our country were the Japanese, consistently depicted as sneaky, inhuman, buck-toothed monsters who threw babies into the air and caught them on their bayonets. The German death camps had been liberated by the Allies and newsreels showed mounds of naked dead bodies, people who had been reduced to skeletons even before they died. We saw pictures of the gas chambers in which innocent people were murdered and the ovens in which they were reduced to ashes.

Blacks were still lynched in the South and black men rightly feared that an advance toward a white woman might result in castration. I have often wondered what those white men felt as they held a black man on the ground, the man hysterical with fear and begging for his life. What was in the mind of the white man who held the black man's genitals tightly in his hands, pulling them away from the body to make room for the slice? Other black men who offended white Southerners were stripped naked, dipped in boiling tar and coated with white chicken feathers. The "tar and feather" punishment caused third-degree burns over the whole body and after hours of agony, the man often died.

Driving through the South also exposed us to other prejudices. My mother was skilled at getting people to talk about their racial attitudes and the Southerners she spoke to seemed unable to spot Jewish tourists.

"A Jew is a Nigger turned inside out," one restaurant owner told us.

The next summer at age eleven, we drove from Brooklyn to Los Angeles. My parents had decided to leave the winter ice and snow of New York for a warmer climate. My father's union had a "shop" there; the foreman, Carl, was an old friend. They had worked together for years in New York until Carl moved to L.A. My father wrote to him asking for a job and Carl responded yes.

It took nine days to drive to L.A. with stops at the Grand Canyon and the Painted Desert. My father started working days to the joy of the whole family and we began to look for a house, an exciting prospect because we had always lived in an apartment. Real estate brokers pampered us by showing us one house after another. We in turn were very polite, feeling somewhat as if we did not belong, as if we were not worthy of a whole house. Finally and with great joy we chose a beautiful home with exceptional grounds that has, I am sure, grown grander and more beautiful in my imagination. My father agreed to turn over the basement to me for a photography studio and darkroom, an impossibility in our four-room Brooklyn apartment. I would also have a bedroom of my own. My father signed the papers and made a down payment.

A few days later Carl called my father into his office. There was a problem. My father was the first Jew ever hired by the company and the other men in the shop were enraged at it. "Either you fire the Jew or we'll go out on strike," they'd told Carl. The foreman said that he had no choice but to fire my father, that he hoped my father would not take it personally and that he had done everything he could to prevent it.

That was in 1946 when religious discrimination was an accepted part of American life. The owner of the house we were to buy kindly returned our deposit when he learned what had happened. We packed our bags and drove the three thousand miles back to Brooklyn where my father returned to his night job. I do not know how it affected my parents or my brother. I thought about it for years, about the darkroom I would never use and the bedroom I would never sleep in. I felt like I had been declared an unsavory immigrant and turned away from Ellis Island.

It seemed to me that there was a similarity between our expulsion from California and the fate of the men in the road gangs from the previous summer. Jews and Blacks were interchangeable, despised merely for existing and subject to the venom of the majority. When we left California I realized that I was as much an underdog as those nameless prisoners working by the side of the road.

My Judaism made me an underdog in society, but accepted in my family. A year or two later, I realized that I had yet another burden to carry, one which made me a pariah even at home—my homosexuality.

Two

Are You Saying that Homosexuality is Normal?

December 15, 1973. On that date the Board of Trustees of the American Psychiatric Association announced that homosexuality had been removed as a mental disorder *per se* from its *Diagnostic and Statistical Manual*. It was the most important achievement of the Gay Liberation Movement. I sat in the Washington, D.C. auditorium of the American Psychiatric Association listening to the press conference, amused to hear reporters ask Dr. Alfred Freedman, president of the association, such questions as, "If it's not a mental illness now, why was it on the list of mental illnesses for the past fifty years?" Since the decision to remove homosexuality as a mental illness was as much a political as a scientific act, the president's logic in answering the reporters' questions was often tortuous. "Are you saying that homosexuality is normal?" asked one reporter. "No," said the president, "only that it's not abnormal."

How extraordinary, I thought. Only a year before these same psychiatrists were holding meetings to proclaim how ill we were. I was witnessing a major change in society brought about by the political pressures we gay activists had exerted. It demonstrated what I had long believed; psychiatric diagnosis stands on a foundation of morality and politics, not science. It was one thing to have always believed it, another to see it in action.

I want to tell that story, how we radical gay activists forced the psychiatrists to remove the scarlet "H" from our lives. Here is how it came about.

On October 8, 1972, the Association for the Advancement of Behavior Therapy (AABT) held its annual meeting at the Hilton Hotel in

New York City. Helen Singer Kaplan (famous for her work in sex therapy) as chair of a panel on homosexuality had invited Bernice Goodman (a social worker) and me to speak as representatives of Identity House (a gay peer counseling center). Bernice was a social worker and I, a psychologist. We were the first openly gay professionals invited to speak at an AABT convention. The panel presentation about homosexuality was held in one of the largest meeting rooms at the convention. Every seat was taken and the overflow crowd stood in the back of the room and along the sidewalls.

The main thrust of my argument was that behaviorists had no right to change the sexual orientations of gay men who felt guilty about their homosexuality since the behaviorists were partly responsible for making gay men feel guilty in the first place. I argued that they should be developing techniques to alleviate sexual guilt. I also proposed the termination of aversion therapy because it put therapists in the role of police and because it established a sado-masochistic relationship between the behaviorist and his gay patient.

Our presentations were well received and many conventioneers chatted with us afterward. We were invited to lunch by Dorothy Suskind, one of the founding psychologists of AABT and Herb Fensterheim who had already published papers about teaching assertiveness training to gay people. They both agreed with our denunciation of the use of aversion therapy on homosexuals and they suggested that I join the association in order to fight against its use.

That afternoon I attended a small workshop led by the psychologist Gerald Davison. I arrived at the meeting early. Only one other person was in the room, a psychologist from the Midwest. We started to chat. He asked if I had heard about the homosexual demonstration of the day before and when I said that I had, he proceeded to tell me how disgusted he was to think that "they" could get away with it without being arrested. He particularly singled out for criticism effeminate men and drag queens he had seen on the streets of New York. He came to the workshop, he said, to learn about Davison's treatment for curing homosexuality.

"You're talking about some of my friends," I said, looking him square in the eyes. He sat shocked for a moment, then left the room. Good, I thought, one less homophobe in the room.

No more than a dozen people attended Davison's workshop. I said very little if anything at all. I was there to observe Davison, to gauge what kind of man he was and where his values lay. I had been told by Terry Wilson, a psychology professor at Rutgers University that Davison was rethinking the value of his previous work.

Davison had begun his career trying to change the sexual orientation of gay college students at SUNY's Stony Brook campus, but he was loath to use aversion therapy. Instead, he had designed an alternative conditioning technique for curing a young man of sadistic sexual fantasies and published the results. He next turned to homosexuality. Gay male college students were placed in a private room and asked to masturbate to a fantasy of gay sex. Just as they were about to ejaculate, they were instructed to switch their imagery to a picture of a naked woman in *Playboy* magazine so that their orgasms were paired with looking at women. That, hypothesized Davison, might cure them. The treatment became known as "Playboy Therapy." It obviously failed. Though well intended as an alternative to aversion therapy, it failed to appreciate that sexual arousal, not ejaculation, defines sexual orientation. Ironically, his treatment reinforced homosexual desire.

I walked over to him at the end of the workshop. "I know who you are," he said. "Let's have a drink." In the lounge, he told me that he had come to the conclusion that his work attempting to change sexual orientation was ill-advised and that he was prepared to repudiate it publicly. It was an extraordinary statement, unique in its honesty, brave in its recognition that it would infuriate many of his colleagues. His point of view about changing sexual orientation was light-years ahead of most of his colleagues in behavior therapy.

Davison had come to believe that *all* treatments designed to "cure" were immoral. He did not believe that anyone's sexual orientation ever changed, no matter what the treatment, but the moral question outweighed the scientific one. Even if there were a sure-fire way to convert gay men and women to heterosexuality, he would oppose it.

The GAA zap was the next day. Richard Quinn, a behaviorist known for his use of aversion therapy on gay men, was giving a lecture at the convention. I recommended to the Gay Activists Alliance (GAA), of which I was a member, that it "zap" (their name for a demonstration) his presentation. The executive committee immediately approved. GAA members were to infiltrate Dr. Quinn's meeting. After he had spoken for ten minutes, we were to interrupt him and inform the audience that we were taking the meeting over to talk about the immorality of aversion therapy, or any therapy intended to make a gay person straight.

I had one worry. The security guards at the Hilton Hotel had a reputation for overreacting during demonstrations. Therefore, I asked a few AABT officers to meet me at Quinn's workshop where I explained what we were going to do. They promised to keep the security guards at bay.

Quinn had just arrived from his home in Belfast, Northern Ireland. Poor man, I thought, he came to New York to get away from the violence back home and ends up the subject of our zap. I introduced myself to him, explaining that I was both a psychologist and a gay liberationist and that the meeting room was peppered with gay radicals (I particularly used the word "radical," so as to intimidate him). I instructed him, as kindly as I could, as to what would take place. I pleaded with him not to make a fuss, because it was going to happen with or without his cooperation. He caved in immediately. Quinn walked to the front of the room, I walked to my seat and the AABT officers stood guard at the door. After Quinn had talked for ten minutes, Ron Gold from GAA stood up. "You've talked long enough, Dr. Quinn. "Now it's our turn."

We chastised the audience for their attempts to convert homosexuals into heterosexuals instead of helping gay people come out. They erupted into fury. Many of them were also opposed to aversion therapy, but they were angry at our interruption of their meeting. During the next hour their anger abated and the two groups exchanged ideas; by the end of the meeting, many people felt that it had been a useful exchange. (Security guards from the Hilton showed up, but the AABT convention officials kept them out.)

In the audience was Robert Spitzer, a research psychiatrist and a member of the Nomenclature Committee of the American Psychiatric Association, the group that formulates and makes changes in the diagnostic system. Spitzer suggested that gay activists take their complaint to the Nomenclature Committee.

An *ad hoc* committee of gay activists, mostly from GAA, was formed to organize the presentation. They were instructed, however, not to identify themselves as an official GAA committee, only as a group of interested individuals because GAA did not want to be seen as cooperating with the psychiatrists. The committee consisted of chairman Ron Gold, Jean O'Leary, Rose Jordan, Ray Prada, Brad Wilson, Bernice Goodman and me. Wilson and Jordan prepared an excellent preparatory written report citing recent psychological research on homosexuality, which was sent to the psychiatric Nomenclature Committee.

Our committee, ruled with an iron hand by Ron Gold, elected to make two presentations to the psychiatrists. Jean O'Leary, an ex-nun, was assigned the first of these, a presentation about the harmful effects of pejorative labeling on gay people in their struggle for civil rights. I was asked to discuss the diagnosis of homosexuality from a professional point of view.

We met often. Each member was assigned the responsibility of fielding potential questions from the psychiatrists. Jean and I were to read our presentations aloud in order for other members to critique them. At each of these meetings I reported that I had not yet finished mine. This announcement was met with displeasure, particularly by Gold, who insisted that my presentation be sufficiently militant and confrontational. But I did not want to play the role of gay activist with the Nomenclature Committee. I knew they would be expecting that and I thought it the better strategy to take a different approach. The last thing I wanted to do at that point was to write something for the *ad hoc* committee's approval.

I decided to spend my time reading about all the diagnostic systems that had ever been invented to classify human behavior in order to understand their structure as documents reflecting the social worries of their times. I began to see these systems as a means of isolating people whose behavior was inexplicable, therefore feared and for that reason condemned.

It was not possible to read this material without chuckling. Most of the diagnostic categories consisted of socially disapproved behavior. The *DSM* from 1968 included such "illnesses" as lying, stealing, the fear of contracting syphilis, or simply being a cranky person.

But I did not chuckle as I learned about the "treatment" some people were subjected to by the medical authorities of the day. I considered them torture. There are many examples. Women were subjected to cliterodectomies even into the last century because they expressed an interest in or enjoyment in sex or because they masturbated. Fortunately only the rich could afford the operation, so most women were spared the physical and psychological scaring from the surgery.

Hydrotherapy was the preferred treatment for many patients at asylums. The patient was tightly wrapped in a sheet or rubber container and placed in a cold bath for a period of hours to days. Also in the nineteenth and twentieth centuries schizophrenic patients were sterilized as a therapeutic treatment, not to prevent procreation. Malaria fever was injected into syphilitic patients (sometimes directly into the brain) in the hope that the high fever would kill the spirochete. Electroconvulsive therapy was its replacement, accomplished by the injection of insulin or the use of electric shock.

And finally, as if one needed further evidence of torture dressed in the mantle of medicine, was the introduction of lobotomy, a procedure that began as late as 1947. As the medical establishment sat silent, men and women were subjected to a pre-frontal lobotomy in which an instrument resembling an ice pick was inserted either through the nose or to the side of the eye and into the brain where it was then wiggled about in order to cause destruction to that part of the cerebrum. By 1951 a total of twenty thousand lobotomies were performed in the United States. The major reason given to justify this operation was bad behavior on the part of the patient; he or she was found to be incorrigible. And sixty percent of the victims of this torture were women, while men in these institutions were in the majority. It seems as if there was a price to be paid for not being lady-like!

It was only professional fashion that dictated a treatment; its usefulness in curing disease was near irrelevant. And nowhere was that more obvious than in the use of aversion therapy upon gay people, a procedure in which an electrical jolt was sent into a gay man as punishment for being aroused by another man. I felt furious reading about these excesses by the medical establishment. I still am.

There was a second and more personal reason that I delayed writing my presentation to the committee; only days before I had brought

William into my home. Fired by passion for him at least as great as my commitment toward gay rights, I was reluctant to sit down and write. We had first met a year before at the Firehouse, the center for the Gay Activists Alliance in New York City. No one at GAA or the ad hoc committee knew that William had moved in with me. I am not sure why we had not told them. Perhaps it happened so quickly, or perhaps I felt so needy (like a child hoarding candy) that I willfully avoided letting anyone know.

There were three months between the December AABT zap and the February presentation to the psychiatrists, time enough for William and me to get to know one another. We talked endlessly about the history of medical diagnosis from the ancient Greeks to the present. In our walks by the Cloisters we talked in turn about pejorative medical labeling, ancient civilizations and historical piracy. It was a period of getting to know each other and to make a connection between our personal values and goals.

Although he spoke with elegance and clarity, William was less skilled in speaking the language of feelings. On the other hand, he was an expert on ancient civilizations, the history of virtually all Western religions, linguistics, literature, English and the arts, including poetry, painting, sculpture, music, opera and ballet. He saw himself as a Renaissance man trapped in the twentieth century. And he was. Although twenty-two years old, he had no educational goals or any occupation. He was, therefore, broke, with no hope of making a living.

He had dropped out of college in 1972, his senior year and had moved in with friends in Brooklyn. He could not contribute to the rent, so they deposited him in the basement on a filthy, smelly, decaying mattress where William read his books beneath a bare light bulb and began the slow process of starvation. "I would have perished there," he said many years later. To placate his roommates I would occasionally arrive with shopping bags of food. At some point I acknowledged that we loved each other, that I wanted him close to me and that even in this desperate situation, he would not ask for my help. Pride was a central part of his character, a kind of twisted inner joy that reaffirmed his status as a victim.

On February 1, 1973, I drove to Brooklyn, collected his few clothes and books and brought William to live with me. He bathed, ate supper, and cuddled in my arms. We talked about Egypt (yet again), about how Hatshepsut, a woman, had declared herself Pharaoh, about how Cleopatra had used her sexuality for political gains—about how much we both wanted to see the Giza pyramids. William said that he wanted to go to Rome, that he owned the best guidebook to Rome ever published. Enthusiastically, butt naked, he rummaged through a tattered shopping bag, found it, and handed it to me. It was "Pausanias' Guide to Rome," written two thousand years ago. He showed me maps of some of the most significant sights on the Palatine Hill, throwing in for good measure racy stories about one ancient emperor or another, especially the gay ones.

As I listened and watched him, I felt so much in love with his voice, his intellect and culture, his body, his kisses and his affection for me that I asked him to stay. He responded by kissing and embracing me, saying the loving words I wanted to hear. Hardly containing his enthusiasm, he opened the Rome guidebook again and said, "And here's where we can get married." He was pointing to the Temple of the Vestal Virgins. I adored him for it. "We'll take a picture together when we get there," I said.

That was seven days before I made my presentation to the Nomenclature Committee to remove homosexuality as a mental illness. I knew what I was doing; knew the implications of "saving" William that February night. I could project the future, both its bright lights and its dark corners. I needed someone to love, to take care of, perhaps as my mother took care of my father. Why not someone, who, for all his liabilities, also loved me?

The presentation to the Nomenclature Committee was scheduled for February 8. I wrote it the evening before, while sitting at my desk pounding away on my old typewriter, William laying on the bed reading. I turned to him often to ask a point of grammar or spelling, yet at the same time I knew that my questions were mainly my way of making contact with him. "I'll read it over when you finish," he said. When he did, he much approved of the sentiments expressed and the strength of my arguments but chastised me for my inability to spell even the simplest words. After his corrections I sat on the bed and read it to him. We talked long into the night about the implications of winning the battle to remove homosexuality as a mental illness. Both of us understood that once the house of moral cards upon which the diagnosis was based fell, that the other sexual diagnoses would follow. We had in mind the group of kinky behaviors that psychiatrists and psychologists called the "paraphilias." Under that classification people who were aroused by a fetish or sado-masochistic behavior or cross-dressing were diagnosed as suffering from a mental illness. From our point of view there was no evidence of anything except violating social mores. Then he took the paper from my hands, placed it on the desk and started to kiss me. I felt overjoyed, filled with excitement, knowing that that night I was having sex with a man I deeply loved and who loved me and that tomorrow I would help to change history for gay people everywhere. Not for a second did I doubt it.

Jean and I presented our statements to the Nomenclature Committee at Columbia University's Psychiatric Institute. The first part of my presentation highlighted the humor one can find within the pages of diagnostic systems, such as the "mental illness" of masturbation. I then tried to demonstrate that the only foundation for the classification of a "Sexual Deviation" was moral, not scientific. I chastised the committee for the role that the psychiatric profession played in the disenfranchisement of, discrimination against, and legal penalties suffered by gay people because we had been diagnosed as psychopathic and sexually deviant. "To continue to classify homosexuality as a disorder," I concluded, "is as valid today as was the diagnosis of masturbation in the 1942 edition. What we hope to convey to you is that we have paid the price for your past mistake. Don't make it again."

We knew that one member of the committee was gay, but wondered whether there were other, deeply closeted gay members, because we worried that our presence might pressure them to vote against us as a way to avoid suspicion. The only members of the committee we were not worried about were the obviously straight psychiatrists. We knew what they were thinking and how to respond to them.

The committee received us cordially. They had all read our written report and they listened carefully to our arguments. During lunch I chatted with Henry Brill, the committee chair, who mentioned some of the impediments to removing homosexuality as a mental disorder from the

DSM. The psychoanalysts formed the biggest roadblock. Psychoanalysts were adamant in their belief that homosexual behavior was aberrant and doomed a gay person to a life of loneliness and depression, often ending in suicide. Only psychoanalysis could save the homosexual from himself, claimed Charles Socarides, the most pompous of the analysts. In 1965, Socarides had wanted the federal government to set up a residential Center for Sexual Medical Rehabilitation (a concentration camp for faggots). Even other psychiatrists were shocked at the idea and no one supported him. During lunch Brill and I talked about the analysts, and gossiped about famous gay psychoanalysts such as Anna Freud and Harry Stack Sullivan. He was shocked at my estimate that between ten to twenty percent of his colleagues were gay. (I now think my estimate to Brill was low.)

A few months later, the Nomenclature Committee, even though divided, voted to recommend the removal of homosexuality as a mental disorder in the next edition of the *Diagnostic and Statistical Manual.* Their recommendation, however, had to be approved by the Board of Trustees of the American Psychiatric Association. In March, Richard Pillard, a gay Bostonian psychiatrist and an active supporter of the removal of homosexuality as a mental illness, convinced the Northeastern New England District Branch to endorse the nomenclature change, making them the first affiliate of the American Psychiatric Association to do so. This was an important step, since it demonstrated that local associations would support the recommendations of the Nomenclature Committee.

I was not privy to the board's discussions, but my understanding from those who were and from Ron Bayer's authoritative account, *Homosexuality and American Psychiatry*, is that most members of the board were sympathetic to the Nomenclature Committee's request, but the removal of homosexuality as a mental disorder represented conflicting moral, ethical, political, and economic values for the board. They sympathized with gay people who had been discriminated against in our society and acknowledged that the medical/psychological profession had contributed to that sorry state of affairs. But psychoanalytically oriented psychiatrists had built their reputations on curing homosexuals and an affirmative vote by the board would represent a slap across their professional faces. It would also have an economic effect upon these and other psychoanalysts, since many gay men would no longer seek treatment in order to change their sexual orientation.

The APA Board of Trustees was now forced to face these problems, and they feared a rebellion by the psychoanalytic members of the association, who were raising petitions against the proposed change.

The Board of Trustees tried to mollify both sides. They suggested that some homosexuals were happy with their lives and had no wish to change their sexual orientation. These homosexuals were called "ego syntonic" and, therefore, not in need of psychiatric treatment. On the other hand, there were homosexuals who were "ego dystonic," unhappy with their sexual orientation, and these homosexuals were in need of treatment. The board removed homosexuality from the list of sexual deviations, and replaced it with "Ego Dystonic" Homosexuality by a vote of thirteen for, none against, and two abstentions.

The annual meeting of the American Psychoanalytic Association was held in New York City the next day. Infuriated by the APA action, Charles Socarides arrived with a petition demanding that the complete APA membership vote on the diagnostic change. Socarides secured two hundred names to his petition, enough to force a vote.

Gay activists knew that a referendum of the APA membership might overturn the nomenclature change. The psychoanalytic group, led by Socarides and Harold Voth, sent out a letter to the membership challenging the board decision, claiming that the association was being taken over by gay activists. To counter this letter, Robert Spitzer and Ron Gold sent the membership another letter paid for by The National Gay Task Force, a new gay liberation group that had been organized by Gold, Bruce Voeller, and Jean O'Leary.

The Gold/Spitzer letter cleverly argued that a professional organization should support the actions of its Board of Trustees. The letter cited many examples of civil rights violations against gay people which had been justified by the misuse of psychiatric diagnosis. The question of homosexuality was left in the background since we were under no illusions about the conservative nature of American psychiatry. Many prominent psychiatrists signed the letter, including the sitting president of APA and all the future candidates for president. The letter did not reveal that it was paid for by a gay activist organization.

Socarides and his rat pack howled when they learned about the letter. They publicly accused APA officers of fraud and demanded an internal investigation, which could not have endeared them in the eyes of these officials. The subsequent investigation repudiated the accusers.

About ten thousand psychiatrists voted in the referendum. Fifty-eight percent supported the actions of the board, while thirty-seven percent voted against. A few years later, due to the lobbying of a number of psychiatrists, particularly Richard Pillard in Boston, ego-dystonic homosexuality was removed from *DSM*.

Ironically, Socarides was an ideal opponent because his abrasive, bull-in-the-china-shop personality offended most of his colleagues. The man's pomposity knew no limits. He taught a course on sexuality at Albert Einstein College of Medicine in the Bronx. One night, Socarides invited a few of his medical students for dinner and proceeded to regale them with his ability to spot a homosexual, "The result," he boasted, "of my many years of clinical acumen." After dinner the three students went out dancing together at a gay bar! Socarides's own son was gay, but we kept the secret, believing it unconscionable to use the son against the father. His son came out years later, and went on to become President Clinton's gay liaison in the White House—which had not the slightest effect upon the elder Socarides's beliefs about homosexuality.

Socarides never forgave me for my role in the APA decision. Some years ago I tried to join the *National Association of Research and Therapy of Homosexuality* (NARTH), an anti-homosexual "professional" organization of which he was then president. In a letter from Joseph Nicolosi, its executive director, who also claims to cure homosexuals, I was rejected for membership because, "We consider your professional views and objectives as too radically opposed to ours."

One of the criticisms leveled against the APA for removing homosexuality as a disorder is that science does not advance by a vote of hands. These critics forget that any list is produced by a group of people who vote for or against it in the first place. Science I learned from my reading of diagnostic systems has little to do with it. More recently astronomers voted on whether or not Pluto was a planet. Every system of classification or diagnosis eventually ends in the process of a vote.

About a month after the vote of the APA Board of Trustees, the television program *60 Minutes* decided to do a segment on the diagnostic change and asked to interview me at the Institute for Human Identity (IHI), a gay professional counseling center I founded. It was an excellent way of publicizing the new normative status of homosexuality to gay people everywhere, especially since the program was the top-rated program on television. It would also publicize the services of IHI. There was one problem however; I was not yet out to my mother who lived in Miami. *60 Minutes* was one of her favorite TV programs and she and her "girlfriends" at her Florida condominium were sure to watch it. I had to tell her first. While the word homosexual or its Jewish equivalent "feygelah" was never mentioned at home, I knew that coming out to her was going to end in a scene but it had to be done.

By coincidence, my mother had decided to visit on just the day that *60 Minutes* was to do the filming at my office. As luck would have it, she arrived on the same day as the show was scheduled to be taped. Because her plane was late, she walked into my office just a couple of hours before the camera crew was due to arrive. I wanted to talk to her immediately, but she announced that she was going to do my laundry! The dirty clothes safely in the washing machine, she finally returned and sat down in my office, as my assistant, Michael Giovinco (who knew what was on my agenda) closed the door and held my calls.

My mother was obviously curious and proud that her son was to appear on *60 Minutes*. I told her that the program was about homosexuality.

"But why do they want to interview you?" she asked.

"Because," I said, "I'm a homosexual."

First a gasp, then a look of shock. She was about to say something when my door opened and the TV crew came walking in (early) bringing huge floodlights, cameras on rolling dollys, and massive coils of electrical wire. My mother sat dazed in the chair as the crew set up; then, without a word, she retired to her quarters and refused to budge.

The taping consumed the next few hours. Morley Safer interviewed me about the nomenclature change and then taped me conducting a "therapy session" with a patient. The patient was a Mormon whose religion condemns homosexuality, and he jumped at the chance to declare his gayness from coast to coast. Finally, Safer interviewed Barbara Gittings, a hero of the early gay rights movement.

After the camera crew left my office, William, Barbara, Michael, my mother and my patient sat and talked about the evening. Barbara knew about my coming out to my mother. She had come out to hers under similar circumstances when she had appeared on the *David Suskind Show* a couple of years earlier. She tried to smooth things over.

"Oh, you must be Charles's mother. I can see the family resemblance," Barbara said under the false impression that she was talking to a rational woman.

"Are you a lesbian?" my mother asked, more an accusation than a question. "Yes," Barbara replied.

"Well," my mother said, shaking her finger in Barbara's face. "Then I think you're sick, too," and walked out of the room.

She went to my bedroom where she called my brother and sister-in-law to tell them what I had "just done to her." To their chagrin, she left the next day to stay with them for the following two weeks.

Airing the program gave gay people throughout the country an important psychological boost, and my mother, who by that time had gotten over the shock, instructed all her girlfriends in Miami to watch "my son, the doctor."

The effect of the nomenclature change was electric. On the most obvious level, the diagnostic status of homosexuality, the change meant that the psychiatric/psychological profession had no justification for continuing to alter an individual's sexual orientation. Sodomy laws in almost all of the states depended upon the medical opinion that homosexuality was perverse, and the APA decision laid the groundwork to challenge these laws. The publicity around the event also encouraged many gay people to come out, as if the APA had given them permission to disclose their sexuality to friends and family. For gay men who hated their homosexuality, the announcement was like an elixir that restored self-esteem.

Shortly thereafter, the American Psychological Association and the National Association of Social Workers publicly supported the APA resolution. Previously, gay people in these professional organizations had been in the closet, but by the mid-1970s these groups had gay caucuses politicking for change.

But how did we create the fertile soil in which to bring about this momentous change? It was the result of the radical gay politics of the early 1970s and its effect upon social change. The emotional reaction of the psychiatrists to our activities put the power of social change into the hands of gay liberationists. We were the ones who manipulated conflict and dissension according to our own schedule and we were the ones with whom they had to negotiate. If one group of professionals or civic leaders refused to negotiate with us, another would, raising dissension between them. In the end, step-by-step, our demands would be met.

We were very different from the previous generation of gay activists. The organizations that came before us such as Mattachine and the Daughters of Bilitus, were assimilationists; they wanted to be perceived by the power structure as good boys and girls. That is why when picketing the White House in 1965 (an extraordinary act of bravery given the times) they had a dress code. Men were required to wear suits and ties and women wore dresses. They wanted to fit in, to say that we are not different than everyone else. Other organizations called themselves "homophile," not homosexual or gay. They welcomed a dialogue with the power structure, but as we later radicals believed, were too complacent to compromise. As the 1970s radical gay movement began, there was little communication between us and these men and women from the earlier generation. They were too careful for our taste. From their point of view, we were too "lefty," and too confrontational.

There is another salient argument to make about the radical gay movement and social change. The Black Liberation Movement taught us an important lesson. Martin Luther King, Jr. saw himself as a moral voice demanding that America change its racist society and his confrontations with the police were well publicized in the media. I remember how angry white people became when he spoke out in opposition to the Vietnam War. Although nonviolent, he was identified as a black *radical* revolutionary who had to be stopped. The FBI watched him carefully including placing a recording device under his bed.

Then Malcolm X, the Black Muslim leader, appeared on the scene preaching a revolutionary doctrine that included the possibility of violence. While King told his followers to "turn the other cheek" if clubbed by police or bitten by their dogs, Malcolm suggested that violence might be the Black Muslim response to violence against them. The Black Panthers also joined the potentially violent Black rebellion. Suddenly, Martin Luther King, Jr. was no longer perceived by white America as a radical. He had not changed his philosophy or confrontational tactics one iota, yet white America's fear of the Black Muslims and the Black Panthers changed their perception of King. *Contrast between groups determines who is perceived as radical and who as moderate.*

The point is that there is a symbiotic relationship between radical and moderate social movements. They need each other although the proposition is repugnant to both of them. Even when fighting for the same cause, radicals invariably perceive moderates as defeatists who would sell the radicals down the drain, while moderates consider radicals to be mentally unbalanced publicity hounds who prevent quiet and effective negotiation. The radical gay movement defined the problem for gays in America, identified the cure, planned and carried out public confrontations. Their members—young, educated, newly employed or not employed at all—had the least to lose personally. But gays in the professions and in business were frightened of the movement. They wanted things done "quietly," without getting anyone upset. Moderate gays would never have come out of the closet and faced TV cameras, the potential beatings on the street by police and the public confrontations. They rightly feared the loss of their jobs and the exposure of their homosexuality to colleagues and family.

The power for social change, therefore, began with radical gay politics. Moderate gay groups became more acceptable to the heterosexual majority because of their contrast to gay radicals, in much the same way as Malcolm made King look like a moderate. Moderate gay groups were much more likely to cozy up with police, politicians, professional and business groups, and to meet with them privately and compromise over goals. The question of when to compromise was always one of timing, something that needed the wisdom of a Solomon. The lesson is that in a conflict between moderate and radical politics, solutions always move toward the center.

Every movement has a *modus operandi*, a manner of working with built-in strengths and weaknesses. This was certainly true of gay militants. We had much strength: we were highly organized with clear goals, an effective hierarchical system for planning and carrying out public demonstrations, and reasonable control over members (at least in public). But our greatest weakness was exactly the same as that of the homophobes. We both shared the trait of self-righteousness, the belief that we were one hundred percent right and that no compromise was acceptable. I understand the problem having suffered from it myself for many years.

Gay militants performed a delicate dance between dissension and dialogue, using conflict as the means of increasing tension. It shocked the body politic, disturbed complacency, shattered icons, and boldly challenged authority. It infuriated the ordinary citizen who saw in the gay radicals an attempt to destroy the values he held dear. From this point of view, conflict is a positive strategy, for out of the competition of ideas, of moral positions, out of anger, and sometimes the desire to destroy, social change may result. It is a lower-scale version of brinksmanship, so effectively used in both international and union/management conflicts. In those examples, the dangers are war or a union strike. With us the potential for violence and the disruption of a meeting or convention was the usual conflict.

The problem is knowing when to stop. Conflict for its own sake is ultimately destructive. In these social conflicts someone has "to blink," hold back and say, "This is getting out of hand." Then the opposing groups, each representing competing social values, can agree that dialogue must replace dissension lest chaos take control, sit down together and come to an agreeable resolution. This is exactly what gay militants longed for. By these tactics, gay radicals made homosexuality a public issue and placed the subject of gay civil rights on the American agenda. Psychiatric groups could always be depended upon to shoot themselves in the foot when faced with conflict due to their inherent self-righteousness.

GAA was not my first experience in radical politics, but it fine-tuned what I had learned earlier as an activist against the war in Vietnam. The gay radical movement was first and foremost a child of the nonviolent movement originated by Gandhi in India and continued by Martin Luther King, Jr. in the United States. Gay liberation, therefore, was laid upon a foundation of morality, upon the proposition that a good society treated its members in an egalitarian manner. The belief that prejudice against gay people was morally wrong provided the glue to bind together a group of people who had previously been isolated from one another, such as street people, transvestites, hustlers, college students and those professional people who joined the movement in the early 1970s. Whatever conflicts existed between their life-styles, and there were many, they forged a union against the homophobic institutions of society.

I have often thought about how to stop a demonstration by gay radicals. I would make every attempt to co-opt the demonstrators. Here is what I would do.

First I would invite them in for tea. I mean this as a metaphor for welcoming them warmly—although if they were standing outside on a cold day, I would certainly provide them with tea and coffee. If they accepted this gesture, I would be halfway to victory over them. I would then join the crowd of demonstrators and ask them about their concerns. After talking in the street for a while, I would invite them into my office/ building/convention to express their complaints to me and a few trusted others. My goal would be to create conflict within the group, to get them talking about me and my intentions, rather than about their complaints. It also would get them off the street, where they can be seen, and into my building where they cannot. Some of them will come to the conclusion (right or wrong) that I am not such a bad guy after all. A few will realize (correctly) that I am willing to make some concessions to their goals, and to do something concrete to fight prejudice against gay people. I would also have picked up the appropriate jargon—I would say gay, not homosexual; homophobia (or heterosexist depending upon which word they used), not discrimination. Adopting the language would help to bind us together, one of my intentions since I would use it to neutralize their effectiveness. I would finally suggest that the gay radicals choose two or three people to join an equal number (equality has symbolic value) of my representatives, and to meet together in the future to make recommendations about change within my office/organization/ institution. What more could they have asked? After shaking hands all around and thanking them for the meeting, I would politely get rid of them.

The object of this grand manipulation is to co-opt the demands of the gay group away from them and onto me. By taking the initiative I take the wind out of their sails. One of the great characteristics of American society is its ability to integrate competing groups and values. That is the goal of co-opting a radical group.

Which brings us to the question of ego. There are people who are capable of separating personal emotional needs from the social goals of the movement. For others every momentary setback becomes a bleeding personal wound leading to a sense of futility. Incapable of compromise, they act as if flesh were being torn from their bodies and brand as a Judas anyone who would accept only half the pie. These people are often the most valued during the early days of a civil rights movement because of their limitless energy, but they end up in conflict with their colleagues because they cannot stop fighting. In order to be successful in the long run, one has to develop the capacity to wear two hats, one public, bellicose and demanding, the other private, softer, still wily, looking for accommodation.

Still, this analysis of the strategies of gay liberation politics does not explain why some gay men and women came to the forefront of the fight rather than others. It is true that every generation of advocates banging on the door of society demanding to be let in stands on the shoulders of those who came before. There must be, however, a personal story to the men and women who led and who continue to lead the battle for gay rights beside the organizational one. Why did I, for instance, welcome a leadership role in challenging authority? It led to no financial advantage or welcome into my profession of psychology. In fact other psychologists and psychiatrists, particularly gay ones, avoided me lest they be tainted by my openness.

There are some events from my childhood that may explain my public opposition to discrimination and unjust social rules. They both involve my parents. Here is the first of them.

In the 1930s and 40s, doctors believed that enemas were a good prescription for fighting disease. I do not know how this bizarre belief originated, but I would like to smack whoever invented the idea in the name of all children of that generation. They also believed that children should get them on a regular basis, whether ill or not. The procedure was as follows. A large rubber bag containing many gallons (at least it felt that way) of warm, soapy water was hooked up to the medicine chest in the bathroom. A long, rubber hose projected from the bottom of the bag, leading to the tip, a hard, black projectile whose *raison d'être* was to be shoved up my ass. Attached to the hose was a clip that when snapped closed, blocked the stream of water. When opened the water flowed freely through the rigid, black rod and into the bowels of the child victim. The child was told to hold onto the oceans of water flooding his colon—hold on, hold on—until one of his parents finally gave him permission to plunk himself on the toilet and fire out the tainted water and all those bad bacteria lurking in his butt. Never mind the screams, howls, cursing, biting and scratching of the child.

I can just hear some people wondering if that explains why I became gay, all those dildoes up my ass. But children often have tricks of their own and vengeance, despite the Biblical injunction, is one of the powers of childhood. Enemas were useful training grounds for my future life. Although I would be less than candid to say that I looked forward to them, they taught me an important lesson at a very early age.

As a child I witnessed the behavior of my parents and eight sets of aunts and uncles. The women were all power-houses lording it over one another and competing for attention and yet still greater power. My uncles sat still, watching ball games on TV, agreeing with their wives, and generally being the passive schmucks they were trained to be. I learned quite early that passivity leads to victimization and I decided not to sit silently by, as my father and uncles did, in the face of a strong but unfair enemy force. Like General Custer's defeat by the Indians, I would "die with my boots on"—or actually off, in the case of the enemas.

It was young, naked Charlie against the grown-ups and I had no intention of losing the battle. My father held me face down on his lap, the bulls-eye squinting meanly up at him. Then, according to their prearranged plan, my mother attempted to plunge the weapon deep into me. First I would squiggle to one side, then the other disrupting her aim. She blamed my father for not holding me tightly enough. "A good beginning," I thought to myself. The ballet continued as I started bouncing on my father's lap, forcefully pushing my butt high in the air, then down again and repeating the process over and over. Even one's mother cannot aim accurately enough to get an ass-hole on the run. In an occasional finale to the family *pas de trois*, I reached up, grabbed the rubber hose and yanked it like hell, tearing the swollen, red bag from the medicine chest. This action led to expressions of shock on the faces of my parents as one of them got clobbered by the bag full of warm, soapy water and bliss on my own, caring not a whit which one the bag landed on, since the overflow drenched us all. They blamed each other for the catastrophe and to me their mutual recriminations were like savoring a dish of Ambrosia. My father may have smacked my ass, but no matter. I had won the battle and they had to give up. Once released, naked Charlie flew out of the bathroom, leaving his parents to clean up the mess.

There were also times when my father or mother held me down so tightly that I could neither squirm nor reach the hose. At such moments, I was unable to stave off the inevitable and even though I would padlock my sphincter tightly, one or the other was able to jab me, while the other released the hose clip. There was nothing I could do then and the water flowed into my bowels. But I was not yet defeated. Their moment of weakness came when I was supposed to sit on the toilet and evacuate the water. Young as I was, my motto was, "If it's shit they want, it's shit they'll get." Squeezing tightly, then unlocking my sphincter with a big squeeze, a geyser rose into the air and settled down on them and me. They did not like this. My father beat the hell out of me, but his violence only proved my victory. They were still left with the task of cleaning up.

These battles were finally too much for them to handle and they stopped giving me enemas. I had won the war. I learned that I could fight my parents, I could fight authority, and I could win. The experience also taught me that my parents and therefore all authorities, are sometimes wrong and that in those cases they should be opposed. From that point on, rebellion against arbitrary authority became a significant part of my character.

For this reason I seldom sought my father's advice. Because he worked a night shift he was not around that much, and when he was, his impulsive temperament was an impediment to communication. On one occasion, however, I did consult with him about a problem I was having in Junior High School. A bully we referred to as "Little Hitler," was repeatedly picking on me. He hit me for no other reason than that it pleased him. He shoved me because he wanted to stand in my spot.

He called me names—"shit-head, fuck-head, prick, fag"—because he had not insulted anyone in the schoolyard for the previous 30 seconds. If he passed me in the hallway and if no teacher was watching, he shoved me into the wall. These displays of aggression were always performed in front of an audience of other kids.

I was all of twelve years old and hardly experienced as a street fighter; nor did I aspire to either frighten or be frightened by other kids. My first line of inquiry was to seek counsel from my fellow schoolmates because they too, had experienced his wrath. "He's going to fuckin' kill you," said one, an honest assessment, if not exactly the help I needed. Another advised me to run faster when Little Hitler arrived on the scene.

I brought my dilemma to my parents. "Stay away from him," my mother said, a thoroughly useless admonition because as every kid knows a bully comes over to you. "Then you move somewhere else." She still did not get the point. My father joined the discussion, telling my mother that it was not my fault that I was being picked on and that she should not blame me for the problem. Then he turned to me. "A bully," he said, "is a coward, who only picks on small kids because he can get away with it. He would never pick on someone bigger, because he'd be afraid to get beaten up."

His analysis was impeccable, but I did not see how it would relieve my problem.

"You have to fight him," my father said. "Go over to him and hit him good and hard in the face. Knock him down. Then fight him as hard as you can. It doesn't make any difference whether you win or lose. Just make sure he gets hurt. Then, he'll never pick on you again."

Has he gone mad? I thought. Didn't he understand that Little Hitler would beat the crap out of me?

"That doesn't matter," he said. "He'll stop picking on you when he finds out that you'll fight back."

Easy for him to say. I wondered why he wouldn't just phone his old Murder Incorporated friends to eliminate Little Hitler. Meanwhile, my mother was screaming in the background not to fight.

A few days later when Little Hitler walked over and pushed me as usual, I socked him hard in the face and knocked him down. He lay on the ground for a few seconds in shock. I was also in shock realizing what I had done and what he was about to do to me in return. Then he jumped up and proceeded to beat the shit out of me. When teachers finally arrived and interceded, I was bleeding from the nose and mouth, my shirt had been torn from my body and I was covered with dirt. By evening I would have a black eye. But Little Hitler also had a bloody nose and his shirt was ripped, although in no way would I suggest that he got as good as he gave. I was a celebrity to my friends, all of whom, though congratulating me for having survived, thought I was out of my mind for fighting back.

At home, my mother went through the usual hysterics, blaming my injuries and torn clothes on my father. He took a steak from the refrigerator and placed it over my black eye—the traditional (ineffective) cure for black eyes in those days. He said that he was proud of me for standing up for myself.

My father was right. The bully never hit me again. My fight in the schoolyard became a metaphor for how I wanted to stand up to all the bullies around me and later to the bully called society. I learned that I did not have to be passive in the face of oppressive forces. I began to defend friends who were weaker than I. It was a moral issue; you do not attack kids who are physically weaker than you. I was no better a fighter, but it was not about how to hurt an opponent. I was delivering the message that I would stand up for myself and for my friends.

As I look back over my life and the political battles I have fought and sometimes won, I have my father to thank for his advice. I wish we had had more discussions like that, but it was not to be.

Charles Silverstein and William Bory at the Atrium
of the Vestal Virgins, The Forum, Rome, 1982.

Photo courtesy of the author.

Three

Black Clouds Swirled in the Sky Above Me

I was not always an indefatigable fighter for gay rights. I was not yet thirty-eight when I made my presentation to the psychiatrists. I had come out a few years before, peeked out rather than come out. The circumstances of my adolescent years explain why I was such a slow sexual learner.

Like so many gay men of my generation, my early years were spent in the shadow of sexuality. My romantic and sexual attraction to men was hidden and all my energies were devoted toward keeping them at bay. There were, however, three young men I loved and my experiences with them profoundly influenced how I would relate to future potential lovers. There is nothing unusual about the following stories; they are typical of gay people from my generation, of secrecy and fear as the motivators of one's life. They are so commonplace in gay people as to be banal for all the pain they cause to a young and inexperienced person. They are about searching for love and sex.

*

I left my house at one a.m. on a cold November night in order to travel undetected to Steve's house. I was sixteen. I arrived at two a.m. and waited on the bench across the street. After a few minutes and satisfied that no one had seen me I walked up the flight of stairs to Steve's apartment. In those prewar buildings, the hallways were long and wide, the floors covered with octagonal white tiles rimmed by simple geometric designs, a bright blue-ish glare everywhere cast by the large, ugly fluorescent lamps overhead. For the next couple of hours I sat quietly alone on the hallway floor outside Steve's apartment, accompanied only by my fantasy of making love to him.

We had met that summer in Boy Scout camp. I was assistant postmaster. The boys, ages fourteen to sixteen lived in lean-tos. After taps I would visit them, sitting on one bed after another, joking with them about the day or gossiping and teasing. I always lingered most at Steve's bed.

At fifteen, Steve was a bit taller than the rest, slender as most boys are at that age. He had dirty blond hair, a broad smile, bright blue eyes, a magnetic, warm personality, and boundless energy. I fell in love, but secretly.

After camp we became buddies. Every Saturday we went to the movies. We attended scout meetings and went on overnight hikes together. We often slept together at his house or mine. That was the most painful, each of us only in his underwear. I bantered with him when I desperately wanted to gaze into his eyes. I pretended to sleep when Morpheus himself could not temper my excitement. At the end of each day, I returned home rejuvenated; I masturbated every night to my fantasy of holding and kissing him.

I wanted to confess my love for him. For hours I would sit on the cold tile floor outside his apartment at night practicing what I would say but I instinctively knew that he was straight and eventually I realized the futility of declaring my homosexuality. I left the hallway and returned home. Yet I would return another night embracing myself in his hallway imagining I was holding Steve. By five a.m. at the latest, I was back at home, undressed and asleep, embracing my pillow. Later it was time to meet Steve for our Saturday together. He never knew how often I spent the night outside his door.

We were both from working-class families, but I aspired to go to college. He did not. I was accepted to New Paltz, part of the State University of New York; attending meant leaving New York City. The idea thrilled me, but infuriated Steve. I was completely baffled by his anger. Now I see that he felt abandoned but back then I could not fathom how deeply he cared for me. He loved me as surely as I did him, although a sexual relationship was never on his agenda.

He did everything possible to convince me to remain in New York. When I refused, he dropped me. He would not meet me or answer my phone calls. In college I wrote him letters, asking him to come up and visit, offering to come back on weekends and stay with him. He never replied. At the end of my freshman year, I phoned him. His voice was distant and icy, his responses clipped and hostile. No, he did not have time to get together that weekend, and he was not sure what his schedule was the next week.

Steve was the first man I ever loved, and I thought about him for decades. There are times, still, when I wonder where he is, what he is like, whether he thinks about those teen years as often as I do.

*

In the summer of 1952, I was seventeen, a Scoutmaster at Ten Mile River Scout Camp. Pete was 16 years old. He was shorter than most of the other boys, but his blond hair, puffed up into an enormous pompadour rose at least four inches above his head. It was his most prized possession, and he combed it compulsively. Pete had an androgynous face, and although I condemned such characteristics in myself, I admired it in him.

About midsummer, thirty of us—twenty-seven boys and three leaders—headed for a three-day trip up Slide Mountain in the Catskills Mountains. At about three p.m. we stopped for the night on the summit of Mt. Wittenberg, a large exposed ridge of rock two-thirds of the way on our journey. It looked out over the entire Hudson River Valley, a breathtaking sight.

Then began the fiercest storm in the history of the Catskills. The wind drove huge pine trees to the ground, lightning struck around us. Hail pelted us like grape shot from cannons. Terrified, we ran down the mountain jumping over huge pine trees that blocked our path leaving our equipment where we had camped.

At the bottom of the mountain a wooden suspension bridge was only inches above the torrential stream that only hours before had been a trickling brook. We lined up on the other side and ran to a nearby house where a wonderful elderly couple sheltered us. We counted heads. Three boys were lost on the mountain. I looked for Pete. He was not there. I walked outside, looking up at the mountain. Pete was somewhere in that blackness, alive or dead or, worse, injured and in pain. Standing in safety, I felt profoundly guilty and began to cry, confident that with the storm as background no one could see or hear me.

At dawn, a party of local people and forest rangers arrived to search for the three missing boys. The rest of us were ordered to remain in our temporary shelter.

"They're coming back," someone yelled. The search party was just a couple of hundred yards away, emerging from the mist that surrounded the forest. First one scout, then another came clearly into sight. Finally I saw Pete alive and well.

Two of the boys, now heroes, immediately started chatting away, describing what had happened to them. But Pete moved quickly through the crowd and headed straight toward me, his eyes looking downward, hands in his pockets. As he stood before me, he placed his head on my shoulders and softly moved it back and forth just barely touching my face with his nose. I put my arms around him and held him tight, and we stood, silent, holding one another. There must have been a point when we realized that we were being observed and we let go and walked toward the house, my arm on his shoulder, his hand around my waist, the tips of our fingers moving minutely against each other's body.

"Got a comb?" Pete asked. His hair was a mess. The words broke the emotional spell which was getting dangerously close to love—at least mine were.

We had yet to spend two more weeks together in scout camp. I was too timid to take the sexual initiative. For the rest of summer, I was in a constant state of emotional arousal.

This happened a year after I had met Steve. Although I continued to see Steve weekly, Pete and I met only sporadically. I wallowed in lonely misery. Given a choice, I preferred the pain of unrequited love to the agony of what I was certain would be rejection. As with Steve, I lost track of Pete when I entered college.

*

In August 1970, the American Psychological Association held its annual meeting in Miami. A graduate student in Psychology, I was eager to hear the papers and seminars about personality theory and psychopathology that would be so important in my life's work. Then thirty-five, I had read many psychology books about homosexuality, but I had no idea what homosexuals were like as people.

I had two days driving down south to think about my impossible predicament: my failing personal psychoanalysis, the women I was dating despite my powerful sexual fantasies about men. All jumbled together they cooked a bitter stew that was impossible to digest.

On the second day of the convention, I noticed a sign that announced a meeting of a new interest group, the Association of Women in Psychology. There, I thought, I would find my kind of people, psychologists who wanted to associate together in order to affect an egalitarian society.

Twenty or thirty men and women attended the meeting, and they all agreed that the time was right to look after women's interests in psychology. I noticed a tall, dark-haired young man, obviously an undergraduate, sitting a few rows away, who contributed many perceptive comments. I could see the minute changes of facial expression as he agreed or disagreed with the others. I realized that he could see me as well, and when our eyes met the connection was made. I felt powerfully drawn to him and I knew that he was drawn to me, although I had no reason to believe his feelings were sexual.

Mark was part of an intellectual elite of students who were, ironically, protesting elitism in America. He read and talked about all the important darlings of his generation. He admired the writings of Wilhelm Reich (a student of Freud) who had invented the "orgone box," become psychotic, and died in a mental hospital. Mark quoted from Mao's Red Book, read everything available about the women's movement, the Black movement, and wanted psychology to help the masses. He even spoke approvingly of homosexuals banding together to demand their rights. Bisexuality was politically correct at the time, so Mark claimed that all people were bisexual. But I did not interpret this as suggesting that he had even the slightest sexual interest in men.

Mark was over six feet tall, with shoulder-length brown hair. His beautiful face could easily have belonged to either a man or a woman, and his androgyny was instantly appealing to me. As our friendship developed, Mark would often sit on the floor, shirtless, playing the guitar, occasionally brushing the hair from his eyes. His body was a wonder, every muscle finely etched. His hairless chest and stomach were flat and well defined, his legs long and muscular, his ass hard. My admiration for Mark's body was all the greater as a contrast to my own which I viewed as unappealing, my face plain, at best. It was the face my father often called ugly. I wondered what Mark's penis looked like; his bulky pants gave no clue. Mark often came into the city on weekends in order to attend radical meetings and he invariably slept at my Inwood apartment. When we shared a bed, I monitored myself carefully, looking away as he undressed to his underwear, keeping secret my increasing heartbeat and breathing. Of course, he had no idea how driven I felt to touch his body, kiss his lips, or to fondle the penis I never saw.

Soul mates give to each other what the other lacks and thus become united. My part was psychological. I was ten years older, worldlier than Mark and already serving my apprenticeship as a psychologist. I easily slipped into the role of mentor who would guide him to self-realization. Over the course of the next year or so, I became the reliable advisor to whom he turned before making up his mind about some issue. I was loving father to Mark's loving son. Mark, however, never took anything without giving something in return, and he was capable of the tenderest moments, even tears during thoughts of sadness. He would even touch or hold me.

I finally decided to tell Mark that I was gay—but not how powerfully attracted I was to him. The opportunity arose one day when he called and asked to stay at my apartment for the weekend in order to attend a radical political meeting in New York City. I was overjoyed when he arrived. The two of us sat and talked in the living room for hours. Finally, I bolstered my spirits for the ultimate acceptance or rejection.

"Mark, I want to tell you something you don't know about me. I'm gay. I've always been attracted to men, sexually."

Mark was always good at getting to the heart of a question. After a long pause, he asked, "Are you sexually attracted to me?"

"Yes."

I do not remember what I said afterward. I had to conceal the intense level of excitement in my body. I probably tried to divert the conversation by talking about sentimentality and friendship.

"Perhaps we should sleep apart tonight."

"I thought maybe we could talk more."

"No, I think we need the physical separation, to sort things out. I'll sleep here on the couch."

"Maybe we should talk more about it now?"

"No, I need time to think about what I want to do."

As I walked toward my bedroom Mark called out, "Could you close the door, please?" Never before in my life, nor since, have I felt so steep a slide into depression. It seemed to me that I had done a reprehensible thing. I lay on my bed, unable to breathe, my chest jammed tight. I looked up at blackness, feeling rejected, helpless, listening intently for any sound from the living room that might give me some sign of what Mark was doing. As long as I heard something, I knew Mark was still there and that we might still be friends in the morning.

Then a different sound: the front door being opened and closing shut. Silence. My chest unlocked, and an awful scream rose out of it. My bed whirled. Black clouds swirled in the sky above me.

*

There was a price to be paid for the insularity of my life, the inability to connect romantically and sexually with another man. I felt so helpless that I came to believe that I was unlovable. My state of unlovability merged with my terror of abandonment and led, inevitably, to a belief that no man could love me as desperately as I would love him. Therefore—and this is the crucial and deadly conclusion—for my own sake and for the little pleasure that I could get out of life, I would have to settle for what I could get and ask for no more.

I had fallen in love with these three straight men, which in the absence of gay alternatives invariably leads to obsessions, then to depression. At various times my every thought was of Steve, Pete or Mark. I repeated things they said to me over and over again. I would touch some piece of clothing or a card they had left in my house. I would look at pictures I had taken of them and cried to recordings of songs that reminded me of them. At night I hugged one of them in my sleep, but woke up in the morning alone. It was a painful way to live, but it was the only way I knew.

The next step in my self-induced torture was to do everything possible to hold onto men I loved. I do not mean I bought expensive gifts, although I might have done that if I had had the money. Instead I provided whatever I thought they wanted, in the hope that they would appreciate my love for them. My gift-giving, mostly symbolic things like doing favors, was an insurance policy against their leaving. Perhaps if I knew some compassionate person to talk to, I might have overcome my sense of isolation and darkness, but talking to someone else about this dilemma was unthinkable.

These days I am heartened and amazed by gay adolescents who do not, will not stop their sexual adventures, even in the face of the direst condemnation, including physical and psychological punishment. How I envy their bravery and determination to search for love. How I wish I had been one of them.

Four

I Rue the Day I Made that Decision

It was after one of those nights outside Steve's hallway that I first sought help. But who could a sixteen-year-old boy talk to? The only person I could think of was our family physician whom I begged not to tell my parents. It was the fastest doctor's appointment I ever had. I told him that I had "homosexual tendencies," the euphemism of the day. He picked up his prescription pad, scribbled something on it and passed it to me. "Go here," he said. Then he quickly left the room. On the paper was written "Mental Health Clinic Kings County Hospital." It was only a ten-minute walk from my house.

Behind the desk of a cold hospital office sat a man in his shirtsleeves, smoking a cigar just the way my uncle did, attending more to what was in his mouth than in the world around him. Two men sat at the far end of the room, notepads on their laps. The doctor introduced himself, but not the others. Between questions he took puffs on his smelly cigar and blew smoke in the air.

I was flooded with fear. I sought treatment because it was supposed to be confidential and here I had an audience. Who were these two men in the corner of the room? My interrogator was oblivious to the fact that I was scared to death. He offered not a word of warmth or friendliness. I do not remember what I told him, but it could not have been much.

At the end of the interview, he told me that I had to see Dr. so and so. He led me and the party of anonymous men down the hall to another office. On a large upholstered chair was a very skinny man sitting lotus style, sporting a Fu Manchu mustache. He never looked at me or changed the expression on his face. In his office was a woman sitting off to the side. She too had a pad of paper on her lap. When I sat down the skinny one said, "So I hear you think you're a homosexual." The words shot through me like a bolt of lightning. He and the other four anonymous observers in the room terrified me. I hemmed and hawed the answer to the question, and to the next and the next. Then, overwhelmed with anxiety and mistrust, I said, "I'm getting out of here," and feeling deeply betrayed bolted from the room.

I began to read books about homosexuality. Professionals were interested only in two questions: What causes it and how can we cure it? The prevailing psychoanalytic theory was that the cause of homosexuality was an overprotective mother and a hostile, distant father. Had these authors been peeking through the windows of my home?

The treatment was also plainly stated. Psychoanalysis for many years would resolve (whatever that meant) the intra-familial conflicts of childhood. A homosexual man could then change his identification from female to male, fall in love with a woman and father a family. It all made sense to me.

Every book, however, contained two ominous comments repeated over and over again. First, treatment was hopeless unless the homosexual were highly motivated to change. His motivation was shown by giving up homosexual sex and substituting sex with women. The second admonition frightened me even more. It was a warning that sometimes homosexuals could not be changed into "normal" people because they were so weak in character that they could not withstand the anxiety aroused by psychoanalysis. For the sake of compassion, said the psychiatrists, we should try to help these unfortunate men "adjust" to their homosexuality. The idea of being "adjusted" burned a hole in me. "These unfortunate homosexuals," one psychiatrist wrote of those unable to become heterosexual, "could learn to tolerate their limitations in life," even though it meant accepting a loveless life, decadent sexuality, deep depression and perhaps suicide. I could hear the condescension in his tone. All I could do was promise myself that under no circumstances would I "adjust" to homosexuality.

I rue the day I made that decision. It fostered a sense of contempt for people who had allowed themselves the freedom to live a gay life. I have often wondered how different my life might have been had I seen "adjustment" as an opportunity rather than as a curse. There are so many forks in the road as we make decisions in life. I thought I saw this fork clearly. One road led to respectability, the other to homosexuality. I chose the wrong one.

Many years later, I walked into the office of a psychoanalyst. I had already graduated from college, but I still had not had sex with either a man or a woman. With some suspicion because of my previous experience in Brooklyn, I told him about the problem. After only a few minutes I relaxed, sensing that he was warmer and friendlier than those idiots from my teen years. I told him that my goal was to become heterosexual and that I would not accept adjustment to a homosexual life. If he had refused my request, I would have walked out. As it was, he agreed that since I was still young, had never had gay sex, and was highly motivated, curing my homosexuality was the obvious goal. With these words, both he and I conspired to spend the next seven years in a futile, guilt-producing, and expensive exercise in sexual repression. I do not blame him for wanting to cure my homosexual desires, any more then I blame myself for demanding it. We were both victims of the heterosexist world in which we lived.

I saw him three times a week. Year after year I lay on the couch and confessed my fantasies, cherished moments of masturbation in which the scenarios provided my only source of nurturance. Then, feeling guilty that my dead father could see and disapprove, I confessed the sin to my symbolic father, the psychoanalyst.

None of the women I dated knew that they were filling a prescription from my therapist. They were as warm and caring as Steve and Mark. I certainly loved, cared for, and wanted them in my life, but I did not desire them sexually. The root cause of our problems, however, was not my homosexuality as my analyst maintained, but pretending that I was heterosexual. When it got too hot in the kitchen, I dropped them.

For instance, in 1968, I was in my third year as a Ph.D. student in clinical psychology and still in the closet. A group of us who were taking our comprehensive exams began talking about what we wanted to do afterward. When my turn came, I announced that I would like to fuck someone all night long—a safe, if adolescent boast, like throwing pepper into the nostrils of bloodhounds who might otherwise sniff out one's real desires.

"You can fuck me all night," Margo said. We had always been friendly in the past, but I was oblivious that she was sexually interested in me.

I was trapped; the Kinsey 6 had convinced his colleagues that he was a Kinsey 1, and now I had to go through with it. "I'll have supper waiting for you when you come home after the exams," she said. "Then, we'll get naked." Just what I wanted to hear! The day after the exams, my fellow students buzzed around me to learn out what had happened.

I told them Margo and I had had a great time. We did not. It was one of the worst experiences of my life. I did not want to be there, did not want to kiss her, to fondle her breasts, to play with her vagina. And I wanted her to keep her hands off my cock, not put it in her mouth—and to stop asking me to "put it in my cunt." Not only was I unable to get it up, I suffered from total anesthesia of my penis. Margo was wonderful, sensitive, and caring. She left the next morning and we never talked about it, a gift of kindness on her part. Later I would envy how relaxed she had been, in contrast to the basket case beside her.

I was an obvious failure as a psychoanalytic patient. My relationship with women only ended in disaster, and my homosexual desire was increasing. I also failed the exams and was thrown out of the psychology program. I was without a profession, without someone to love and still alienated from my family. It was as if I had been walking a road and come to a sudden dead end. I could not go forward or backward or find a direction that might clear up the haze that surrounded me. (A year later I would enter Rutgers University, where I completed my Ph.D. in psychology.)

I particularly liked and trusted Betsy, a consultant to the psychology program, and chose to tell her the whole story. She listened carefully as I reviewed my failed history of psychoanalysis, and my equally failed sexual relationships with women.

"What homosexual experiences have you had?" she asked.

"None," I answered.

"Why not?"

I sat in my chair dumbfounded. No one had ever before asked me that. Her question presupposed that having a homosexual experience did not make me bad. When I left her that evening, I was determined to stop my psychoanalysis and come out as a gay man.

I was ready. But how, where?

Five

Can I Help You Off With Your Pants?

I've often wondered what a straight boy feels at puberty. When he wakes up in the morning with come in his underwear, does he feel proud because it marks another notch toward manhood? What happens next in the straight boy's life? Through his own invention, or by learning from classmates, does he start jerking off? When he curls his toes, throws back his neck, the seizure overcomes him and he spurts out milky fluid on his belly, does he feel the full power of his masculinity? For him, the experience of puberty is like a growing flower and at the proper time, the buds unfold naturally, revealing their full inner beauty. The flower is his sexuality. He would not dream of calling it his "heterosexuality." He is too immature to understand that there are other flowers in the garden. They too have waited until their time to bloom and their buds will also open naturally, revealing different, but just as immutable sets of colors. One of these flowers is homosexuality, but I could hardly have thought of it as a flower at the time—more as a poisonous weed.

All that changed the day Betsy asked, "Why not?" She was curious that a gay man of thirty-four had not yet had sex with another man. It had the effect of giving me permission to be a homosexual—if only I knew what that meant. I was determined to find out. My path was unusual. I bought a new pair of skis that winter, and broke my leg the first day I used them. This dreadful accident had me confined to a plaster cast that began above my toes and ended below the hip. My leg, confined for nine months, looked like a leftover from a concentration camp, but with the aid of a physical therapist knowledgeable in the tortures of his profession, I nursed the weakened muscles back to normal.

During this period, I was obsessed with trying not to fall down flights of stairs or slip on the ice, and to hobble fast enough to please cab drivers.

Broken leg or not, I had to fulfill my obligations, which at the time included working full-time at Lincoln Hospital Mental Health Center in the Bronx and teaching part-time in the Psychology Department of City College.

One night a colleague invited me to dinner. Her husband, a journalist, was writing an article about sex ads in newspapers. He had an enormous collection of *Screw* and *The East Village Other*, and I started reading them after dinner. Page after page of enticing sexual come-ons made my head swim. The testosterone-producing cells in my testicles, quiescent since the days of the fracture, came to life and chugged out testosterone while I sat and read all the delicious things men wanted to do with each other.

I was overcome by lust. The previous six months had corked my sexual drive tightly under the plaster. Now that cork came popping out, as if from a bottle of champagne, and I bubbled up, giddy, intoxicated, filled with sexual energy. I determined to do something about it that night, hastily excused myself and ran (so to speak) home.

Taking a shower, I began to cry, grateful that the sound of falling water masked the sounds of my tears, as if I could hide my sadness and fear from myself. I was terrified of what I was about to do. I told myself that if I do this thing, have sex with another man, there would be no turning back. I would become one of "them." The beast would be let out of the cage, and once sensing freedom would never return to his prison. I realized how successfully I had kept myself in ignorance. For instance I did not know where to find other homosexual men. Even if I found them, how should I act? I realized the full significance of my ignorance of gay life. But the flow of testosterone would not be stilled and I dressed and drove down to Greenwich Village where I heard gay people congregated.

"Now what?" I said to myself, leaning on my crutches on a corner of Greenwich Avenue. I barely realized what an absurd sight I must have made. Then I noticed a waiter behind the counter of a coffee shop. He was obviously gay; even I could tell that. So I walked in, sat by the counter, and ordered something to eat.

"I'm from out of town and I'm looking for a gay bar. Any around here?"

"Just go to Julius's around the corner," he said.

I stood for a few seconds on the threshold of the bar, my left trouser leg ripped almost to the waist to accommodate the cast, and noticed all eyes turned toward me. Then, as if by some prearranged signal, they all turned away and continued their conversations. I stood in shock. There were so many of them.

At the bar, a number of men engaged me in conversation. My absurd appearance was a conversation piece and I was grateful to those men who chatted me up. Then a pleasant looking man, about my own age, came over and introduced himself. His name was Don, and I soon learned that he was an elementary school teacher, as I had been for six years before entering graduate school. With that in common, we talked for about an hour. He was charming, attractive, and seemed to like talking to me.

I racked my brain for a way of enticing him home.

"I have some really terrific pot," I said. "It's great shit. Why don't you come home with me and we can smoke it?"

As I look back upon that night, I see the steps of my dance, and I wish they could have been different. I should have said, "Don, you have beautiful eyes, and your lips are as enticing as the song of the Sirens. I want to make love to you." I could hardly have said such words. I was about to have my first homosexual experience, but it would be years yet before I learned to love the homosexuality in myself and in other gay men.

"Yes, where do you live."

I lived in the section of Manhattan called Inwood, the most northern neighborhood on the island. Don followed behind me in his car as I led him up the West Side Highway. While driving I wondered how we could have sex together with the cast on my leg. After we parked our cars, Don complimented me on how well I negotiated the steps leading to the door of my small apartment.

We walked down the long corridor leading to the living room.

"What a charming place," Don said, lying outrageously.

Then, standing in the center of the room, with a great flourish, I flung aside my crutches, and attacked him, frantically pulling off his shirt, opening his belt and pulling down his pants. "I guess you haven't had it for a long time," said the good-natured Don, obviously taken back by the suddenness of my attack and feeling not a little foolish standing in the center of a strange living room with his pants around his ankles.

"You have no idea," I replied as I pushed him down onto the couch, at which point I almost lost my balance and toppled over him. Sitting next to Don, I tucked my right hand under the waistband of his underwear, holding onto it tightly, while simultaneously propping my plaster cast across his legs, preventing his retreat in any direction.

The experienced Don slowed me down and reminded me of my promise of "great shit." The marijuana smoked, our bodies relaxed, he removed his pants and sat there in his underwear, while I looked long and hard at his body.

In ecstasy I rubbed my fingers gently across his chest, feeling the hairs that made up the dark line running from chest to navel and down to the top of his waistband. I touched his erection through his soft cotton briefs, at once feeling naughty and excited. Silently, he reached down and took them off.

"Can I help you off with your pants?" he asked. Only then did I realize that I had not yet taken off a stitch of clothes. I was too mesmerized by touching Don to remember to get naked myself. He slowly unzipped my fly and negotiating around the plaster cast, pulled off my pants, while at the same time I tore off my shirt. Then we retired to the bedroom, Don holding on to me so that I would not fall. I could have walked by myself, but I savored his taking care of me.

There are a limited number of sexual acts that can be performed with someone in a large plaster cast. We kissed a lot. I felt like a geographer mapping new territory, exploring first with my fingers, then my tongue. Don shifted his head down to my crotch, slowly moving his tongue across my hard dick, which, try as he might was impossible for him to suck because the edge of the cast rubbed painfully across his face. He started to masturbate me—difficult, but possible—gently taking my hand and placing it around his cock. We kissed until both of us came, and I gloried in the sounds of our ejaculations, especially my own, a series of groans no other man had ever heard before.

Don wanted to spend the night and that pleased me. We cuddled and talked until he rolled over (something I could not do) and went to sleep. I lay awake for hours. From time to time I touched his body—no place in particular, just spots here and there—lingering wherever I wanted in the joy of knowing that it was permissible. While he was awake, even after sex, I held his penis in my hand looking at it as if it were some newly found artifact from an archeological dig. Now as he slept I looked down at him, held his genitals in my hand, kissed his lips, touched his chest, then sat up and continued to look.

What a needy person I was that night and for a thousand nights yet to come. "What have I done to myself?" I screamed inside my head. All the years I had condemned my homosexuality and curtailed my passions appeared before me as if I were living a nightmare. While I gazed upon the gentle Don sleeping comfortably beside me, I remembered the hundreds of hours I spent with Steve and how successfully I censured my every action, never once telling him how much I loved him. I thought about Pete and the closeness we shared, never once talking about sex. And Mark too, whose abandonment had not yet healed in me.

Watching Don sleep that night, I decided that I would become a catalyst for change, for the acceptance of homosexuality in society so that other gay people could be spared the pains of my generation. I had no idea how to go about it, but somewhere inside of me I knew that even though feeling incomplete as a man, feeling as if there were a part of me yet unformed, I would heal myself and dedicate my professional life to healing others.

I started that night. The hours with Don had demonstrated how tender and considerate a gay man could be, so I wanted to understand why I was so prejudiced against homosexuals. In today's jargon, I asked myself about the root of my homophobia. Who was I afraid to disappoint? The answer phrased this way was clear.

I saw a vision of myself, a child of eight, returning home from a classmate's birthday party. I entered my apartment and held out my hand toward my mother, showing her the cup of candy with the colored crepe paper around it and the colored pipe-cleaner handle. "It's for you, Mommy," I said, proving yet again that I was a good boy, always ready to deprive myself of my needs to make her happy. In the cup were a variety of candies, nuts and raisins, all for her. There was nothing for me. This was the model of how I had deprived myself of passion, of love, how I vowed never to give in to my dreams. There was no homosexuality in the cup of candies, only a child's love for his mother who had declared him her personal property and to which he, in his innocence had acquiesced. Now the grown man realized what a terrible bargain he had made, how devoid of love he was and how desperately alone he felt.

At the root of my homophobia stood my parents. The more I wanted to please them, the more I hated the homosexual part of myself. Good boys were not queer. Good boys did not want to suck cock, or eat out a man's asshole, or fuck or any of the things I longed to do. My homophobia protected my parents, particularly my mother from shame. The self-hatred I felt for so many years had to be a reflection of what I believed they felt about being homosexual, being queer, being a fag. That was intimately tied up with being a man and my failure on that score was all the more humiliating to me.

In the morning I told Don about watching him sleep, about touching his body and kissing him everywhere I could reach. He asked why I had not woken him up if I wanted more sex. I said it was not sex that I craved. I do not think he understood, but why should he? I barely understood myself. I did have the good sense to tell him that the night had changed my life. I took his phone number, even though I knew I would never call. I was not yet the liberated man I aspired to be. We said our good-byes over breakfast and I let him walk out of my life.

Six

What Do You People Want?

The summer of 1970 was one of the low points in my life. I was never going to change into a heterosexual man. It was only months before that I had sex with Don. I now knew that there was an underground homosexual community in New York and where to find it. I learned from my experience with Don that men could be tender and caring, traits that formed the foundation of my night-time fantasies. I was finally prepared to come out and to learn what other homosexual men were like.

The gay activism of the 1970s is always attributed to the match that was lit at the Stonewall Inn, a seedy, Mafia-controlled bar on Christopher Street in Greenwich Village. Its habitués were the underside of gay life, hustlers and transvestites who assembled there because they felt it a sanctuary against the outside world and its potential for violence. At one a.m. on June 28, 1969, the police raided the bar and the riots began. It was our shot heard 'round the world. I did not hear the shot. I was still in the closet that weekend.

In December 1969, a dozen gay men met to found the Gay Activists Alliance (GAA), an organization devoted to fighting for the civil rights of gay people. Tom Doerr designed the Lambda as the symbol of gay liberation. For us it represented the harnessed energy of political activism. We also adopted Frank Kameny's slogan "Gay is good." One of the founding members was Marty Robinson (Tom Doerr's lover), who wrote an article for the *Village Voice* titled, "The Cure for Homosexuality is Rebellion." The rebellious tactics of GAA were in the spirit of nonviolent confrontation and in the years of its activism the organization never initiated violence or responded violently even in the face of provocation. GAA became the most successful gay activist organization of the 1970s and it was with them that I began my new life.

The GAA advertised their meetings and dances in the *Village Voice*. I read these announcements for weeks, intrigued by the notion of attending yet frightened by the idea of being seen at a public meeting. But only months before I had had sex with Don, and I remembered the promise I had made to myself to become a gay activist. I knew that I had to come out.

During the summer of 1971, I went to one of GAA's Saturday night dances. The cast had been off my leg for months and I was able to walk without a cane. I drove down to SoHo and parked far away from the building. SoHo was then a neighborhood of deserted streets lined with factories and warehouses, dark except for the occasional light from an artist's loft, not the posh, trendy area studded with art galleries and expensive restaurants it was later to become. Getting out of the car, I looked down the dark street and observed a long line of gay men, many in cut-offs and tight T-shirts waiting to enter the building. They all seemed so happy, so friendly. And they were constantly touching one another. It terrified me so that I turned around and drove back home. When I got there, I thought about the night I had spent with Don and how much I wanted to be a part of that line waiting to get into the Firehouse.

The following Thursday night I anxiously walked into the Firehouse to attend a meeting of the membership and instantly felt a sense of community. I watched with wonder, alternately attracted and repelled, as gay men touched each other, kissed or walked arm in arm. Most of all I noticed how joyful everyone seemed to be.

The Firehouse was literally an old firehouse, no longer in use, sold by the city to a private party, rented by GAA and converted into a meeting and recreation hall. The building had four floors. Each one had its own character, thus creating four distinctive environments. The main floor (where the fire trucks used to stand) was a huge open space in which the Thursday night general meetings and the Saturday night dances were held. Hundreds of people came to the meetings but over a thousand arrived every Saturday to dance from 9 p.m. to 2 a.m.

Below the main floor was the basement, a mostly filthy, dark, damp, dingy place, where, during the dances one could find kegs of cold beer, cases of soda, and men standing around drinking and socializing. Things could get very cruisy down there on Saturday nights.

A narrow, metal, spiral staircase connected the main to the second floor. It got very crowded on this stairway during the dances since men were simultaneously climbing up and down. The second floor was quieter than the two floors below. Coffee and tea were served there for those who did not like beer or wanted a break from the noise. Around the room were small wooden tables and chairs. There were couches with stained and ripped upholstery and broken springs, some in such decay that they sat on the floor, the legs having been broken off years ago. Quiet conversations were the rule here, and during the Saturday night dances the chairs and filthy furniture were all occupied by couples or small groups. The second floor was also used weeknights for members to socialize and for committee meetings.

One evening, a number of friends and I were sitting in the back of the room. Other gays were sitting at the wooden tables, closer to the stairway. Suddenly a clanging noise rose from the circular staircase. Everyone turned toward the stairway, waiting to see who was climbing up so slowly and banging the metal sides of the staircase. It was the most unusual sound we ever heard there and everyone started to laugh.

Finally up to the landing rose a blind, orthodox Jewish man in his twenties, dressed in black, wearing a yarmulke, a full beard, and tapping with a long, white cane. Tap, tap, tap, tap went the cane as this most unusual sight negotiated his way along the side of the long wall. The room became deadly silent, all eyes following the strange apparition. Did he know he had walked into a place filled with faggots? Did he think he was in a synagogue? The man tapped a few more times then made a beeline to one of the tables. The men sitting there remained in their chairs even after he banged into their table, watching mesmerized as he touched the head of one of the guys, who though bug-eyed, remained still. The rest of us went into paroxysms of laughter as the interloper made his next move, which was to grab the guy's balls and hold onto them tightly. The intruder was pushed away. Undaunted, he grabbed the crotch of another man at the table. (By that time we figured he wasn't looking for a synagogue.) On the street a man like that would be in danger, but not at GAA. No one tried to hurt him. On the other hand, no one wanted to be groped by him either. What followed was a bizarre scene of a group of gay men running tip-toe from one end of the room to the other carrying their shoes in their hands. Finally defeated at not being able to bag any more genitals, the man in black went clanging back down the staircase and out the front door.

The top floor contained the administrative offices of the organization. Like the other floors, it was just a large, open narrow space. It was also the least welcoming of the four floors in the building. At one end a wall and a door made an office in which the various papers and records of the organization were kept, helter-skelter, thrown about with a minimum of care. Very little publicly happened on this floor. Periodically cliques of GAA officers met up there to plot some strategy against a homophobic group or against another faction in GAA.

On only one occasion did I spend time there. There had been a series of homosexual murders in New York City. A serial killer would go over a trick's house, tie and gag him, then burn the poor man to death. The police wanted to catch the killer and assigned two undercover cops to cruise the bars. They came to us for "training" on how to cruise. As a trusted psychologist member of the organization, I was asked to participate in the training, which consisted of a couple of hours in the office. (The police were also in touch with me a number of times afterward for consultation.) One of the cops was very good at it, but the other, younger and more attractive was nervous as hell, perhaps because he was actually being cruised by everyone else in the room. We never heard from the police again. To the best of my knowledge the killer was never caught. For a while afterward, I received phone calls threatening my life if I continued to help the police, but I believed that they came from fellow GAA members always willing to pull pranks on each other. Nothing was ever secret in the organization for long, and local gossip (what we called "trashing") absorbed most of the nonpolitical socializing.

In the spirit of "participatory democracy," the rules of the organization promised any gay person the right to speak at a meeting. To balance out this act of generosity, the meetings were conducted strictly according to Robert's Rules of Order. Hundreds of chairs were set up on the ground floor of the Firehouse and to these meetings came the membership, almost all men, mostly in their twenties and thirties. In those chairs sat some of the brightest and most socially committed, but also some of the strangest people I have ever met. Our colorful gang included street people who battled the police at the Stonewall, transvestites, and gay men stoned out of their minds (or as we said in those days, "Ripped to the tits"). Here are a few examples of some of our more colorful members.

We had a lot of members named John. One of them had a dog that accompanied him to the Firehouse. Afterward, we found dog feces on the floor. John refused either to pick it up or to curb his dog. The problem was finally placed on the membership meeting agenda. For two hours, hundreds of members argued whether John could be excluded from the Firehouse on the grounds of dog shit. The vote of the membership reaffirmed his right to the building as a gay man, dog shit or no dog shit.

Bill, a quiet fellow, appeared at the Saturday night dances stark naked and carrying a plastic see-through purse. One night one of the lesbians presented him with a gift, a woolen, knitted penis cover for his genitals. "It's to keep you warm, Bill," she said. Some of us begged him to wear it, but he just dropped it into his purse.

There was "Little John Basso" (nee John Wojtewicz). Many of us were invited to his wedding to Liz, his transsexual wife-to-be (even though Little John already had a female wife and child). He asked to be married in the Firehouse, but after long discussions about whether the couple should be aping heterosexual marriage, the executive committee refused. (I was invited to their three weddings, since Liz didn't show up for the first two. Little John wanted a military ceremony, so he asked us to wear ROTC uniforms.) In order to pay for Liz's operations he carried out the most bizarre bank robbery in New York City history. Holding the staff of a Brooklyn bank hostage, he bought them pizzas and at one point herded them into a room and absentmindedly left his guns with them. The press dubbed him "the gay bank robber." The film *Dog Day Afternoon*, starring Al Pacino as John, was an accurate portrayal of his erratic personality.

Early in my tenure at GAA, I joined an ad hoc group that wanted to repair the piano on the second floor. We each contributed one dollar a week to a fund that was held by Roger, a recent immigrant to the city who was crashing at my Inwood apartment. Week after week we turned over about twenty dollars or so. After a few months, during a membership meeting I noticed how sad he looked and how red his eyes were.

"What's wrong, Roger?" I asked.

"I'm in excruciating pain. I have to get to the hospital as soon as possible. I'm dying of cancer," he said weakly. I was shocked. He had been taking some pills during the meeting and I asked him what they were.

"Medicine for my cancer," he said his face and body now somewhat uncoordinated. "I can't take this pain any more. Please help me."

Already a veteran of GAA's parliamentary system, I stood up and shouted, "I move the agenda be suspended for a point of personal privilege." This was generally done only for something dire and everyone could see something serious was going on. All eyes in the room turned toward me and, truly a rare moment in our chaotic meetings, all conversation stopped.

"Please listen to Roger. He has something very important to say," I announced.

Roger stood up feebly, one arm around my shoulders for support. His voice, barely audible, carried in the hushed room. He told everyone how much he loved them and how his family had thrown him out of the house when they learned that he was gay. He talked about his new family at GAA and how they had given his life meaning. With a brilliant sense of timing, he fell silent for a moment, then announced that he had cancer and expected to die shortly. He burst into tears. There was not a dry eye in the house. Everyone knew the pain of discrimination and while the organization could be quite nutty at times, they were also the most compassionate group of people I have ever met.

"Take me to the hospital," Roger said to me still leaning on my shoulder, but less steady than before. As we passed through the meeting room, members embraced and kissed him, cried in his arms. "Thank you, thank you," Roger said to each of them, still crying himself.

I drove to Roosevelt Hospital, where Roger claimed to be a patient. After I reported his condition to a sympathetic nurse in the emergency room, she took him into an examination room immediately. Within fifteen minutes a doctor came out to tell me that I could take my friend home. "Home?" I asked, confused. "But he's dying of cancer."

"No, he isn't," the doctor said with a smirk. "First of all, he's never been a patient here. And he's a drug addict, not a cancer patient. Here are the drugs I took from his pocket."

There they were: Tuinals, a favorite of barbiturate addicts. That is what he had been swallowing during the meeting; hence his wobbly condition. It suddenly became clear why Roger had volunteered to hold the money. It was left for me to return to the meeting and inform the contributors about what had happened to the money. (In *Under the Rainbow*, Arnie Kantrowitz wrote that Roger was "a down freak who gobbled barbiturates like they were bonbons.") We regretted losing the money, but also felt sorry that drugs had destroyed Roger's life. When I threw him out of my apartment, he angrily accused me of ingratitude because he had not stolen any money from me (yet). We lost contact with him until a few years later when we learned that he had become the treasurer of a gay liberation group in Florida. The piano was never repaired.

The transvestites at GAA formed a group they called Street Transvestites Action Revolutionaries (STAR). In it were drag queens like Marsha Johnson and Sylvia Rivera both of whom participated during the Stonewall rebellion. One day I received a call from some of Marsha's friends, saying that she had been sent to Manhattan State Hospital for psychiatric observation. Marsha regularly stood on street corners and talked to the moon, but that day she claimed that the moon answered. I agreed that communicating with the moon was no reason to lock her up. Marsha was always warm and friendly to everyone and she was never dangerous. "What do you want of me?" I asked. They wanted me to go to Manhattan State and take her out. I tried to explain about hospitalization and legal procedures and why I could not discharge her.

"You're just uptight, man. Fuck that. We'll get her out."

They drove to Manhattan State, found Marsha, grabbed her and drove off. (So much for hospital security.) Just to rub it in, they called me back to report that Marsha was home, surrounded by friends, "No thanks to you, man."

Occasionally, Marsha deliberately got herself arrested in the wintertime, or so she claimed so that she would not have to be homeless in the cold. Her body was found years later floating in the Hudson River. The police labeled her death a suicide, but many people believe she was pushed into the river.

For years we had been pressuring the New York City Council to pass a law making it illegal to discriminate against gays in housing and employment. Each day we filled the Council chamber with bellicose GAA members shouting gay liberation slogans. We were not good boys and girls. When someone spoke against the bill we shouted, "Gay is angry." Our intention was to create a militant and defiant presence in order to scare members of the Council who denied us our rights. Once, when the Council chairman decided to terminate the hearing because of our confrontational tactics led by Arthur Evans and Marc Rubin, we blocked the path of the Council members and told them they could not leave the room. "You can leave the room when every gay person has his civil rights, and not before," shouted Arthur. Police filed into the chamber itching to beat us up. In the end, the Council members retook their seats and continued the hearing.

At one of these hearings I was bored by the repetitiveness of the speeches, and I walked outside into the large hallway on the second floor of City Hall. There I met Beebee, one of the quieter drag queens at GAA. Beebee was short, slightly overweight, always wore a blond wig, and was hard to rouse to anger. "Where's the ladies room?" she asked and I pointed down the hall. She walked over and tried to enter, but was stopped by a cop stationed at the door.

"You're not a girl," he said. "Go to the men's room."

Ever polite, Beebee turned and walked to the men's room, where, once again, the cop stationed there stopped her.

"You can't come in here. You're a girl," he said.

She went back to the ladies' room, then the men's room again. It was obvious the cops were playing their own little game.

Anyone with experience in gay liberation politics knows you don't fuck with a drag queen. Beebee calmly walked over to the stairs, lifted her skirt, pulled down her panties, whipped out her dick—and pissed on the steps. The cops rushed the poor girl, who was not quite finished with her business and she ended up pissing on their shoes (or was it in them?).

"You're under arrest," they shouted.

I rushed into the Council chamber and yelled, "They're arresting Beebee." About forty or fifty GAA members charged into the hall. We grabbed her, somehow pushed the cops away and re-entered the Council chamber and kept Beebee with us for the rest of the day. She proved the old adage that, "You can't beat City Hall, but you can piss on the steps."

There were others: the Tamali of death, Buree woman (who was not gay, just friendless), Snake Man, Quasimodo. Every GAA member has his/her own list. While we all laughed at the antics of these colorful members, we also recognized that they had been damaged and rejected by society because of their homosexuality. For that reason alone, the ethos of the organization demanded that we give them a home.

Many of these strange people ran for office during our annual elections. "Nomination Night" was held in a spirit of anything goes and any member, no matter how bizarre, could run for office. In fact, the more bizarre the better. The membership turned out in full force and the most insipid gossip (mostly sexual) about candidates was publicly announced on the floor and the repartee between members provided a never-ending series of belly laughs. The atmosphere was something between a town carnival and the burning of Christians in the Coliseum. The stranger the candidate, the more the membership applauded.

One election for president particularly stands out in my mind. Running for office was a psychotic fellow who claimed to be a member of the Swiss Guards, only he called it the "Swish Guards." I cannot remember his name, nor can any of my friends. I do not think he knew it either. His speech was a word salad, a series of verbalizations with no meaning whatsoever, punctuated with great flourishes of the arms. When finished he received a standing ovation from the membership. Also running that night for President was another John (he called himself "Crystal Vision") who complained that street people were not being treated with dignity, and Bruce Voeller whose overly serious speech was greeted by a chorus of snoring sounds. Bruce was elected in a landslide, but he was so furious about the frivolity of the organization that he, Ron Gold and Jean O'Leary left to form the National Gay Task Force.

GAA was not a community center. It offered no services to its members. It was deeply dedicated to fighting for gay civil rights. Underneath the zany behavior of its members was a serious well-reasoned ideology and the techniques to bring its goals to fruition. The ideology at GAA was in synchrony with the leftist values of the 1970s. Capitalism was tainted by greed and selfishness; the accumulation of money and property, in contrast to a concern for human welfare, were the signs of capitalistic decay. On the other hand, GAA had to pay rent and the phone bill and buy beer for dances. Therefore, we charged an admission fee of two dollars for the dances. The result of the conflict of values was an irresponsible accounting system. The first year the treasurer was found with his hand in the till. Unwilling to trust the police and the courts, GAA held its own trial and ended up by suspending the treasurer's membership. (The former treasurer threatened to run for president in the next election, saying that stealing the money was our fault because we let him.)

Some outsiders saw us as arrogant. We believed that we were the vanguard of a new society free from the discriminating restraints of the past. We were convinced the world was about to turn in our direction and we would be the first to give it a good spin. We believed that gay love relationships in all their variety were going to set the standards for cultural change and that gay love would eventually lead to sexual freedom, which included the right to frequent sexual partners in a day when easily cured venereal diseases were the most serious malady. But we rejected sexual role-playing as an imitation of oppressive heterosexual marriage, in favor of sexual egalitarianism in which versatility was the standard. We also rejected the apparel of the businessman as conformist and substituted long hair, denims, work shirts, mustaches and beards.

The manipulation of words and symbols was a crucial part of the strategy of radical gay politics. The most important of these was rejecting the word "homosexual" and substituting "gay." Homosexual had too many emotional connections to it such as mental illness, jail, effeminacy and sex. The word "gay," on the other hand was virtually unknown by the general population (and by many homosexuals as well) and did not carry historical baggage. We all called ourselves gay and demanded that everyone do the same. By calling ourselves gay, we were defining our own identity.

The word "homophobic" is another example of using words to reinterpret the world. It has very little meaning from a psychological perspective, especially because of its use of the word *phobia*. It was a brilliant political conception first publicized by the psychologist George Weinberg and used so effectively that people believed it to be a significant psychological term. Its political function was to attack institutions or people who depreciated gays. The people who beat us on the streets or called us fags were no longer merely prejudiced. They suffered—and here is the brilliance of the term—from a mental illness called "homophobia." We provided a medical diagnosis to balance the scale that had previously been tipped to our detriment. "Homophobia" was as effective in going on the offense against discrimination as the word "racist" was to the Black Liberation Movement and "sexist" to the Women's Liberation Movement.

We had a number of techniques for fighting discrimination against gay people. We did this by means of our "zaps," by our good relationship with the press and through the annual Gay Pride Day march, now a June tradition all over the world celebrating the anniversary of the Stonewall riots. But we did not call them "parades" as they do now. Parades have a celebratory air about them, suggesting a time for fun and frolic. We were not celebrating, we were marching for our civil rights, exhibiting ourselves to a shocked heterosexual audience and shouting for other gay people to come out of the closet. This was not accidental. GAA did not want their marches to deteriorate into the parades they have now become.

The first march was held in June 1970. I attended the second march in 1971 and vividly remember the rush of energy and enthusiasm I felt standing with my brothers and sisters in gay liberation waiting for the moment when our leaders would give the order to begin. We had mixed feelings about starting out at Christopher Street where the first few marches began. While we were overjoyed to be marching for our rights, many of us worried that some violent straight men might attack us or worse a speeding car come crashing into us. (The first few marches went up Sixth Avenue, but we only had half the street. Cars continued driving up Sixth Avenue on the other half and some came dangerously close to us.) We greeted each other with friendly kisses and "Happy Birthday," as if we had started life anew at the Stonewall.

There were not a lot of drag queens in those first few marches, except for members of GAA like Sylvia Rivera, Marsha Johnson, and the two Beebees. But there was "Rollerina." For years Rollerina received thundering applause from the marchers. A conservative male stockbroker by day, at the marches he turned up in a long gauzy dress, a woman's hat, wearing heavy horn-rimmed glasses and roller-skates (hence his name).

And in his hand was a long baton with a five-pointed star at the top—like a fairy godmother. Rollerina skated his way back and forth among the marchers, occasionally throwing his baton in the air (and never catching it) to cheers from the crowd. Even though he never said a word, his dependability spurred us to shout our slogans all the louder. "Two, four, six, eight, we don't want a fascist state," was one. "Out of the closets and into the streets," was another. There were lots of signs, too. My favorite was "Avenge Sodom and Gomorrah."

The march up Sixth Avenue ended in Central Park in what we called a "Gay-In," thousands of gay men and lesbians lounging (and fondling) on the lawns and speeches from gay activist leaders. It was a wonderful place to cruise.

Demonstrating in public was an ideological requirement. Prior to the radical gay movement, homosexuality had been like a plant kept in a dark closet, never to be seen or allowed to grow. Out of sight during the day, homosexuals moved in the shadows of nightfall hiding not only from the punishing society at large, but also from each other. The publicity created by the gay movement was the metaphoric sunlight that helped to transform our feelings about ourselves as it did the perception of us by the wider society. We measured the success of our actions by the amount of favorable publicity, not whether we won a particular battle. Our Public Relations committee made sure that our demonstrations were well covered by radio, newspapers and television.

As an institution, the media is rarely interested in values or morality. They want news and a bunch of queens creating a ruckus at a bureaucratic office or a business was news. They wanted to show the faces of homos, even name them and in contrast to the gays of previous generations, we gave our names, our organization and a phone number where people could reach us.

We gave the media what they wanted through our zaps, demonstrations (oftentimes humorous) against homophobic people, agencies and businesses. GAA was good at using symbols, and this was nowhere more apparent than during the zaps. Since some of our members were themselves members of the press or worked in public relations, they understood the needs of the media, deadlines for copy and supplied reporters with a constant stream of press releases and information even before the zaps occurred. Prior knowledge was required for the press to show up at the right time with cameramen. Our Public Relations committee, chaired by Ron Gold, was so efficient and supplied such well-written copy that it was sometimes published word for word. Zaps were meant to create publicity about discrimination against gay people. The humorous zaps were a way to reduce the potential violence that might be used against us.

Many of these zaps occurred before I joined GAA. In February 1970, the police of the Sixth Precinct arrested one hundred seventy people in a raid on the Snake Pit, a gay bar in the Village. Only a few customers were detained including a terrified twenty-three-year-old illegal immigrant who jumped out of a second-story window in the precinct, only to be impaled on a metal fence below. The precinct was subsequently picketed for one night.

The police were also hassling the street people and hustlers who frequented the Village and GAA decided to come to their aid (not that they asked). GAA members by the hundreds turned up at the corner of Greenwich Avenue and Tenth Street, many wearing our blue shirts with "GAA" emblazoned in gold on them. The hustlers in whose name we were fighting, were obviously terrified by the spotlight we were turning on them and by the police arriving in droves ready for a fight. When we arrived, the hustlers fled the scene, probably angry with us because we had scared the "Johns" away preventing the hustlers from making their night's rent.

The Women's House of Detention, next to the Jefferson Library, was just across the street. (It was later demolished and replaced by a garden.) The imprisoned women shouted their encouragement to the gay men in the street and then started sending down long, burning rolls of toilet paper. The police started to get nasty and violence was in the air. But GAA was founded on nonviolence, so President Jim Owles asked that everyone wearing a GAA shirt remove it or turn it inside out. The demonstration did get violent however and some cars were overturned.

When *Harper's* published an essay by Joseph Epstein wishing all homosexuals off the face of the earth, a group from GAA took over the magazine's offices. Zappers brought coffee and donuts to distribute to the staff telling the secretaries that they did not have to go back to work until after GAA held a meeting with Midge Decter, the editor of *Harper's*. (A good dose of *chutzpah* never hurt.) An unsatisfactory meeting with Decter was held, but the point was made. Gays were not going to put up with homophobic articles in her magazine (which did not stop Decter from writing and publishing more hateful articles herself in the decades that followed the zap).

When the Household Finance Corporation announced that it would not lend money to homosexuals, GAA zapped HFC's midtown offices. "Are you proud you don't give loans to homosexuals?" yelled Arthur Evans. When the officials refused to talk, the other demonstrators yelled, "Answer the homosexual!"

Into the Manhattan County Clerk's office walked a wedding party consisting of two grooms in tuxedos, two brides in wedding dresses and an entourage of well-wishers, all members of GAA. The grooms and brides applied for marriage licenses. When they were refused, the County Clerk's office was taken over for a wedding party. Two wedding cakes appeared, with two grooms on top of one cake and two brides on top of the other. Pieces of cake and coffee were distributed to the staff. When the police arrived they were also offered coffee and cake. The demonstration ended after the press took pictures and interviewed the brides and grooms.

Fidelifacts was a firm on Forty-second Street that gathered information about the private lives of prospective employees for businesses. One of the firm's representatives had once said of potential gay employees, "If it walks like a duck and quacks like a duck, it must be a duck." During the street demonstration against Fidelifacts, Marty Robinson wore a duck costume, while other GAA members handed out literature and talked to passers-by.

Perhaps the most amusing demonstration I attended took place one Saturday night at the home of Saul Sharison, Chairman of the General Welfare Committee of the City Council, who had prevented discussion of our civil rights bill. Announcements were made for everyone to remain at the Firehouse when the dance shut down. Then a thousand or more strong we walked through the streets and collected at Sharison's home. When we arrived there the police were waiting for us. They had been informed about the zap. (Despite supervision, a couple of demonstrators were beaten by the police anyway.) We marched in full voice, chanting and yelling—by then it was about three a.m.—until we woke up everyone in the neighborhood. The media had received press releases in advance about why we were picketing Sharison's house and the goals of GAA. While some of us continued chanting loudly, others pasted GAA stickers all over the lobby of Sharison's building. Then a small group of volunteers was chosen to jump over the police barricades so that press photographers could get action pictures for their papers. We affectionately dubbed them the "Suicide Squad." Over the barricades they went and the police "arrested" them; the pictures were taken and everyone went home. It made a hell of a story in the papers the next day.

Not all of the demonstrations ended peacefully. One evening in 1971, a group of demonstrators returned to the Firehouse after a zap in Hauppauge, Long Island. Within minutes, Ethan Geto walked in to report that while he was attending a dinner of the Inner Circle, an annual meeting of New York City power brokers, drag acts derisive of gay people were being performed. A bunch of GAA members left to crash the dinner and chastise them for it. When they did so, Michael May, president of the Firemen's union, attacked Morty Manford and Jim Owles. He threw Jim down the escalator. Although police officials (including the police commissioner) witnessed the attack, no one tried to stop May or subsequently arrested him. Jim (who was taken to the hospital) and Morty were arrested, but no one at the dinner would testify against May.

Another public act of GAA was hounding politicians running for office. In 1970, Arthur Goldberg was running for governor of New York. He had formerly been a Justice on the United States Supreme Court and our ambassador to the United Nations. While he was speaking on a street corner, a group of GAA members demanded to know whether he would support civil rights laws for gay people including the repeal of sodomy laws. When he said that he would not, they shouted at him so vehemently that he retreated into his limousine and drove away. (He later endorsed GAA's civil rights platform.) Later that month, five GAA members staged a sit-in at the office of the Republican State Committee, demanding that Governor Nelson Rockefeller support gay rights. They were arrested and dubbed the "Rockefeller Five."

Mayor John Lindsay was hounded virtually everywhere he went by a group of GAA members, who kept demanding that he support gay rights. At the one-hundredth anniversary of the Metropolitan Museum of Art in 1970, a dozen or so GAA members including Jim Owles, Arnie Kantrowitz, Arthur Evans, and Marty Robinson got on the receiving line and when they shook Lindsay's hand would not let go and loudly said, "When are you going to support gay rights." They also disrupted his TV show. In June 1971, a group of GAA members chained themselves to a desk in City Hall to protest Thomas Cuite's blocking of the civil rights bill. At another City Hall demonstration the same year, GAA founder Arthur Bell, an openly gay reporter for the *Village Voice*, was listening to homophobic comments being made by Council Member Matthew Troy to reporters. Arthur walked over to Troy, called him a bigot and kicked him in the ass.

The psychiatric establishment was particularly vilified by gay radicals and for good reason. Behind our anger at them for how they had harmed us was a deep sense of hurt at being rejected because we were members of the class "homosexual," rather than for our individual assets and limitations. Many gays identified with the pink triangle worn by homosexuals in Nazi concentration camps.

So motivated to fight psychiatric oppression in the 1970s, some gay people showed up at psychiatric meetings unannounced and often leaderless. One meeting stands out in my mind. On April 6, 1976, the New York Academy of Medicine had planned a psychoanalytic meeting on the topic of changing homosexuals into heterosexuals, featuring two arch enemies of gay people, Irving Bieber and Charles Socarides. When word got out about the meeting, hundreds of gay men and women showed up spontaneously and covered the entire floor of the Academy of Medicine lobby with their bodies. There was no attempt to stop anyone, but occasionally analysts attending the meeting fell onto the prone demonstrators. It was a bit of a mess, but very effective for a leaderless demonstration. The chair of the meeting who was also the chair of his psychiatry department was infuriated and demanded to know, "Who's in charge here?" In fact no one was, something he refused to believe. As he continued to demand a representative, people pointed to me, perhaps because of my professional standing.

He and I stood among the bodies and talked. He self-righteously insisted that I order everyone to leave something I would not have done even if I had the authority to do so. I explained that demonstrators were participating as individuals. I tried to explain how angry we were about psychiatry's contribution to the oppression of gay people. He was not interested in the discussion, only in getting rid of us. He threatened to call the police and have all of us arrested.

"Well, if you feel you must, then go ahead," I said, offering him a dime for the phone booth. I knew his was an empty threat since psychoanalysts were much too cowardly to create conflict and scandal. He became very angry at me for calling his bluff.

"What do you people want?" he shouted.

"Gay people are lying on the floor because they want to be heard. That's what we want." I then suggested that since the meeting consisted of a panel presentation, why not invite an openly gay person to join the panel. I was sure that the demonstrators would accept the compromise, get off the floor and listen quietly to the panel.

"That's extortion. You're a fascist," he yelled at me, "and I won't do it. This is a closed meeting and no homosexual is going to sit on the panel." With these words he turned around and walked up the stairs to the meeting, a perfect example of self-righteous stupidity. He was not wrong about the accusation of "extortion," but what did that have to do with it? If he had not been overwhelmed by his own sense of outrage, he might have welcomed a gay person on the panel (preferably someone irrational, or better yet psychotic) demonstrating a sense of openness and fair play to his colleagues. I tend to believe that he was blinded by the fact that the people creating trouble for him were fags and dykes, usually perceived as powerless. To give in to them would have reduced his sense of power and masculinity.

The meeting began late and the audience was peppered with gay people from the Gay Socialist Action Project, a different group than those who were lying on the floor downstairs. As he started to introduce the panel, one gay person started to read from a prepared statement, followed by others. The chair finally decided to call off the meeting and the analysts like lemmings, quietly left the meeting. The rigid behavior of the chair of the meeting played right into the hands of the radicals.

In general, professionals, while skillful enough at their own internal politics are clueless when challenged by radical movements who play by a different set of rules.

I loved every bit of these political shenanigans, including the internecine battles within GAA. They represented my apprenticeship in militant gay politics and I studied its strategies as keenly as I did my psychology textbooks. People like Jim Owles, Arthur Evans, Marty Robinson, Arnie Kantrowitz, Arthur Bell, Morty Manford, Pete Fisher, and Marc Rubin were my teachers.

We gay radicals had much in common. We were angry at our second-class status and willing to fight it publicly. Our finely tuned sense of right and wrong bound us together. Formal religion, however, was distasteful; we saw in it both a source of discrimination against us and the hypocrisy of the clergy, some of whom denounced us as sinners during the day but had sex with us at night.

The Vietnam War was our training ground in social change. I had been one of the leaders against the war at Rutgers University and I led the New Jersey student strike that demanded we leave South East Asia. One of my responsibilities was protecting students who were arrested by the police. I had worked with ACLU attorneys, with Rutgers law students, I argued daily with the State Police and local prosecutors. In the next few years, many student activists brought their newly learned political skills (and moral beliefs) into the neophyte gay civil rights movement. This is why 1970s gay liberationists rejected the assimilationist agenda of previous gay organizations. We knew how to fight.

No doubt many of us found the energy to fight society as a substitute for our parents, particularly our fathers. Whatever the reason, fathers, police, politicians, and psychiatrists were all branches of the same tree that stood for hate, violence and discrimination. We were grandiose in the way all social movements must be and we felt invincible.

I enthusiastically joined whatever demonstrations I could and served on a variety of committees. You could find no more enthusiastic recruit. It was easy to identify with GAA's political aggressiveness. In fact it was the most therapeutic experience of my life, far more effective than my wasted years of psychoanalysis. It changed a timid, self-loathing homosexual into a radical gay man fighting alongside his friends for self-respect and civil rights. Still, social shyness does not simply evaporate.

My personality was divided between the public and private me. The public Charles was an aggressive social activist competent to join any team planning political actions. The private Charles was socially awkward. Accordingly I planned my own treatment.

The Saturday night dances were an important component of my strategy. The two-dollar admission fee entitled one to the full evening's activities, all the beer and soda you could drink, and all the coffee or tea, together with occasional cookies or chips. The coat check was free, but many people threw their coats on the floor in a heap that rose in the air like an ancient Indian burial ground. Vee Mulqueen and Mick Ortiz were the popular D.J.s, even if they overplayed The Rolling Stones. The ground floor vibrated to as many as a thousand gay men wildly dancing. You could virtually dance with anyone you wished, or take your partner and join another couple, dancing as a foursome, then dance with one from the other couple and back to your own partner again. The dance floor was an organic structure of many parts, each communicating, if only briefly with its other parts. Chuck Ortleb (the future founder of *Christopher Street* magazine and the *New York Native*) and I were dance buddies for a while long before either of us became involved in publishing.

The Firehouse had no ventilation system. As the night wore on and the temperature rose dramatically in the non-air-conditioned surroundings, shirts came off and the odor of perspiration permeated the building. The air became so humid that glasses fogged over in the jungle-like atmosphere and clothes became drenched in perspiration. The odor of sweat was erotic, as were the glistening bodies of shirtless men. Very few men could remain on the dance floor all night no matter what their energy level and taking a break was usually necessary. Overheated men went downstairs to drink beer and socialize, although the heat in the basement was just as stifling as on the floor above. Many men negotiated the spiral staircase to the second floor, occasionally stopping en route to look down upon the kaleidoscope of hundreds of arms waving in the air, connected to gyrating bodies in motion and the frequent orgiastic screams of pleasure uttered by the men below to the music.

During Saturday night dances the coffee room on the second floor became my home. We had only a small staff there, probably no more than six people working in whatever shifts we agreed upon for the night. Co-workers invited friends and potential tricks into the room, thus creating a social circle all our own. We could have arranged things as self-service. Instead we turned the spigot of the huge coffee maker inward so that we had to pour the coffee for whoever wanted it. This allowed for conversation, gossip, and cruising. ("Would you like to come home with me after the dance?" I asked one gorgeous man. "Do you have a sling and harness?" he responded. I hadn't.) We also had the opportunity of inviting a potential trick into the room or sitting with him at a table. The very physical structure of walls, a door and counters protected the private side of my personality. I used the coffee room as my place of safety, venturing onto the floor of GAA as I made friends, learning how to cruise and how to entice someone home after the dance.

One Thursday evening during the spring of 1972, I was sitting with some friends on the second floor. A few students from Queens College joined us. I knew most of them. One, however, I had not seen before. He was at least six feet tall, thin, with brown hair that fell over his shoulders and down to his waist. His face was beautiful, androgynous, and so youthful looking that I could not ascertain his age. I was instantly reminded of Mark. He smiled at me as we were introduced. We shook hands.

"My name is William," he said. Perhaps we chatted for a minute or two. His bearing was elegant, his eyes flirtatious, his manner reserved, tentative. I took him as shy. It was instant infatuation and I felt like a shard of metal being uncontrollably drawn to a powerful magnet. They left as quickly as they arrived, their college friend with them. After a few steps he turned around to look at me and for a few wonderful seconds, we gazed into each other's eyes. Then he bowed his head ever so slightly, turned and rejoined his friends. I was mesmerized.

Seven

The Surgeons Drilled Through the Skulls of Their Victims

Although we did not know it at the time, GAA's October 8th 1972 zap of the behaviorist convention was a watershed in our fight for full civil rights. We walked into the Hilton Hotel resolved to create publicity about the unfair treatment of gay men and women. We had no way of knowing that some behavior therapists were already questioning the value and ethics of their colleagues' work.

In the 1970s, aversion therapy was the behavioral treatment of choice for people diagnosed as sexually deviant, which included but was not limited to homosexuals. It was the conditioning technique used to treat a gay man in order to transform him into a heterosexual. Nor was it confined to the United States; aversion therapy was well established in Great Britain, Germany, and to a lesser extent throughout Europe. It is worthwhile to describe this procedure because young gays today have no idea what tortures gay men were subjected to in previous generations.

Behaviorists believed that a homosexual man got that way by *learning* to be gay, not by identifying with his mother as the Freudians claimed. One had only to cure homosexual *behavior* using conditioning techniques and the "problem" would be gone forever.

The basic principle was to provide a painful stimulation to a homosexual at the same time as he looked at pictures of attractive nude men or men having sex together. If a gay man associated painful stimulation with gay sex according to the behaviorists, he might be cured of his homosexuality and turn instead toward women for sexual satisfaction. Unfortunately this naive interpretation of sexuality persisted even in the face of repeated failures.

The most popular treatment was *electrical aversion*. While looking at pictures of nude men having sex the patient was jolted by a charge of electricity through electrodes attached to his hands. (Some gay activists claimed that the electrodes were placed on a gay man's genitals, but that was not true.) In another technique the gay man was injected with a drug that made him vomit constantly while at the same time watching a film of men having sex together.

In the vilest conditioning study ever perpetrated on a gay man, a psychiatrist at Tulane University named Heath *implanted electrodes into the man's brain*. A naked female prostitute hired for the "treatment" lay on a bed in another room. The gay man was then placed in the room with the prostitute and the electrodes connected to a shock machine. While Heath sent a small charge of electricity into what was then called the "pleasure center" of the man's brain, the prostitute tried to seduce him. This was supposed to cure the man of his homosexuality! The patient (victim) did not have sex with the prostitute. Heath's description of the treatment did not report the extent of cerebral damage caused by the treatment, nor do we know what happened to the uncured man after he left the laboratory.

In an experiment reminiscent of the medical horrors perpetrated by Nazis, but in the 1970s, a few German surgeons went even further. Their patients were prisoners and inmates of mental hospitals diagnosed as sexual deviants. *The surgeons drilled through the skulls of their victims, inserted an instrument into the brain through which they destroyed a part of it.*

Their published studies are chilling to read. Their criteria for choosing victims was solely the patients' being imprisoned for a sexual crime including homosexuality. (In one case, a man was operated on because he masturbated too often.) Fortunately other sex researchers in Germany accused the surgeons and the sex researchers who worked with them of unethical conduct, raising so great a voice against them that the government prohibited the surgeons from continuing their "research." We have no information about the physical and mental condition of these men after the mutilations.

Congruent with the prejudices of society, behaviorists of the day believed that homosexual men were deficient in masculinity. They reasoned that if they could increase our maleness, our sexual orientation would automatically change, so they set about to butch us up. They did this by injecting patients with testosterone, one of the male hormones associated with masculinity. In fact the hormone is highly correlated with sex drive. To the doctors' dismay not only did they fail in their efforts to cure their patients, but ended up creating a group of particularly horny gay men!

Two questions cry out to be answered. Why did the behaviorists do these horrible things to us? Second and more important, why did gay men volunteer as subjects for aversion therapy? These questions would consume a considerable amount of my time for both personal and professional reasons. I had been one of those men who out of self-hate had imprisoned myself in the hands of psychoanalysis for seven years in order to be cured of my homosexuality. I knew that it was only a matter of chance that I had been entrusted to an analyst rather than to a behaviorist. I too might have volunteered for aversion therapy had it been offered to me. If I could understand it in others, perhaps I might understand it in myself.

Aversion therapists saw themselves as responding to the demands of homosexual men. Out of compassion for the pain of these men, for the depression of their lives, for the sake of their families and as an alternative to imprisonment, they searched for a treatment that might cure deviant sexuality. One would occasionally find them writing about a patient from a small, rural town, a married man for instance erotically attracted to teenaged boys who feared exposure and arrest. These isolated gay men often said that they would kill themselves unless they had relief from their homosexual fantasies. Some of the behaviorists with whom I talked said, "What would you have me do, tell him there's no treatment, and send him out to be either arrested or kill himself?" It was because of these concerns that some therapists called me a fascist when I demanded that they stop using aversion techniques on gay men, techniques that I repeatedly characterized as torture.

Gay men volunteered for aversion therapy in large numbers thankful for the opportunity to be made "normal." (It should be noted that of the thousands of people who volunteered for aversion therapy, only a handful were women.) Of the dozens of men I have met who were treated, not one questioned the rightness of his decision at the time.

Guilt makes one feel bad, but shame, worthless. So shamed were some homosexual men that aversion therapy, though extreme in its methods, looked like a medical elixir that might restore their sense of pride and fill the loneliness they felt within. It was a perfect match between the aversion therapist who saw himself in the role of a healer and the homosexual weighed down by a life of shame. Both parties in this conspiracy thought the gay liberationist a madman, a coldhearted ideologue insensitive to their pain.

I sympathized with both therapists and patients. The therapists were not acting out of an evil intent, yet I knew that their treatments were ill conceived and doomed to failure. Their patients were going to remain sexually attracted to men no matter what the treatment. While the conspirators saw themselves as cooperating in the name of mental health, I saw their venture as an exercise in sado-masochism.

And it was so naïve, such a simple-minded view of human sexuality— that conditioning could reverse the course of sexual attraction. The techniques were designed to create a sexual vacuum, sexual ethnic cleansing in the place of homosexual desire.

"We only treat gay men who feel guilty about having sex with a man," one researcher said to me

"Then why don't you treat a gay man's feeling of guilt, rather than his homosexuality?" I responded.

I further meant to shatter the pretense of altruism underlying aversion therapy. It was fraudulent to maintain that therapists wanted to relieve guilt. "Suppose a man came to you saying that he was a 'hit man' for the mob, but now that he's killed a dozen people, he's starting to feel guilty. However, he can't quit because he has a family to support. Would you help him feel less guilty? Or your patient might be a man who feels guilty because he molests little girls. Would you help him feel better about it?" The truth was that aversion therapists like analysts before and after them only helped people when their wishes coincided with social mores. If not, they judged the behavior abnormal and attempted to cure it.

I relived the events at the convention for the next week or so, momentarily taken aback by the warmth shown toward me by many behaviorists. I thought they had been kind given that I had come there to disrupt their meeting, chastise their ethics and challenge their treatment of gay people. A few gay professionals had come out to me, but for professional reasons (read fear) they could only root from the sidelines. The straight ones on the other hand, had not the slightest reservation about being seen publicly with me and often encouraged their colleagues to sit with us and join our discussions. But it took me a while to understand the meaning behind the invitation to join AABT. I finally realized that they wanted *me* to champion the battle against aversion therapy. Davison who was about to put his professional reputation on the line, was prepared to co-lead the attack. Other behaviorists were ready to support us.

My participation in the nomenclature change had been as an outsider politicking for change. In the battle over aversion therapy I was a lightning rod, a psychologist member of AABT publicly recognized as a leader in providing counseling services to gay people. At my side were many heterosexual behaviorists who had been waiting for someone to take the lead in order to stop any treatment whose goal was to change homosexuals into heterosexuals.

The role of an activist in these two conflicts was different. Gay activists often interrupted APA meetings, called participants insulting names and willfully ignored the rules of the psychiatric establishment. Dialogue in radical activist terms can only occur after dissension and conflict has created two sharply opposed and hostile camps. But when you choose to work from within a professional group, you accept its traditional procedures for raising issues and resolving conflict. Otherwise other professionals in the group, including those who agree with your position will be offended and jump off the wagon. They are willing to disagree with their colleagues, but they will not be party to personal attacks and enmity.

*

Three weeks after I made my presentation at the behaviorist convention I bumped into William again. It was in the Ninth Circle (a gay bar) on Halloween evening, 1972. He was dressed completely in black;

his face powdered pure white—an obvious vampire costume. He was again with friends from Queens College. William told me about spending the previous summer in England and chitchatted about life in London. As he talked I longed for him to invite me to join him and his friends, but he did not and I was far too shy to suggest it. Then moving backwards, bowing slightly, he said good-bye and walked out into the streets on one of the most festive gay holidays of the year.

From then on I saw him frequently at the Saturday GAA dances. One evening he walked up to the second floor kitchen. By this time all the other coffee servers knew that he was mine to serve. After coffee we danced together downstairs, but only one dance a night, because when it ended, he would abruptly disappear into the crowd promising to return—which he never did.

Everything about William excited me. He looked a bit like Mark with long hair that draped to his waist; but his attitude was frivolous, while Mark's was dreadfully serious. He was slim and moved with flair and subtlety, except on the dance floor where he let loose a reservoir of passion, energy, and sweat. During our short discussions, his tentativeness and reserve, the aura of elusiveness about him was tantalizing to me: he fired my imagination and my sexual fantasies.

Occasionally I watched him dancing. He was very popular on the dance floor, men constantly asking to dance with him. I imagined that not a few of them wanted to get into his pants (as I did). Most of them were politely refused. The others, like me, got one dance and then he moved off into a sea of twirling, screaming bodies, gone as if through a time tunnel to another reality. I admired William from afar, feeling tantalized and scared at the same time. At age thirty-seven I was famished for attachment. I wanted to be part of William's life since the first night we met, wanted him still as I watched him handle his popularity with deftness.

I was fifteen years his senior and I used that as an excuse for not asking him out. I feared his elusiveness, that if I risked asking for a date he would disappear through the time tunnel and I would never see him again. I satisfied myself (or at least pretended to) by chatting for a minute or two while serving him coffee, watching him with friends and by our short occasional dances.

One Saturday night William walked up to the Firehouse's second floor for a cup of coffee. He asked if I was allowed to leave the kitchen and join him at one of the tables. He knew that everyone who worked there bounced around during the night depending upon each one's mood, his or her desire to talk or dance with friends or to cruise. But he would never have made a direct request; that was not his style. The question was more alluring than a request. "I can for some people," I said, trying to respond in kind. We sat together drinking coffee at one of the decrepit tables and after a few minutes, William's knee rubbed against mine. I felt very bold when I invited him home and his assent filled me with anticipation.

We talked for a long time in my living room. I learned that William was studying Chinese and Russian in college. We talked about the history of China and its ancient system of examinations and about Confucian philosophy. We listened to Gregorian music as we began our sex play on the living room rug. He was much more experienced than I, more relaxed about sex and just as passionate as I had imagined. Afterward we continued talking about China and about his favorite Russian poets. With sacred music still playing in the background we fell asleep in each other's arms. He left the next morning saying that he wanted to see me again. He would not, however, make a date. He said he never dated anyone because he did not like planning. We would simply run into one another at the Firehouse at a Thursday night meeting or at the Saturday night dances and he either would or would not go home with me. A bit obsessed I searched for him, trying to determine whom he might be going home with (instead of with me), but there were no others. Although men were constantly propositioning him, William had an extraordinary ability to avoid them. It only made me want him more and always search for him when I was in the Firehouse. Slowly we began to spend more weekends together.

William joined me in the struggle against aversion therapy by editing my papers and he often accompanied me to behaviorist conventions or quiet dinners where I engaged in dialogue with advocates of aversion therapy. Other activists usually argued that aversion therapy was ineffective. That was not my strategy. I had long since learned the lesson that treatments exist because society approves of them, not because of their effectiveness. I continually cast aversion therapy as a punishing arm of society, albeit more benevolent than the penal system that sent gay men to jail. Aversion therapy reinforced shame, ending in a deeper sense of hopelessness. I knew that I was asking some psychologists and psychiatrists who had built their reputations on treating sexual deviants to reject their own work. They were not bad men; they were merely wrong. I respected how difficult it would be for them to turn their backs upon their professional pasts.

Gerry Davison was elected president of AABT in 1974. William and I listened to his presidential address on the immorality of changing sexual orientation, thereby fulfilling his promise made to me the day we first met. It created a stir and not a few colleagues openly discussed whether he might be a closeted gay man himself. He was also director of the clinical psychology program at Stony Brook and invited me to give a colloquium to his department.

I was editor of the *Journal of Homosexuality* and I chose to use its pages to create a dialogue about the therapeutic treatment of homosexuals. In 1974, Gerry, Dave Begelman (another behaviorist), and I presented papers against treatment, while psychologists in favor responded. At the 1975 AABT convention, we held a panel for the authors to further discuss the behavioral treatment of gay people. The goal of these papers and presentations was to make aversion therapy unacceptable. As aversion therapists had helped to present gay people as pariahs in society, I wanted to make them pariahs in our profession.

Cyril Franks one of the founders of AABT, had been head of the psychological clinic when I was a graduate student at Rutgers University. He was also a friend. Cyril was editor-in-chief of the AABT journal *Behavior Therapy*, the leading organ of research in behavior therapy, sent to and read by AABT members and behavior therapists throughout the world. One day in 1974, Cyril handed me a book and asked whether I would like to review it for *Behavior Therapy*. The book was *Deviant Sexual Behavior: Modification and Assessment*, by John Bancroft a British psychiatrist, professor at Oxford University and one of the world's most prolific proponents of aversion therapy. It was obvious that Cyril was joining the campaign against aversion therapy. Cyril is himself British and friendly with Bancroft. I had deep respect for Cyril for being willing to anger his old friend. "Take as much space as you need," Cyril said, an extraordinary statement from any editor, but especially of a psychological journal where articles are routinely pared to the bone.

I read Bancroft's book very carefully filling the margins with notes. Aversion therapists studied conditioning techniques not people and the book lacked an understanding of the personalities and sexual behavior of gays. It contained a number of egregious statements. For instance homosexuals, according to Bancroft, classified women into two categories; women who are like one's mother or sister and prostitutes. "It is not uncommon for homosexuals to enjoy heterosexual relationships but only with the second category of woman," wrote Bancroft.

I realized that neither Bancroft nor any other aversion therapist ever outlined the perfect test for changing sexual orientation by the use of conditioning theory. Take two groups: one homosexual, one heterosexual and change the homosexuals into heterosexuals, and change the heterosexuals into homosexuals. Then change them back again. "If you can do that," I wrote in the margin, "I'll give up my fight."

My review was published in 1975 and it hit Bancroft very hard. I suggested that aversion therapists were social engineers in the hire of conventional morality. I refused to let him off the horns of the dilemma of providing a therapy for someone without first proving his behavior abnormal—the same argument we used so effectively against the psychiatrists in the battle over the mental status of homosexuality.

Cyril invited Bancroft to respond. I was delighted with that decision. I wanted the ball in the air as long as possible because it would help to keep the public dialogue going.

Bancroft went right to the heart of my criticism, identifying me as part of the Gay Liberation Movement and accusing me of arguing for "an alternative form of repression (that) makes a mockery of the sexual freedom of the individual that most liberal minded people ... would value." His next point demonstrated how well he understood my campaign. "It is therefore important," he wrote, "that, at the present time, there should be some therapists who are prepared to resist the stigma that Silverstein and others like him are trying to impose on them...."

He was right. I wanted to stigmatize aversion therapists. All in all I thought, a superb response. The issues were laid out for behavior therapists to judge for themselves. Bancroft later became director of the Kinsey Institute and a friend of gay rights. He has subsequently become very prolific in his research about human sexuality.

By then gay caucuses were organized in all professional associations, including AABT; professionals were coming out of the closet and confronting colleagues who claimed to cure homosexuals. Government grants to cure homosexuals were more difficult to obtain. Sex research in biology was steaming ahead finding anatomical differences between men and women, gay and straight, implying that much of human sexuality was programmed before birth, therefore normative. Within a couple of years, aversion therapy faded away into history.

Aversion therapy would have run its course and ended without the intercession of Gerry Davison and me and our colleagues in behaviorism. I would like to think however, that we hastened its demise by a few years; that some gay men were spared electricity running through their bodies, that a multitude of men who were taught that they were bad were given the opportunity to start getting their lives back together again—as gay men.

Eight

Excuse Me, Mr. Rockefeller, but Could You Loan Me a Dollar?

While participating at a GAA zap I thought that there must be something more effective that I could do as a gay man in addition to yelling gay slogans in the street. Sometime in 1971 I joined a disparate group whose goal was to organize a counseling center for gay people in New York City. The first meeting was attended by the usual collection of 1970s radicals: pot-smoking hippies, drag queens, radical feminists, gay liberationists, a few professionals and the usual quota of certifiable lunatics ("crazies," as we called them). Forty of us sat in a large circle (the better to emphasize "participatory democracy") scanning the room for like-minded others with whom to develop an ideological/political alliance. My eyes met those of a similar-aged woman with blonde hair. She spoke often about the therapeutic needs of gay people with great sensitivity and caring. When the meeting ended we introduced ourselves. Her name was Bernice Goodman; she was a lesbian social worker with a private practice in New York City. We quickly formed both an emotional and professional connection.

The organizing group went through a number of transformations, each filled with acrimony. Finally five of us came together to organize a peer counseling walk-in center for gay people in New York. They were Bernice, Sidney Abbot, Barbara Love, Tina Mandel, and myself. We shared a sense of moral outrage at society's unrelenting discrimination against gay people. Sidney and Barbara (who were lovers) had considerable experience in the women's movement. (Their book, *Sappho Was a Right On Woman*, was published in 1972.) Tina had been a long-time member of the New York chapter of Daughters of Bilitus and Bernice was one of the few openly lesbian therapists in the city. (Rose Jordan, also from DOB, joined us almost immediately thereafter.)

We decided that our respective skills were sufficient to constitute ourselves as a Steering Committee under the name Identity House (called I House) suggested by Barbara. The women asked me to serve as director. After feigning refusal and even though I was still a poor graduate student I accepted, thus committing myself to an almost full-time, unpaid career in gay psychology. There could not have been a better partnership than among the five of us as we set up our service.

I House was a walk-in peer counseling center where gay people could talk about their problems with another openly gay person. No fee would be charged, although contributions were welcomed. If professional treatment was required, clients were referred to our consulting staff, a small group of mostly gay professionals. Second, I House would serve as a training institution and thereby legitimatize peer counseling as an appropriate form of treatment for gay people. Volunteer peer counselors would be supervised by the therapists, who were to exchange their *pro bono* supervision for referrals from the center.

We clearly had a "marketing" strategy in mind. Gay people had so often voluntarily entered psychoanalysis to change their sexual orientation from homosexual to heterosexual. For most of this century they had no alternative or heard another voice telling them that they were okay. We were going to be that voice and we would tell them that a gay peer counselor or therapist was better suited to their needs than a homophobic straight one. We believed with the fervor of religious converts that gay people would eventually reject oppressive psychiatry and switch to what eventually became known as "gay affirmative psychotherapy." During this organizing phase, the five of us appeared on radio, TV and in newspaper articles.

Father Robert Weeks invited I House to set up operations in the basement of the rectory of the Episcopalian Church of the Holy Apostle on West Twenty-eighth Street. A year earlier he had allowed the Gay Liberation Front and afterward the Gay Activist Alliance to meet there. This unsung heterosexual hero of the New York City early gay therapy movement gave us space on weekends and allowed us to install our own phone. We advertised in the *Village Voice*, at the time the only newspaper in New York City that carried explicitly gay advertising. Each night both a man and a woman sat on duty ready to talk to people in person or on the phone.

As a gay service organization I House was far ahead of its time. We had no models of gay counseling, nor were there public or private funds available to us. Our only source of income came from donations contributed by people counseled in the walk-in clinic. With that small sum the organization had to pay a minimal rent to the church, advertising and the phone bill.

I House was a perfect reflection of the gay political ideologies and conflicts of the early 1970s. Gay people distrusted professional therapists in that decade. The nonprofessional founders of Identity House were suspicious of, and feared the intentions of *any* professional, including Bernice and me. At the same time they were dependent upon us and other therapists to train and supervise them. This conflict simmered for over a year.

I House operated on the principle of "participatory democracy" and a consensus was required to formulate all policy. This organizational structure led to an extraordinary number of internal conflicts, which in retrospect were probably unavoidable. Participatory democracy allowed any person to take up as much time at a staff meeting as he or she wanted, to attack anyone and to hold the floor until being shouted down by someone else. As a result, important decisions were often postponed because we did not get to them. As chair of the meeting I was not allowed to curtail discussion because that would have been "elitist," an ideological insult. ("Vertical" organizations were devalued because someone would be in charge. Ideological purity demanded a "horizontal" structure that led to chaos.) One meeting of the Walk-In Center staff, chaired by Don Sussman, a peer counselor, was held in his apartment. The yelling became so loud that it echoed off the building across the street and Don's neighbors phoned in angry complaints and banged on his walls. Afterward, Don resigned as director of the Walk-In Center.

Staff meetings regressed into exercises in anarchy and mean-spirited vituperative attacks, much of them directed against Bernice and me. We were accused of being "elitists" and unsympathetic to the process of participatory democracy, both of which were true. Our refusal to allow peer counselors to become therapists without academic credentials only alienated us even further from most of the peers. The split between professionals and non-professionals accelerated over time. Finally, in the summer of 1972, Sidney and Barbara announced that they had reserved the trademark "Identity House" in their own names. Sidney and Barbara would turn over the trademark only if Bernice and I dropped our plans to make the organization more professional. It was a neat power play.

It was just at that time that I escaped New York and the conflicts at I House by attending two conventions in Hawaii. I had never been there and decided to leave a week early, stay with gay friends for a few days, attend the annual meeting of the Association for Humanistic Psychology (AHP), and afterward the annual convention of the American Psychological Association (APA). I spent the flight from New York to Oahu reading newspaper accounts of Little John Basso's bizarre attempt to rob a Brooklyn bank in order to pay for his girlfriend's transsexual operation.

The next day I received a phone call from a man named John. He had been referred to me by a social worker on Waikiki. John wanted to discuss an important problem in an organization he coordinated. When he arrived at the Hilton he explained that he was "in charge" of the drag queens on Hotel Street. A number of conflicts had recently occurred among some of the girls which threatened the survival of the group. Since I was "such a prominent gay psychologist," he wondered whether I would volunteer my services to assist his group.

Up to that moment my only experience with drag queens (except for those in GAA) had been the times when Nathan Frank had taken me to the Gilded Grape, a transvestite bar in midtown New York where a group of men pretending to be women hustled another group of men pretending to be straight. I had not the faintest idea where Hotel Street was, or even if it was a street or the name of a club, and could not tell if this man was the head of a gay organization or a pimp having problems with his stable. So I said, "Yes." I couldn't wait to meet the girls. Zaralaya, clinical director at I House, agreed to help run the group.

Hotel Street is in downtown Honolulu, an area never visited by tourists, nor will you find it listed in any guidebook about Hawaii. It is only two blocks long and its claim to fame is massive prostitution and a series of decadent bars. It was on Hotel Street that the sailors of every country collected when their ships were in port. They got drunk and picked up women for sex. By a compromise worked out years before, female prostitutes had their turf on one of these two blocks and its bars, and the drag queens (also prostitutes) claimed the other block. This geographical division was known and respected by the habitués of the street while the transient sailors were under the impression that a girl is a girl is a girl.

The main objective of these prostitutes was to swindle as much money out of the sailors as they could—legally if possible, or illegally if that would fetch a greater sum. The sailor invariably offered to buy the lady a drink intending to get her drunk and have sex with her for nothing. By arrangement the bartender put no alcohol in her drink and she was paid a commission for every drink that was ordered for her. Within a short period of time the sailor was drunk and the lady ready to make her next move, which was to proposition him. The deal struck, they went to a nearby rooming house where he was required to pay for a room and where she also got a commission. In the room the sailor drank more liquor. If he was not sufficiently drunk, she might drop a "Mickey Finn" into his drink. Within a short period of time he would fall asleep. In either case, when he woke up, his wallet and anything else of value he possessed might be missing. Presumably there were times when the girls met young men who actually turned them on and with whom sex was personally satisfying, but as every working girl knows you can't make a living that way.

John and I agreed that his group could hold a meeting the next day in my suite. At about ten a.m., twenty drag queens dressed in shorts or pedal pushers walked into the Hilton Hawaiian Village Hotel. They were obviously very excited about being given the opportunity to speak their minds. (I later learned they were worried that the Hilton would not let them in because the year before they had held a meeting at another hotel and ended up blowing every bellhop on duty.) Along with them came a few men, that is to say, males who claimed to be men. "They're our butch queens," explained one of the drag queens. "We're here to protect our women," said one of the butch queens in an accusatory tone. In the lexicon of the Hawaiian drag queen of the day there were no homosexuals and no gays—only queens.

"We don't want any men at our meeting," the drag queens shouted. I hardly knew what to make of the fact that I, an obvious butch queen, had been given a special dispensation. Throwing conventional logic to the wind I agreed with them and we banished the boyfriend butch queens to the large terrace where they stayed for the remainder of the meeting. I did not, however, forget how these people were testing our limited concepts of maleness and femaleness.

The girls complained about many things, mostly petty squabbles among themselves. The subject of John was assiduously avoided even when I inquired and I had the distinct impression that they had been instructed not to discuss him. In the two meetings I had with the girls I never found out exactly what his relationship was to them, nor the power that he seemed to exert over their lives. But they talked freely about their lives on Hotel Street.

The police were well aware of the activities on the street and in the bars. Perhaps they unofficially condoned it because the area was so well circumscribed geographically and they did not have to worry about the activities interfering with the tourist economy. It also kept most of the drunken sailors downtown. But the police did have one means of harassing the girls. By law every drag queen when dressed as a woman on the street, was required to wear a button that read, "I am a boy." At night, when the girls were working, cops occasionally checked to see if they were wearing their buttons. Passive-aggressive behavior was the drag queens only weapon and so they strapped the buttons to their underarms. When a cop demanded, "Let me see your button," he found the drag queen's underarm shoved into his face.

The sailors were under the impression that they were with women. What happened, I wondered when the clothes came off? Did sailors feel betrayed and angry when their searching hands found a hard penis, rather than the expected vagina? "Oh, we all work it out OK," said one of the girls to a chorus of agreement. "I just take his hand away and turn on my stomach," said another. The only sailors who might become aggressive were the "haoles" (pronounced "howlee"), the Hawaiian term for mainland Americans. Some of the girls told stories about being beaten by American sailors when they discovered the deception.

When I went to Hotel Street that night the transformation of the girls into denizens of the night was amazing. Most of them spent hours grooming, putting on their makeup and elaborate clothes. I would not have been able to recognize them individually if they had not run up to me and said hello. "Where's your button?" I joked. "Right here, baby," and the underarm wafted my way. I chatted with a number of them for a few minutes and then left them to ply their trade on the cute sailors in tight pants out for a night of action.

A couple of days later, the American Psychological Association convention began. There was one panel on homosexuality during the conference. Sitting on the panel were four psychologists, none of them gay, two of whom, Harold Greenwald and Albert Ellis, were my friends. Just before the panel discussion began, a gay colleague mentioned to me that he had overheard a psychologist saying, "I have to leave now and go to the fag panel."

In the audience were a number of gay psychologists although we did not know each other yet. The panel members made their presentations, describing gay life in the usual pejorative ways. At the end of the panel the chair asked if there were any questions. Furious, I jumped to the microphone and asked why there weren't any gay psychologists on the panel. The chair said, "There aren't any in APA."

"Well, you're looking at one!" I responded—and thereby became the first gay psychologist to come out on the floor of the American Psychological Association. Since I had already asked one question, the chair asked me to sit down. I refused saying that I intended to stay at the microphone long enough to balance out the panel's prejudice against homosexuals. I gave a critique of the bias of the panel and asked both Howard and Al to tell the audience whether they ever had any homosexual experiences and how they felt about them. (In retrospect, I am shocked at the rudeness of my demand.) Howard replied that he *had*, but did not like it, while Al said that he had enjoyed the experience. Neither was very descriptive. My boldness encouraged a number of other gay psychologists in the audience to speak up, although few identified themselves as gay. During the rest of the conference, closeted gay psychologists chatted with me about their problems coming out and expressed their wish for a gay subgroup within the organization.

That evening I attended a cocktail party given by Howard. "Why did you tell people you're a homosexual?" he asked.

"Because I am," I replied.

"But I've known you for years," he said, "and I know you're heterosexual." There was nothing I could say to convince him otherwise. He concluded that my announcement was a ploy to seduce women! How painful it was for him to learn that I was gay.

When I returned to New York, Bernice and I decided that we had had it with Identity House and resigned. We agreed that the internal conflicts would only serve to destroy the organization and its services to the gay community. We believed that the gay community needed a full-time counseling center, staffed with legally qualified professionals. We yearned for an elitist organization with efficiently chaired meetings. Don Sussman, the former Director of the I House Walk-In Center joined us. With fifteen hundred dollars seed money provided by Steve Temmer, a gay businessman (who also provided start-up money to the magazine *Christopher Street*) and organizational help from Rick Rosin, a gay advertising executive, we rented a seven-room apartment at West Eighty-third Street and West End Avenue. Fifteen hundred dollars does not go a long way, especially since more than half of it went to pay the first month's rent and security.

On June 1, 1973, The Institute for Human Identity (IHI) opened its doors to serve the psychotherapeutic needs of the gay community. (IHI was the first full-time gay counseling center to open in New York City, but it was not the first in the country. That honor goes to the Homophile Community Health Center, organized by Rev. Don McGaw and Dr. Richard Pillard in Boston. Counseling centers also opened later in Seattle, Los Angeles, Philadelphia and Pittsburgh.) I was IHI's full-time director and Michael Giovinco (from GAA) the full-time Administrative Assistant. We were each paid a salary of fifty dollars a week. Because of the inadequate salary, William and I took the master bedroom for our private quarters. Many gay and lesbian therapists who had shunned Identity House because of its hostility toward professionals volunteered their services to IHI three or more hours a week. Therapy fees were turned over to IHI to pay expenses. Within the first few months, all the clinic's available therapy hours were booked.

We tried to inform the gay community about our services in a number of ways. Advertising was always a problem because there was virtually no local gay press in 1973. We had to be inventive. Perhaps the most humorous way we created publicity for the clinic was to use "the trucks" in Greenwich Village. At night gay men wandered into the area to have sex. On weekends one could find hundreds of men along Washington Street having sex.

On a few Friday and Saturday nights, William, Don Sussman, and I drove to the Village, set up a folding table on the sidewalk and served coffee and cookies to the sexual adventurers. Along with each cup of coffee went an IHI brochure. This led to conversations about the counseling needs of gay people. We later saw "the trucks" written on several intake forms as the referral source for new clients.

Some of IHI's services were unique. For instance, we advertised a natural childbirth class for lesbians and their lovers in the *Village Voice*. The ad drew a large number of homophobic phone calls, but it also piqued the interest of newspaper reporters who wrote about IHI's class and our counseling center. (One evening, a new client who was looking for the bathroom opened a door and saw a pregnant lesbian on the floor, with a nurse standing over her. Then she opened a second door and found William, who had just taken a shower, standing stark naked in the bedroom. "What kind of place are you running here?" she asked the receptionist.)

We quickly filled a therapy group for lesbian couples and another one for male couples. These groups were unique in 1973. We also advertised for a group of heterosexually married gay men and our phones did not stop ringing for two weeks. Unfortunately all of them were looking for sex with other gay married men, not for a support group. "What do you do in this group?" was the most common question asked over the phone. "What!" most of them exclaimed after a description of the support group, "You just talk?" Click. A few of the married men offered money if I would find them tricks.

IHI had a lot of visibility in the media because we were the only professional homosexual service in the city. Since we answered the phone in person during the day, media people knew we would respond to their needs in a timely manner. Some of the visits I received from the media were priceless.

One day I received a call from an enthusiastic woman who said that she wanted to visit me with a colleague to talk about the problems of the "Cosmo girl." What the hell is a Cosmo girl? I wondered. I had heard of *Cosmopolitan* magazine, but I did not put the two together. "Maybe it's the name of some new drag queen in the Village," Michael Giovinco, my assistant, suggested.

The appointed day and time arrived and into my office walked a woman who explained that she was an editor from *Cosmopolitan* magazine. "You read Cosmo don't you?" she inquired.

"Yes, of course," I said, "every week," oblivious to the fact that it was a monthly magazine Accompanying her was an obvious gay man as her co-interviewer. "I want to ask you about a problem that the Cosmo girl has dating men," she said. It still did not dawn on me that a person could be identified by the name of a magazine she reads. I was also mystified by their belief that as the director of a homosexual counseling center, I would have something intelligent to say about the dating habits of young heterosexual women.

"The Cosmo girl has a problem dating men in New York City," she explained. "Every time she finds a warm, sensitive, caring man and falls in love with him, he turns out to be gay. What suggestions can you give the Cosmo girl for finding out if her boyfriend is a homosexual?"

I thought the whole thing a put-on instigated by some of my friends, but none of them would have known what a Cosmo girl was any more than I did. These people were serious. I wanted to say, "This is the stupidest question anyone has asked me in years." Still, I answered the question honestly.

"Why doesn't the Cosmo girl ask her boyfriend if he's gay?"

"Out of the question," they said. The Cosmo girl needed a way to establish her boyfriend's sexual identity without his being aware of it.

"The Cosmo girl should take a walk with her boyfriend on a crowded street," I said. "Then she should watch his face. If he looks at more men's asses than women's, he's probably gay."

After a moment of silence they left my office. Both William and Michael rushed in wanting to know what had happened. When I told them, neither believed me.

I came in contact with many well-known sex researchers and

clinicians during my tenure at I House and IHI. We were often on panels together or talked socially during conventions. I first met John Gagnon, one of the best known sociologists in America, over pastrami sandwiches at an international conference on sexuality in Montreal in 1973. He has been a friend ever since and we meet every once in a while to dish and trash some of our colleagues. Jesse Helms often attacks John on the floor of the Senate because of John's long history of conducting research on human sexuality, which subject Senator Helms prefers be kept undercover lest the country's adolescents learn something useful. The research started with Kinsey years ago; together with Bill Simon, John devised the theory of "Sexual Scripts," to explain how people learn sexual behavior. It is an alternative theory to those that explain human sexual behavior from a biological point of view.

One day in the late 1980s John called to ask if I would like to be a consultant to a weekend program on the presentation of sexuality on television. He could pay my way to California and expenses at the conference which would be attended by representatives from all the networks and television programs. "I don't know anything about television," I told John. "What do you want me to do?"

"Nothing," he said. I think he really wanted some familiar intellectual company in the low-brow land of sitcoms.

The conference was held at the Ojai Valley Inn in Southern California. Those who remember the old Ronald Coleman movie *Lost Horizon* may remember the beautiful scenery that surrounded Shangri-La. That was Ojai valley. The inn used to be restricted (no Jews allowed), a fact that did not go unnoticed by the many Jews associated with Hollywood and television who attended the conference.

The weekend was funded by John D. Rockefeller III, who, although quite old, attended the conference accompanied by three young attractive women "secretaries." All elegantly dressed they did not inspire confidence in their ability to take dictation; but why not, virtually everyone agreed. Had I his money, I would surround myself with as many male "secretaries."

The resort was composed of relatively small cottages with dimly lit dirt trails connecting them to the public buildings. I was walking one of these trails one evening, when in the distance I saw a tall man walking toward me. Sure enough it was John D. III himself —and alone. It is not often that one has the opportunity to meet the heir to one of America's most notorious robber-baron empires. I suppose anyone would be at least a little impressed, especially someone like me brought up on the streets of Brooklyn. This is a magical moment, I thought, an opportunity that will never again occur in my lifetime. I had an irresistible urge to throw the man to the ground and steal his wallet. I did not care that the tabloid headlines might read "Psychotic Sex Doctor Attacks Tottering Rockefeller at California Resort." Of course it was just a fantasy. But I had to do something. As he approached, I said, "Excuse me, Mr. Rockefeller, but could you loan me a dollar?"

"I never carry any cash on me," he said.

"A check will do."

He silently walked away and disappeared into the darkness. Another missed opportunity!

During my tenure as director of the IHI, Helen Singer Kaplan invited me to join her sex therapy training program at the Payne-Whitney Clinic in New York. Helen directed one of the most important sex therapy training programs in the country. Trainees were assigned to small clinical teams. Mine included a short, enormously friendly woman with a heavy German-accent, Ruth Westheimer. She was not yet the famous Dr. Ruth. As a child Ruth and a thousand other Jewish children had been sent by their parents out of Germany for safety's sake. The parents intended to follow shortly thereafter but were instead taken to the Nazi extermination camps and killed. Ruth lived with foster families in Switzerland and London until she went to Israel where she fought in the 1948 War of Independence. Sitting on a Jerusalem roof with a rifle that was probably as tall as she, Ruth sniped at Arabs. She was wounded, but not seriously. After studying at the Sorbonne in Paris, she came to New York where she earned a doctorate at Columbia University.

Ruth did not have clinical experience and she was terrified of doing initial interviews and treatment of patients. I tried to calm her fears when she was assigned her first initial interview which was always held in the presence of the clinical team. I arrived at our office with flowers for her. She was thrilled with them and they helped alleviate her anxiety over the impending interview. There was no vase in the room, so we walked into

Kaplan's office where we found one. Ruth did fine at her initial interview of a patient.

Helen had what seemed to me to be ambivalent feelings about homosexuality. On the one hand she invited me to join the training group so that gay people with sexual dysfunctions could be helped by a gay therapist. On the other hand whenever a visitor arrived she introduced me as the "homosexual" psychologist. Toward the end of my training, according to Helen, the director of Psychiatry at Payne-Whitney ordered her to drop me from the training program because I was a homosexual. I was perplexed since the psychiatry department had been known for decades to contain a preponderance of gay psychiatrists. She explained that the complaint was that I was openly gay. If I had been in the closet the director would not have objected. Helen refused to drop me, agreeing that the department would have been better off if all the gay members were open about their sexual orientation. A year later, however, she wanted to offer treatment for gay men who wanted to go straight. In my discussions with her, she refused to see the incompatibility of these attitudes.

Ruth said hello and good-bye to virtually everyone she met at the Payne-Whitney clinic whether she knew them or not and got upset if they did not return the courtesy. Payne-Whitney is a famous institution housing many psychotic people and patients could sometimes be found sitting on benches in the lobby. Ruth would often wave at them, say hello and wait for a response. "They're catatonic schizophrenics, Ruth," I'd say, pulling her along. "They don't wave at people."

After the training sessions, Ruth would customarily drive me back to my West Side office at IHI. During one of these rides she complained about her insecurity as a clinician. "Why don't you volunteer to work at IHI? We'll provide supervision for you," I said.

"Great," said Ruth in her lively German-accent. "Let's go right now, and I'll start." She came to my office that day, joined our staff, and did not object when I informed her that she had to be supervised by a lesbian.

We were then having problems with our landlady who wanted to raise our rent astronomically. Like Ruth, the landlady was a survivor of Nazi Germany. I reasoned that Ruth would get a better deal for us than if I attempted the negotiation. It worked like a charm; our new lease gave us only a negligible increase in rent. Ruth worked at IHI as a clinician until her midnight radio program made her the darling of college students which catapulted her to national fame. She has remained a good friend to IHI over the years.

We received a lot of strange phone calls at IHI including telephone masturbators ("phone freaks," as they were called). "What are you wearing?" or, "Do you have a big dick?" were common openers. Michael, who answered the phone (and Jeffrey after him) was wonderful with them, trying to coax them to come in for therapy. If another call came in at the same time, Michael put the masturbator on hold. Sure enough when Michael returned, the phone caller was still there, waiting patiently to tell Michael the next outrageous story. Neither Michael nor Jeffrey ever got any of them to come in and they never succeeded in getting him to jerk off with them—at least not at work.

Police and FBI agents sometimes visited me. One cop arrived at my office wanting to question me about a murder. Cops would sometimes ask questions about patients being seen at IHI. They were never hostile when I reminded them that these records were confidential. While the police often interviewed me at my IHI office, the FBI visited me at home after William and I moved out of IHI and into an apartment of our own. Early one Sunday morning in 1975, my door buzzer woke me up. Standing in my underwear I opened the door and was greeted by two impeccably dressed FBI agents who asked if they could talk to me inside my apartment. "Come back after ten minutes, when I've made some coffee," I said and closed the door. Ten minutes later they rang again. The coffee made (William still sleeping in the bedroom), I showed them into the living room. They showed me pictures of a young boy who had disappeared and asked if I knew anything about him. The question infuriated me. We gay liberationists were fighting against the assumption that homosexuality and child molesting were related. I asked why they had come to my apartment and they claimed the visit was "routine." They asked if anyone else was in the apartment and when I said that my lover was asleep in the bedroom, they asked whether he would come out to be interviewed.

"Tell them to go fuck themselves," said William, who rolled over and went back to sleep.

"He asked me to tell you to go fuck yourselves," I conveyed to the two

FBI gentlemen. I then explained why I was angry: their assumption that when a boy disappears on the street, homosexuals must have something to do with it.

"Then what's this doing here?" one asked, pointing to the *Children's Book of Verse* sitting on the coffee table. I had given the book to William as a birthday present only a couple of days before. It was his favorite book as a child and he often reminisced about it, sad that it had long ago fallen apart from use. The night I gave him the book, he read his favorite childhood poems to me, tears in his eyes, loving me for finding it. Now the book was being looked upon as something dirty, a potential sign that a missing child might be secreted somewhere in the apartment. I refused their request to look around. I had had enough. They had interrupted my sleep, accused gay men of being child molesters and contaminated the intimate feelings the book of verse had brought to me and William. I lost it. "You guys in the FBI should be the last people to harass gay men, considering the fact that your boss Hoover, is the biggest closet queen in America." Looking straight at the younger of the two agents, I said, "You can't live with a woman unless you're married to her, or you'll be fired. You can't even fuck her because Hoover thinks that's immoral, so you have to pull your *putz* every day, while Hoover and his boyfriend Clyde go home and suck each other's dicks." He turned a pastel blue while the other remained calm in the face of my outburst. They left immediately thereafter and I heard no more from them. I admit to being a bit scared afterward, knowing that I had been unnecessarily mean and would end up in a nasty FBI file. It was a time when the gay community was dishing about homophobic closet queens like Hoover and Tolson.

There were two other poisonous closet queens of the day. The first was Francis Cardinal Spellman, Roman Catholic Archbishop of New York. I know two people who claim to have had sex with him and another who was invited to "Franny's" parties, where he learned that Spellman had a reputation for liking chorus boys. Rumor had it that he often showed up at the stage door in his chauffeur-driven limousine waiting for his garcon de jour.

Roy Cohn rose to fame on the coat tails of Senator Joseph McCarthy, who claimed to have found Communists and homosexuals in and out of government. Cohn claimed that the army and the State Department were riddled with homosexuals who posed serious security risks and should therefore be fired. Yet it was common knowledge that Cohn was a "bottom" with a large sexual appetite and who held gay parties in his house. One of his biographers claimed that he carried an "industrial-sized" bottle of Vaseline with him. Two of my patients were invited to his parties. Even on his deathbed when he was infected with HIV, Cohn denied that he was a homosexual or that AIDS was killing him. At this last stage of life he actively lobbied for the Catholic Church against the gay rights bill we had introduced into the New York City Council.

We all understand people's need to be in the closet. What is not acceptable is the sexual and moral hypocrisy of people like Cohn and Spellman.

Since William did not work, we spent a considerable amount of time together. He became party to my every professional activity. He came in contact with everyone on the staff on a daily basis and attended staff meetings. He seldom spoke which lent an air of mystery about him and more than one colleague described William as an enigma. "Half the time," William wrote in his journal, "I have nothing to say, and the other half I think my ideas too precious to tell another." William lost his shyness, however, when presented with humorous situations as in the following event.

One day while still at IHI, I received a phone call from a well-known female colleague inviting me to lunch. She was going out with a man who she suspected had "a homosexual side." No Cosmo girl she asked him and he denied it, but she did not believe him. If I was wondering why she was confiding this information to me, she quickly explained. She thought that with my help she could test her theory. Could I arrange for a young man to make himself available for a night in bed with her boyfriend? Then, in the morning, "Mabel" (as we will call her) might find out if her boyfriend ("Frederick") was or was not a closeted homosexual.

I should have responded, "Of course I can arrange that, Mabel, but these guys are very expensive. They charge three hundred dollars for the night." Then I could have split the money with whomever I got to hustle Frederick. As it was and lacking the facility of taking care of myself financially, I said, "Huh!" Not an elegant response. I was shocked at Mabel's bold, controlling manipulation (although later I wondered whether Frederick might have manipulated Mabel to arrange it). I said I would get back to her the next day. When I returned home I told William about the proposition. "I don't know if I want to do this," I said.

"Yes!" he said jumping up and down and roaring with laughter. He disliked Mabel because of her frequent suggestions to me to dump him. "And," William continued, "We have to be there when they get together." The whole proposition seemed like wonderful theater to him and he had every intention of enjoying the show. But whom could we trust to be discreet for all our sakes? We knew exactly whom to call. We had a friend, "Marty," with whom we socialized and had occasional threesomes. He was a very sweet, warm-hearted guy and we enjoyed his company with or without sex. With only a little coaxing, Marty agreed. I called Mabel and we set the date.

When William, Marty, and I arrived at Frederick's apartment, Mabel was already there. Frederick was an attractive, charming man and seemed perfectly relaxed. The five of us chit-chatted, had drinks, then went out for dinner in a nearby restaurant. Frederick paid the bill. Afterward the five of us went back to his apartment and plopped down in the living room. There followed a few minutes of inane conversation. Although inexperienced as a procurer I thought it about time that the lovebirds be left alone to work things out for themselves. I stood up, stretched my arms, and yawned. William followed my lead. Mabel did not budge an inch so we sat down again, not a little confused about what the hell was going on. A few minutes later we repeated the yawning routine and once again Mabel acted as if she were glued to her chair. A more aggressive approach was obviously called for.

"Okay, Mabel, time for us to leave," I said.

"Good-bye," she said.

"You're leaving, too," I commanded.

"No, I'm not," she said in just as commanding a tone. "They can go in the bedroom and I'll wait here until they're finished. I won't disturb them."

William and I lifted her off the chair, brought her to the closet, helped her put on her coat, walked her out the front door, put her in a cab and went home ourselves.

"What happened?" we asked Marty the next morning, expecting he would paint us a detailed description of the sex between him and

Frederick. He refused. Damn. The only thing he told us was that he did not think it was Frederick's first time in bed with a man. Mabel and Frederick parted company some months later, but I was not told why; nor did I ask. I was glad to see the end of the theater of so many manipulations.

William first met my mother during my tenure at IHI. Their relationship went through a number of stages. He saw her rather than met her, the day the *60 Minutes* camera crew arrived at my office early in 1974. She did not notice him since there were so many people in the office that evening.

The next year she returned to New York for her annual pilgrimage to her sons. "I'll be here for four weeks," she said. She slept in our bedroom while William and I slept in my office. After a few days she noticed that while other people came and went, one man appeared to be there all the time. She also noticed that he and I spent time together after the others left. Occasionally they would pass each other in the long, narrow hallway that led from my office to the bathroom. While passing and without a word between them, they walked with their backs to opposite walls, staring at the other, then moving on. My mother had been with us for about a week and neither had said a word to the other.

"Don't think I'm stupid," she said to me one day. "I know who he is. He's your boyfriend."

"Would you like to meet him?" I asked.

"No," she replied in her most indignant voice.

Nor did William relish the opportunity to meet her. He had heard my stories about growing up, about how powerful a woman she was and about her vendettas. The thought of spending time with her terrified him. When I tried to arrange for the three of us to have supper together one night, first William refused ("How could you do this to me?"), then my mother ("You're just trying to hurt me!"). Each of us ate alone that night.

The ice between them was broken a couple of days later when I took my mother to a party being given by a gay friend. During the party someone offered her a joint. "Are you crazy?" she indignantly said. We three left shortly thereafter.

She repeated the story as we walked back to IHI. "What kind of stupid ass was that jerk to think I'd want to put that filthy, smelly thing in my mouth," she exclaimed.

"He had no respect for you," said William, uttering the first words between them. He followed that by saying, "You're absolutely right; he's a stupid ass." And by the time we arrived at IHI, the two of them had bonded on attacking the stupidity of my colleague and the stupidity of every other person my mother disliked, at least as many of them as she could get in during our short walk.

The next night we went to dinner together. Walking back from the restaurant on Amsterdam Avenue, my mother commented on the age of the buildings. She was representative of a generation that preferred wall-to-wall carpeting to rugs, painted walls to woodwork, post-World War Two architecture to anything that preceded it. "Look how old that building is," she'd say, pointing to a fine brownstone across the street. "They should burn it down."

"And that one, too," responded William, pointing to the one next to it. As they walked down the avenue, they consulted with one another as to which of the buildings should be burned, torn down or spared. A few minutes later, I pointed out that they had agreed to burn down virtually every building for blocks on Amsterdam Avenue. "Good," my mother said, "they can put up projects."

My mother also had a new ear to listen to her vendettas. As kids at home my brother and I learned how to turn ourselves off to her endless complaints. (No response was necessary anyway.) If, during her visits, my mother started complaining, I would walk out of the room having heard enough of it. On the other hand William remained, listening to her repeat the stories yet again and furious at me for leaving him alone with her. "So walk out," I said. "She won't notice. She'll just continue talking until someone comes back into the room or she gets tired and goes to sleep." That he thought rude, refused to do it and continued to accuse me of abandoning him.

"I love you dearly," I said, "but I will not stay in the room after my mother starts bitching." William complained because he ended up spending more time with her than I. This was because I was working with patients, while he was unemployed and therefore, available. Exasperated, he yelled, "You're driving me to get a job."

William was extremely sympathetic toward me during my mother's illnesses in the 1980s. My weekly trips to Miami to care for her upset him as much as they did me. While I was complaining about the problem one evening, William said, "It's okay if you want to bring her to New York to live with us." He had sensed, incorrectly, that I wanted to take care of her. I thought it as loving a suggestion as one could ask for. I declined the offer.

"I'm going to miss her," William said after we buried her ashes at the funeral. He had come to love her aggression, her wish to burn every building that offended her and most people as well. He adored listening to her complain about "the laughing hyena" in my building or one "stupid ass" or another. He admired her lack of compassion for, or remorse in her hostile treatment of people. He cherished the times they sat together in the living room comparing notes about my liabilities.

Finally, in 1978, I resigned as director of IHI. That was the end of my days as a leader in gay liberation and I went into private practice and continued to pursue my writing.

Nine

Hez Gotta Schlong Likea Schmulka Bernstein Salami

After six or seven years, William and I agreed to stop being monogamous. I was the more jealous one, envious of his ability to attract men. He had not the slightest worry about my having outside activities, considering it no more than "scratching an itch," but he did worry about my sociability and propensity for attachment.

I was under considerable pressure in 1982, and wanted to get away and do something kooky if only for a few days. Friends suggested a gay whorehouse in the Dominican Republic called the Hotel Victoria. It sounded exactly like the kind of frivolous vacation I was longed for, far from gay liberation and the emotional needs of my patients.

"Go and have a good time," William said, delighted to get rid of me and have the apartment to himself, adding that he hoped that I would have sex with as many boys as I wanted, and admonished me to "bring back pictures." I assumed that he would also go out, but I knew that most of his time would be spent at home quietly reading. I packed the Polaroid camera I had bought the day before in order to keep a record of my experiences, along with lots of cheap underwear to give the boys as presents, as instructed by my friends.

The Hotel Victoria was an ugly three-story building in downtown Santo Domingo with twenty to twenty-five rooms. "Standard" rooms cost eighteen dollars a night; "deluxe" rooms fetched twenty dollars. All rooms had private bathrooms, air conditioners, at least one lamp containing no less than a twenty-five-watt bulb and dreadful mattresses (but no bugs, as far as I could tell). A deluxe room had a door on the bathroom; standard rooms did not. I splurged for the extra two bucks.

A small "restaurant" on the second floor contained three tables seating a total of twelve people. The food was tasteless at best, yet there were men who took all their meals there so as not to miss out on any sexual opportunity. I met men who had been in Santo Domingo for two weeks and had never left the hotel. After one meal I knew that I would eat my meals out; after all, there were twenty-four hours in a day, time enough for tasting food and boys.

The third-floor roof was actually quite pleasant. It had just been converted into a swimming pool surrounded by tables and chairs under thatched "mini-roofs." It was a quiet marvelous meeting place for both the "grown-ups" (as I called them) and the attractive Dominican boys who paid one peso apiece to spend the day at the hotel in hopes of making the money back (and more) by bedding one of us Gringos. The boys were also required to produce identity cards to prove that they were at least eighteen years old. The hotel existed at the sufferance of the police and would not allow pederasts to bring in underage boys.

When God gave out physical attributes, he did not do it equitably. For all-around attractiveness, the Germans cannot be beat ("God's little joke," William mused). The Scots were given the most perfect asses (not that they knew what to do with them the year William and I were in Scotland). To the Dominicans he gave large, beautiful penises that hung snugly over their testicles like those drawings of male genitalia in anatomy textbooks that make one wonder whether they are the sexual fantasies of the artists. I did not know about this physical attribute until I arrived at the Hotel Victoria.

My first afternoon at the hotel I met Morris, a middle-aged fellow Brooklynite who had not lost his accent. He asked me if there was a scientific name for the large Dominican penis. "It's called the *Projectus Ethiopicus*," I said. And he believed me. "Take out ya *Projectus Ethiopicus*," he would say to some Dominican boy he had chosen to fuck him.

Morris had spent the previous week at the hotel. He pointed out every boy he went to bed with, told me the size of the boy's penis and what they did in bed—information I had not asked for. That was one of the wonderful things about Morris; he gave you all the relevant information before you asked. Morris got fucked at least three times a day. "Oh! my God, Oh! my God," I often heard him yelling from his room as I walked through the hall. Being the perfect Jewish mother he took it upon himself to make sure that I would end up as sexually sated as he. He particularly wanted me to meet "Deep Throat," a young man who had become a veritable legend at the hotel, whose oral skills were so widely acknowledged that the grown-ups spoke about him in hushed tones. I had fantasies of being swallowed whole, only one arm still free trying to grasp hold of something—anything—in order to prevent me from disappearing completely down his python-like throat.

"We're goin' ta da disco ta fine Deep Throat," Morris said one night. The local gay disco was a long taxi ride from the hotel. It had a very small dance floor and a terrible sound system, but it was filled with well-dressed, sexy, energetic, friendly Dominicans. Deep Throat was nowhere to be found.

"I'm gorna get ya a numba," Morris said, inspecting the dancing crowd. "See dat one wit da white pantz? Hez gotta schlong likea Schmulka Bernstein salami." Morris held his two index fingers a foot apart for emphasis, just in case I had never seen a Schmulka Bernstein before. He was off in a flash taking my silence (or rather ignoring it) as permission. Seconds later Jose appeared at my side, the outline of his Schmulka Bernstein prominent underneath his white pants. Morris pushed the two of us onto the dance floor and Jose immediately started nibbling on my neck and rubbing at least a pound and one-half against my leg.

Despite the fact that I had told him not to arrange for me to have sex with Jose, Morris informed me that Jose would arrive at my hotel room at four p.m. the next day.

"You don' speak Spanizh," he said, "so I taught you wuz jus shy. So now enjoy em."

"I thought I spoke English to you, Morris," I replied, but resigned myself to the date.

Just as we were about to leave the club Deep Throat arrived. Morris went into overdrive, charged through the dancers and spoke to him. When he returned, Morris said, "Deep Throat's cummin' to yer rum at five p.m. tamorrah."

"But Morris, Jose's coming at four."

"So what? Thro' em out at five."

"But suppose I like Jose and want to spend more than an hour wid—I mean, with—*him*?"

"What's dat got ta do wid it? What's wrong wid ya?"

We simply looked at each other both speaking English but without a language in common.

Jose did not turn up the next day and (thankfully) Deep Throat arrived twenty-four hours late while I was out sightseeing.

I met most of the *muchachos* at the pool. Almost none of them spoke English so the grown-ups who spoke Spanish interpreted everything relevant, including information passed around about the boys sitting in our group: the size of their *Projectus Ethiopicus*, who liked to get fucked as well as to fuck, their skills at blow-jobs (with Deep Throat as the unfair standard). The grown-ups were usually fun to be with since virtually all the boys were available every day to everyone.

There were many sexual connections made around the pool. While I stood in the water at one end for instance, one of the boys would stand on the diving board at the other wearing Speedos that looked like they had been painted on his body. He would dive off the board, swim underwater until he reached me, put his hand up my bathing suit and tickle my balls. He might also go down on his knees and pull off his bathing suit (no mean feat), to give me an idea of the merchandise he was selling. No sex was allowed at or around the pool because it was lower than the surrounding buildings and from which we might be observed by neighbors. The boys were advertising only; they strictly obeyed the rules. If I wanted him we went to my room where the boy always showered before and after sex, then spent as much time with me as I wanted.

There was a Merengue Festival in town one morning and I decided to see it. The other grown-ups thought I was ill—or bizarre for going. I hired Elliot as my guide and we walked to the waterfront where the expensive hotels were located. There we had an outdoor lunch and waited for the parade to begin. It started with a contingent of the National Guard (all twenty of them), followed by the National Baton Twirlers (all twenty of them). Like all the Dominicans, the baton twirlers were energetic and had no trouble throwing the batons high in the air. Try as they might, however, they lacked the skill to catch them. The locals having been to Merengue Festivals before, ducked when the batons started their downward trek. Elliot, sweet boy that he was, pushed me down and covered my body with his and made no complaint as one of the batons hit him square on the back. The rest of the parade was less interesting. A number of National Guardsmen cruised me as we walked around the waterfront afterward.

Back at the hotel Elliot and I took a shower together then lay in bed. I pretended to be interested in learning how to count from one to ten in Spanish. With each number I licked a different part of his body, the numbers nine and ten centering on his genitals, front and back. He got the point and we had sex, then took a nap with Elliot cuddled up against me. I made it a practice to keep the air conditioner on high, since the boys were unused to it and cuddled all the closer.

A couple of hours later I sat at the pool and announced that I planned to go to the Botanical Gardens the next day. Morris and the others stared in disbelief. "I cand undastand ya," Morris said. I invited him to join me at the Botanical Gardens the next day. "I give up," he concluded. "Maybe ya nod a real fag!"

I was having exactly the kind of vacation I had longed for. Still, I thought of William constantly and phoned him daily. I spent at least an hour each day at the pool writing a journal chronicling my activities, the *muchachos*, my observations about the grown-ups: all as a gift, a long love letter to William. The grown-ups, in turn, were astonished by my behavior. They remained of good cheer, however, and continued to talk to me—except for the pederasts, some of whom worried that I was a cop taking notes on them.

"There are dreams for sale at the Hotel Victoria," I wrote to William. Men from around the world came to Santo Domingo and an unfortunate few fell deeply in love with the local boys.

"She's frum London," said Morris as he noticed me spying upon an elderly man sitting with a beautiful boy at the other end of the roof. "She's in love. The *schmuck* tinks he cun ged a visa for da kid an bring em back ta London to liv wid em. He cand get da kid out, and even if he could, why wud a young guy stay wid an ol guy like dat? Da Brit'z headed for a fall."

Morris was right. He knew the difference between getting your rocks off and love. The morning the Englishman left he promised the boy to begin working toward getting him to England, and thus made his island adventure one of the most painful experiences of his life. The boy who was willing to say or do anything to get out of the Dominican Republic knew that he would receive a series of expensive presents for at least a year.

"That will never happen to me," I wrote to William. "I know who I love. I talk to you or write down my thoughts and conjure you up in my mind and have you close to me. Ten years has not been enough. I want you always."

Morris left the same day and I missed him immediately.

Eddie was Swiss, an educated and cultured fellow in his thirties who worked six months a year and spent the other six months traveling from one gay vacation spot to another. He had been coming to the Hotel Victoria for years and he knew the whereabouts of every gay whorehouse in the world. He did not think me odd for reading at the pool; he even brought some books of his own.

Giorgie was his sidekick, a twenty-one-year-old boy from Santiago who sat at the pool listening to Eddie's Walkman. Giorgie lived with Eddie in the hotel and ate all his meals with him, never wavering from his side, never violating his loyalty. Eddie spoke Spanish; Giorgie spoke no English. For two days after Morris left, Eddie, Giorgie, and I took our meals together, visited the restorations going on in the city and talked about the hotel, its scene, and what was to become of Giorgie after Eddie returned to Switzerland.

"He does everything," Eddie said of Giorgie's sexual versatility, "but I know he's straight. I want him to get out of this place and go back to Santiago and marry some local girl. I don't want him to end up jaded like a lot of the boys here." Eddie was convinced that Giorgie was an innocent who had fallen into the Hotel Victoria only because he needed cash to live on the streets. Fortunately he had found Eddie to take care of him.

"Bullshit," said Steve, one of the pederasts. "I saw him here last year. He found someone else to take care of him for a couple of weeks. There's nothing innocent about him. He's just a nice, sweet Dominican boy."

Innocent or not, Eddie was going to put Giorgie on the bus to Santiago with lots of *pesos* in his pocket and a new wardrobe of neatly folded clothes packed in his new luggage.

At dinner my last night, Eddie said that Giorgie wanted to have pictures of us as a memento. Back at the hotel I brought out my Polaroid and Eddie took three pictures, one for each of us. Eddie also told me that Giorgie wanted to come to my room later in order to say good-bye.

I was rather pleased with myself as I packed. I had had my kooky vacation. There was not the slightest gay consciousness in the place: no political discussions about civil rights, negotiating with the media or clarifying the gay agenda. No one worried about the relationship between gender role and sexual identity. The only agenda was sex—by contract, to be sure—the grown-ups talking endlessly about what boy did what, the *muchachos* gossiping about what Gringo wanted what. What a variety of men I met at the Hotel Victoria. Some were a mother lode of psychological disorders; others, more settled with themselves, took this sexual slice of life in stride. I had spent far longer thinking about my love for William and missing him than having sex with these charming young men. And I was escaping the Hotel Victoria without falling in love and making a fool of myself. I was ready to go back to New York, to return to William and to all the responsibilities I had put on the back burner four days earlier.

A knock on my door jarred me out of my reverie. It was Giorgie coming to say good-bye. He handed me a piece of torn cardboard, the backing to a shirt I thought, upon which were scrawled his name and address, some of the words crossed out, then spelled correctly on the next line. I taped it into my love letter to William that also held a dozen pictures from naked boys to flowers in the garden. We stood there with no language in common, wondering how to communicate our feelings without words.

"I miss you," he said.

Giorgie must have asked Eddie to teach him those words. He must have practiced them over and over as he walked to my room. I took him in my arms, kissed him, stroked his head, felt his arms around me—and melted.

"I miss you," I said.

"Photo," Giorgie whispered and took off his shirt and lay on my bed.

I searched for the Polaroid camera that I had only minutes before packed in my bag. Finding it, I took the last of my pictures in the Hotel Victoria.

Giorgie unbuckled his belt suggesting that he wanted to please me by posing nude. His seduction was perfect, lying there like a beautiful Greek statue. Eddie knew, *had* to know, why Giorgie wanted to say good-bye by coming to my room. He *had* to know that Giorgie wanted to kiss my body and spend the night in my arms. *Had* to know how I wanted him! How I wanted Giorgie naked in my bed—first for the picture, then to touch his beautiful face and chest, to lay my hand on and stroke his cock while I kissed him with all the passion that was surging inside me.

What a fraud you are I said to myself while staring at Giorgie, the first button of his pants now open. You've fallen in love, idiot, like you promised not to do. The zipper was halfway down when I raised my hand signaling Giorgie to stop.

"No," I said—the hardest no I have ever uttered. But I preferred the temporary feeling of longing to the far more painful good-bye had I allowed myself to be seduced. I had no way of knowing how hurt he felt, or how he interpreted my behavior. He stood up and dressed. Intensely I watched him pull up his zipper, buckle his belt, put on his shoes and button his shirt. He walked over and stood beside me, kissed and embraced me. I only touched his back, too scared to hold him.

Giorgie left my room. I placed the picture of him bare-chested in my love letter to William and finished packing. On the flight back to New York, I wrote William all about that night, ending, "I love you. Don Carlos."

At home William and I sat on our couch and I read him my love letter from Santo Domingo—all forty legal-sized pages of it—stopping only to show him the pictures of naked young men on my bed and the grown-ups sitting around the pool. He commiserated with me when I read the last section about Giorgie and he looked long and hard at the picture.

"You were always a sucker for a cute boy," William said his arm around my shoulder.

"Like you," I replied, as I kissed him.

I handed him my love letter when I had finished reading. He read the whole of it again silently, as I sat and watched his face, noting his chuckling and occasional comments about the pictures. Finished, he cuddled into my arms and kissed me, saying, "The best present I've ever had. Let's have Morris over for dinner."

"I want to read it again," William said a minute later, "but by myself this time, alone." He left the living room.

Later that night William stood before me nude, saying, "Let's see if I'm a better lay than any Dominican!"

And of course he was.

Charles Silverstein
Director of Institute for Human Identity
circa 1990.

Photo by Michael Leonard. Used by permission of the photographer.

Ten

Indirection? I'll Never Get Laid

In 1973, I received a phone call from Nathan Frank. He and his partner were starting a new company that would specialize in publishing professional journals. Their first venture was to be the *Journal of Homosexuality*. Given that Nathan and his partner were investing their own money in the company, starting with a gay journal was a brave act on their part. Nathan asked if I would be its founding editor. He had come to me because I was an out of the closet psychologist and because of my affiliation with IHI. With the encouragement of friends, particularly Cyril Franks, I agreed. I was allotted the sum of twenty-five a month for expenses, including phone bills, stationery, envelopes, and postage.

I planned to announce the publication of the journal during the 1973 annual meeting of the American Psychological Association. After renting a suite at the hotel in which to hold meetings, William and I flew to New Orleans. Posting notices about an interest group meeting was complicated because the convention is spread out among many hotels, with tens of thousands of psychologists traveling from one to another via special buses hired to transport them. Literally thousands of notices are tacked onto bulletin boards. A novel strategy was needed to inform attending psychologists about the journal and how to get in touch with me. Reasoning that there was one place where every psychologist had to visit, we taped the notice above every urinal in every convention hotel. Female friends taped the notice in the ladies rooms. Within a couple of days every psychologist at the convention had seen the notice—many times. I was flooded with phone calls from researchers and clinicians, both gay and straight, interested in contributing papers to the *Journal of Homosexuality*. These potential contributors and I held a number of meetings in my suite during the convention; it was a daring step forward by many otherwise closeted psychologists. I also sought input from psychologists who had made their reputations by trying to cure homosexuality, particularly the behaviorists who advocated the use of aversion therapy.

The first issue of the *Journal of Homosexuality* appeared in Fall 1974 and contained nine papers and three book reviews. John Money contributed a paper on transsexualism, Thomas Kando a paper on sexual conservatism among transsexuals, Ted Reiss a fine review of test data on female homosexuality. The historian Vern Bullough wrote about how homosexuality had been transformed from a perversion into a medical illness. Eugene Levitt and Albert Klassen from the Kinsey Institute wrote survey articles on attitudes toward homosexuals as did Al MacDonald and Richard Games who did some of the finest work (ever) explaining the psychological foundation of homophobia. Mike Serber from Atascadero Hospital in California submitted a paper about his successful treatment of homosexual pedophiles. Two other historical papers about buggery in the British Royal Navy by Arthur Gilbert and Colin Williams (also from the Kinsey Institute) were published. Three books were reviewed. Gerald Davison reviewed a book written by the sociologists John Gagnon and William Simon. Violet Franks, the psychologist wife of Cyril, reviewed a book about male and female homosexuality written by Saghir and Robbins. The third book by Kinsey Institute researchers Weinberg and Williams, was reviewed by Al MacDonald and Ray Evans. They were an all-star group of contributors and the journal was off to a good start.

Mike Serber was one of the psychiatric heroes of the 1970s. He had been appointed to the staff of Atascadero State Hospital in California, a residential treatment facility for pedophiles and rapists. It was actually a prison since all of its inmates had been convicted of felony sexual crimes. He soon found that some of the inmates (gay and straight) were being given electric shock treatments as punishment rather than as treatment. When the institution ignored his complaint, he gave the story to the press and he was summarily fired. The storm of publicity over the Nazi-like treatment of inmates at Atascadero and the firing of Serber led to a new administration and Mike was rehired and appointed Clinical Director.

Mike was a foe of aversion therapy. In its place he designed the most sophisticated and successful treatment program for gay pedophiles ever seen. He reasoned that homosexuality was not the problem; it was the age group that were attractive to them. His program reinforced their good feelings about being gay, but worked to develop sexual interest in adults rather than teenagers. The program was very successful but it was terminated shortly after Mike's death from cancer. Mike suffered from terminal lymphoma. He was in extraordinary pain, but when he asked for more pain killers his doctors refused saying that he might become addicted to them! "What assholes" he said to me. "I'm going to die and they're afraid of addiction." Fortunately one or more of his colleagues brought drugs to the hospital for him use in order to have a peaceful death.

I sent my mother then living in Miami a copy of the first issue and, after skimming through John Money's paper on transsexualism, she called to express her fear that I was going to have my genitals cut off and grow breasts. I assured her that it was not in the cards. (On one of her visits to New York, she became curious about what I was writing on the computer. Looking over my shoulder, she read for a minute, and then said, "Oh! the same old shit.")

Nathan Frank, my publisher, had a warm personality and a good sense of humor. His clothes never varied: a pair of jeans, a white tee shirt, a wide-brimmed canvas hat and metal rim glasses. He occasionally asked William and me to join him in making the rounds of some of Manhattan's gay bars. He liked gay bars with—shall we say "character"—and we wandered from the Gilded Grape to Dirty Edna's to God knows where.

One day he secured an Accujack from the manufacturer, saying that he wanted to have it reviewed in the journal. The Accujack was a jerk-off machine consisting of a large motor out of which projected a long tube that could be connected to any of a number of hollow plastic sleeves. You attached one of the plastic sleeves to the hose, put a bit of lubricant in the sleeve and placed it over your penis. Turning on the switch created a vacuum in the sleeve that rode up and down your penis, which, the manufacturer claimed, would get you off. It was even claimed to make your erection larger than normal.

"I'm not finished testing it yet," said Nathan who already had the machine for the past three months. I actually feared that he had fallen in love with the damn thing and lost the ability to relate to other men sexually. Eventually he brought the machine to my house and gave it to me "for review." William was appalled that I allowed the three-hundred-dollar erotic vacuum cleaner into our house at all. Ignoring the demands of scientific investigation he said, "I'll do it to you for nothing." Of course I tried it, but I had the greatest difficulty feeling aroused by the damned vacuum cleaner, frightened that it might short out and send bolts of electricity through my dick. But throwing caution to the wind I placed one of the sleeves around my penis and turned on the machine. The sleeve came to life, going up and down my penis in one of the most unerotic experiences of my life. It soon popped off (instead of getting me to pop off) demonstrating how important mental imagery is to sexual arousal. Nathan took the machine back soon thereafter. (In 1998, Bill Andretti reviewed the up-to-date Accujac in *The Guide*, writing one of the funniest reviews I have ever read.)

Nathan gave me a great deal of freedom as editor, but unfortunately he seldom paid the monthly twenty-five dollars promised. My salary at IHI was minimal and I simply could not continue without at least my expenses being covered. In 1978, I resigned as editor.

In 1976, while still director of IHI, I was approached by Frank Taylor, formerly editor-in-chief at McGraw-Hill Publishing Company, to write a book for parents who learn that a son or daughter is gay. He came to me for three reasons: my affiliation with IHI, my editorship of JH, and the fact that I was openly gay. I had never written a book, but Taylor offered to provide editorial help. *A Family Matter: A Parents' Guide to Homosexuality* was published in 1977, the first book for parents of gay children.

Some of the McGraw Hill salesmen were offended by its presentation of homosexuality as an acceptable lifestyle and refused to offer the book to retailers. McGraw Hill's editor-in-chief was embarrassed by the immature actions of his salesmen, especially since the book was well received by the press. To compensate, Taylor saw to it that I was scheduled for a comprehensive publicity tour.

A book tour is both exciting and maddening. The exciting part is being treated like a celebrity. On the negative side were cities in which no books were available in bookstores so that the publicity was virtually useless. Many authors tell the same story; it had nothing to do with homosexuality.

Publishers' publicity departments try to get their authors booked on every form of media they can on the assumption that getting the greatest exposure increases the sale of books. I was booked for six or more appearances a day; in the evenings, I would fly to another city, then start all over again in the morning. The tour took me to fourteen cities in which I made one-hundred twenty-eight appearances. The hectic pace is not for the timid, but call-in programs gave me the opportunity to joust with listeners who were opposed to civil rights protection for gay people. The problem was that I knew nothing about many of the programs on which I was scheduled to appear—nor about their hosts.

One day I walked into the reception room of a radio station in the South, announced who I was and sat down. After a few minutes I sensed that something was wrong. Then I listened to the music. A commercial came on for "Jesus Christ, our Savior!" The McGraw-Hill publicity department had me, a Jewish faggot from New York, booked on a Southern Baptist radio station. (Anyone familiar with anti-Semitic prejudice knows that "Jewish," "faggot," and "New York" are redundant.)

"I haven't read your book, yet," said the host of the program as she introduced herself, adding, "I just want you to know that Anita Bryant is a good friend of mine. We should all be thankful that she's doing God's work. Now I want to ask you something before I agree to interview you."

In the 1970s, Anita Bryant, a well-known singer and former Miss America was the advertising voice for Florida orange juice. She was spearheading a campaign claiming that homosexuals molested children, which was how a child was "recruited" into gay life. She also accused us of murdering children by swallowing semen, proving that she wasn't the brightest bulb on the block. Bryant and her Baptist cohorts eventually succeeded in forcing a referendum overturning a civil rights ordinance for gay people in Dade County, Florida.

Here it comes, I thought. She is going to ask me if I'm queer, or whether I think homosexuals molest children. I decided that I would not be rude and answer her questions honestly, even if she threw me out afterward.

"I want to know whether you think children should come out?"

"Yes," I said, resigning myself to being given the heave-ho. "I think children should definitely come out."

"Oh! I'm so pleased that you said that! Let's go now and record the interview." With my unread book tucked under her arm, she led the way into the studio.

I didn't get it. No friend of Anita Bryant who has a program on a Southern Baptist radio station could be in favor of homosexuals coming out of the closet. She introduced me to the radio audience and specifically told teenagers to listen to what I had to say. After a few questions I started to catch on. She meant "coming out for Jesus" and suppressing your homosexuality. There could not have been a wider gulf between us.

If I explained the confusion, I thought, she would throw me out. So I responded to her questions with answers that had double meanings and I never criticized homosexual desire. An alert listener could hear the gay-positive side. I have no idea if she read any part of my book afterward. If so, I am sure she did not air the program.

I prepared for my 1977 tour of the South by reading all of the prohibitions in the Bible against homosexuality, even memorizing some of Leviticus. Armed with these quotations, I felt prepared to slay the prejudiced Philistines on radio and TV, naïvely thinking that scholarship, compassion and logic could break through the impenetrable skin of bigotry. On one program or another I would mention the problems of translation or interpretations changing through the centuries, only to be met by the demand that I call myself a sinner and deliver myself into the hands of Jesus. They were always angry and hateful toward me. In 1977 I was not smart or mature enough to emotionally accept that the rivers around Manhattan are like moats keeping us separate and distinct from the narrow-minded provincialism one finds in much of the rest of the country. Nothing in my experience including discrimination for being Jewish, prepared me for the expressions of hatred against gay people I encountered in the South and the Southwest.

"I think we should do the same thing with you faggots like Hitler did to the Jews."

"You should all be put in front of a firing squad."

"You're nothing but scum. Go back to New York."

The callers always identified themselves as Christians and foretold that all "fags are going to burn in hell." Although fundamentalist

Christians claim to "love the sinner, but not the sin," the fury and hatred in my callers' voices made it quite clear that they hated us.

I had similar experiences in Houston in 1992 when I was promoting *The New Joy of Gay Sex*. On a call-in radio program, people said: "I hope all of you people get AIDS and die; If you come to my neighborhood, I'll kill you; I'd like to put all of you in a building and burn it down." Perhaps the most frightening voice was that of an elderly women, screaming at the host for allowing me on the program. When I tried to respond to her, she yelled, "I'm not talking to you, you fag bastard!" Every one of these callers began their attack by saying, "I'm a Christian.")

William joined me on the 1977 West Coast tour for *A Family Matter* and we took the opportunity to meet people and go places we had never been before. We spent an afternoon with Evelyn Hooker the psychologist who, in 1954 did the first study to show that gay men were not different than straights on psychological tests. From L.A. we went to San Francisco, then to Portland where I met with gay groups. From there we drove to Timberline Lodge on Mount Hood for a few days occupying the Honeymoon Suite and where I took a picture of us lying naked in the honeymoon bed. After speaking engagements in Seattle we drove to Mount Rainier and walked its mountain trails. William was awed by the mountains and the canyons, but terrified by the heights.

Finally we flew to Vancouver, in part for William to meet my former dissertation adviser. William arrived wearing his most hostile costume, a red bandana on his head, sun glasses, an expression on his face as if to kill. He was hostile to Canadian immigration and the immigration officer refused to admit him. I was furious at him. It was only by the intercession of my advisor who came down to the airport and personally vouched for us that we were allowed to enter.

I also wanted to buy a piece of New Guinea art in Vancouver. I had bought a few pieces on previous trips to Vancouver. I bought a wonderful shield, five feet long, made by New Guinea headhunters to add to my collection. It was a vintage piece with arrow holes in it. (I told everyone in New York that it was owned by a queer headhunter who had to defend himself against tribal homophobes.) The gallery owner wrapped it in cardboard so that I could take it on the plane. We had to change planes in Toronto at three a.m. in order to get back to New York and we were virtual zombies by the time we presented ourselves before American Customs. The customs officer okayed our baggage, including the shield, but we were so tired that we were unaware that our baggage was on a conveyor belt and was about to drop it into the bowels of the airport destined to ride cargo. Our cherished shield was in danger of being damaged.

Adrenaline poured into our blood vessels. William leapt onto the moving chute, attempting to grab hold of the brittle shield, while the custom officer and I tried to grab his legs in order to pull him back. We only caught his untied sneakers and ended up holding them in our hands, while William disappeared into the black hole below. One can only wonder at the baggage handler's shock when at three a.m. he saw a man falling through the chute headfirst.

"I'm on a no frills fare," William said nonchalantly as he picked up the (unbroken) shield, dusted himself off, and walked out the exit door. Within a couple of minutes he appeared before us, the shield tucked under his arm. "Are you impounding my sneakers?" he said to the speechless customs officer who returned the one he was holding. He grabbed the other one out of my hand and berated both of us for holding him back in his rescue of the shield.

Since *A Family Matter* was written for parents, quite a few mothers called, by and large young women who wanted their children to grow up emotionally healthy. What they feared most was that they might do something to cause a son or daughter to become homosexual. The mother would mention something that she did or did not do. Every mother mentioned something different and asked if that could make her kid gay. It became obvious that their fears had nothing to do with homosexuality. These women were suffering from feelings of guilt about their mothering skills and theorizing that what they perceived as their errors would scar their children for life. They were simply inexperienced mothers who had been fed the psychoanalytic notion that mothers cause homosexuality. I did the best I could to relieve their anxiety.

Frank Taylor was also the American representative of the London firm that published the international bestseller *The Joy of Sex*. The London firm of Mitchell Beazley made a fortune with Alex Comfort's book and thought that they could repeat their success with *The Joy of*

Gay Sex. Given the times, Mitchell Beazley and Taylor agreed that only New Yorkers could write the book. Taylor asked me if I would do Joy. I thought that my strength, however, was as a psychologist and counselor to the gay community and that I would need a co-author, a skilled writer whose sex life was more varied than my own.

One of the writers interviewed by the publisher was a struggling young novelist named Edmund White. His first novel *Forgetting Elena* had been a critical success in 1973, but he was having trouble finding a publisher for his second. I was also his psychotherapist. During therapy sessions Edmund reported his conversations with Taylor (who knew nothing about our therapist-client relationship). Edmund, in turn, did not know that I was the other author. Then he told me that Taylor called him to say that he had been chosen ("in the debutante contest," as he called it) and was trying to find out who the other writer was. It came as a shock when I revealed that it was me. I also stated that the ethics of my profession prevented me from being both therapist and colleague. If he accepted the job, which I encouraged him to do, we would have to terminate our therapeutic relationship. He could seek therapy with someone else.

At first Ed was upset and angry that he was forced into a choice of either losing badly needed income or his therapy. Ed now jokes about the dilemma, saying, "The need to pay my rent exceeded my need for therapy." He has also written about our therapy together and book collaboration in some of his writings.

It turned out to be an excellent collaboration. Ed is a Midwestern WASP with a strong literary background and I am an assimilated Brooklyn Jew whose strength was in psychology and psychotherapy. Fortunately we held compatible gay political beliefs. Ed had been at the Stonewall the first night of the riots. We decided to write the kind of book that we would have wanted to read ourselves as adolescents, a guide for men coming out. We reasoned that our book should have a wider focus than just sex, that it should also advise the reader about life in the gay community and the majority of passages in the finished book were of a nonsexual nature. Ed and I lived just a few blocks from each other so it was easy for us to meet frequently, talk, and trade essays for critiquing.

William edited everything I wrote. He was skilled at understanding the meaning of what I wanted to say and like a good woodsman with a chain saw, cut away the unnecessary brush in my papers and books. He was unrelenting in his demands for brevity and clarity and his lessons in that regard have remained with me. But he was dead set against my writing *The Joy of Gay Sex* because he feared that it would inform straight people about our sex lives, an idea he found intolerable. He much preferred that homosexuality (at least the sexual side of it) be kept secret. The only aspect of the work that pleased him was meeting and becoming friends with Michael Leonard whose color plates for the book we both admired, and who became a cherished friend.

Ed and I agreed that the book should be sexually stimulating. Toward that end we wrote six masturbation stories. We also wrote openly about the "kinkier" varieties of sex, such as bondage and water sports and we tried to be wise older brothers to teenagers who were struggling with their homophobic families.

Our relationship with the publishers, however, was strained. They exuded as much contempt for writers as they did for homosexuals. This seemed odd to us since some of them were gay. The publishers were worried that the public outcry against gay people created by Anita Bryant would seriously affect sales and that books might be confiscated by local officials and governmental customs services. It is very expensive to fight censorship battles, and it was made clear to us that Mitchell Beazley would not defend *Joy* in court.

The Joy of Gay Sex was a "packaged" book—a book prepared and printed by a packager then sold to a publisher who puts his name on it. Mitchell Beazley, a London firm, sold the books to Crown Publishers in the United States and Crown sold them to bookstores. Attorneys on both sides of the Atlantic scrutinized our manuscript and they forced us to defend our text on many occasions. For instance, the publishers objected to a section on sexually transmitted diseases, maintaining that disease is a turnoff. Ed and I would not relent on this issue and we wrote an informative essay on STDs after consultation with the CDC and experts in infectious diseases. When the British publishers critiqued our essay, we asked whom they consulted, only to learn that they took advice on STDs from a dentist!

Worries about censorship and confiscation led to the removal of all the masturbation fantasies Ed and I enjoyed writing. The lawyers also objected to the word "shit" and went ballistic over our essay on "bondage" which they pared down to one short paragraph without our permission.

The publishers were terrified when they read our essay on teenagers and rejected it out of hand because it did not condemn sex between teenagers and adults. They wanted us to write that sex between the generations was sick and immoral. The publishers may have been overreacting to the Anita Bryant scare, but in the end Ed and I dropped the essay rather than publish lies or make some gay men feel guilty about their sexual fantasies.

One day Herb Michealman the editor-in-chief at Crown summoned Ed and me to an audience in his office. By this time our patience was wearing thin. Ed refused to attend having had enough of censorship, while I planned my confrontation strategy.

Why were we writing the word "cock" instead of "penis?" Herb inquired.

"Because a cock and a penis are not the same," I responded. "Your penis is part of your anatomy. Your cock is something you fuck your wife with." Herb was shocked, but "cock" stayed in the book. He was actually a kind man and while he worried about the possibility of legal action against the book, he was uncomfortable in the role of censor.

Ed and I reacted to the publishers' interference in our individual ways. I was confrontational; Ed was subtle. It was the publisher's custom to come to New York and after a long, tedious dinner at an expensive restaurant to hand Ed and me a list of rewrites to be completed by the next day. Ed and I much preferred to have dinner by ourselves and do the rewrites instead of wasting time with them. Finally at one of these dinners I told the Mitchell Beazley people that I did not want to have dinner with them anymore. When asked why, I said that I did not like them and saw no reason to suffer through more tedious meals. Ed thanked me profusely afterward because he could never have done that.

On the other hand Roger Hearn, the English editor of the book (Frank Taylor was the American editor; we also had two editors-in-chief as well as two sets of lawyers to please), a heterosexual man, said that he wanted to learn more about what homosexuals were like. He wondered whether we might suggest a place where he could go and "observe" them. Since he was already in the presence of two notable homos, we understood that he wanted to watch fags having sex. Ed pinched me sensing the venom that was about to shoot from my lips and with all his Midwestern charm said, "I know just the place. It's called the Toilet. But don't worry about the name, it's not so bad." In fact the Toilet represented the height (or depth, depending on your point of view) of decadence in 1977. (The Mineshaft was its replacement in the 1980s.) The whole place was literally a toilet. One wall featured a large number of "glory holes" through which men put their penises for those on the other side to play with, or suck, or do whatever they wished. A naked man could also lie in a bathtub while other men urinated on him, often in groups. Ed gave Hearn instructions on how to get there and when to go.

Our British editor walked into the foul-smelling place at the appointed hour. According to his account to us the next day, at one point he needed to urinate. He walked over to someone and asked where he could find the toilet, not yet comprehending that anywhere in the Toilet was a toilet. The man opened his mouth. Shocked, Roger walked away and searched for a "bona fide room with urinals and toilet seats." He found a room with toilet seats, on each of which sat a naked man his mouth agape. Too much the English gentleman, Roger went to a sink ("It was filthy") and started to urinate when one of the seated men rushed over and put his open mouth under Roger's stream of urine. Roger ended up pissing in the sink, in the man's gaping mouth and on himself and he left the Toilet immediately thereafter. As I listened to Roger tell his story I winked at Edmund, appreciative at how well he had solved the problem of heterosexual condescension. I could never have done that.

The publishers' fears of legal troubles over the book were not unfounded. In the United States the chain stores carried the book under the counter so that straight customers would not be offended. Some libraries bought the book to a chorus of objections by the religious right, who often had it removed. (As late as December 1995, the presence of the book in the Clifton, New Jersey library was challenged by the religious right.)

In Winnipeg, Canada, a local newspaper reported how a woman in a rush looking for a copy of the *Joy of Cooking*, picked up *The Joy of*

Gay Sex by mistake. When she got home she opened the book (to "F," in order to make a fricassee?) and was profoundly embarrassed by what she saw. She called the police, who, upon her complaint raided the store and confiscated all copies of Joy. The whole affair had been trumped up by the police. Fortunately, the court ordered the books returned.

Joy was translated into German, Italian, Swedish, and French. Copies of the American edition were also exported throughout the world. A French Canadian firm published the book and sent thousands of copies to Paris, where French customs seized and shredded them. Thousands of copies of the American edition were imported into Britain, where they were seized by Her Majesty's Customs in London and burned. (In 1982, the British also banned my book, *Man to Man: Gay Couples in America*.)

Banning books is a complicated matter. When a book is prohibited from being published or distributed in a country, the publisher and the bookstore are both liable for criminal prosecution. Even if the book is not banned, (as *Joy* wasn't) and homosexuality is legal, the book can be declared "obscene" by the Customs. In that case, it cannot be imported into the country.

When Jearld Moldenhauer, owner of Glad Day Book Shop in Toronto, ordered copies of *Joy* from the United States, Her Majesty's Customs confiscated them even though homosexuality and anal intercourse are legal in Canada. At great financial risk, Moldenhauer sued for the return of the books. I volunteered to testify at the trial. The Customs officer testified that pictures and descriptions of anal intercourse were on the prohibited list for entry into Canada. When asked if he had considered the educational or cultural value of the book, he said, "That's not my business."

In my testimony I gave the history of the book and the reasons for writing it. I also noted that the book was part sex manual and part counsel for young people entering the gay world. The Crown pointed out that there were nine pictures of anal intercourse in the book. It was all quite polite, the Canadians not given to dramatics in the courtroom as we are here. A number of Canadian professionals also testified in favor of the book including Ronald Langevin, an eminent sex researcher from the Clark Institute of Psychiatry in Toronto.

In what must be counted as one of the finest legal decisions for gay people, Judge Hawkins wrote: "To write about homosexual practices, without dealing with anal intercourse, would be equivalent to writing a history of music and omitting Mozart. The books were ordered returned to Glad Day Book Shop.

Even with these legal wins, a system of *de facto* censorship existed almost everywhere in the United States, including our largest cities. It was after all 1977 and there could not have been more than a few gay bookstores in the whole country. Many gay men were simply too intimidated to ask a clerk for the under-the-counter book.

Even though Mitchell Beazley was a British firm, *Joy* was never published in England. *Gay News*, a London-based gay newspaper, had published a poem in which the author imagined giving a blow-job to Jesus on the cross. Mary Whitehouse (their Anita Bryant) sued the paper for blasphemy under a law that had not been invoked for ages. The paper was subsequently closed down and gay people came in for a great deal of criticism. Mitchell Beazley was understandably afraid that the same thing would happen to them if they published *Joy* in Great Britain.

Ironically it was the case of a heterosexual man that resulted in overturning British Customs laws against pornography. Around 1987 he bought a mail order life-size inflatable female doll with a hole for a vagina. Customs confiscated it because sex toys were prohibited for import. The man turned to the European High Court to rule on the dispute. Since Great Britain was joining the European Common Market, it was ordered to apply the same liberal standards for importation as the rest of Europe. The straight man got his fuckable doll back and it meant the end to the censorship of gay materials.

An added bonus for working on the book was meeting and making friends with the British artist Michael Leonard who painted the exceptional color plates at the beginning of the book. Irish in background, British in manner, Michael was raised under the Raj in India. His father was an officer in the British army and a probable spy during the period known as the Great Game, the surreptitious conflict between Great Britain and Russia for control over Central Asia. In 1978 William and I visited Michael in London. Michael asked William to model for him.

Both Ed and I received a lot of fan mail after the publication of

The Joy of Gay Sex. Gay men from all over the world wrote to us about suffering from the pain of discrimination and from the pernicious effects of hiding in the closet. Two letters stand out. The first was one from a teen-aged boy in San Juan who asked me to mail him a dildo, a request that I ignored because our agent feared legal problems. The second was from a London organization having an auction for a non-profit gay group. They asked if I would send them a pair of old used underwear! They emphasized the importance of the used condition—not new or freshly laundered. I sent it to them but never learned how much my underwear fetched in the auction.

By the late 1980s, the AIDS epidemic had already killed tens of thousands of gay men. The original *Joy of Gay Sex* was out of print and I thought that a new edition, updated for the 1990s might influence young gay men to avoid unsafe sex. Edmund was working hard on a new novel and therefore not available. I searched for a new co-author, eventually asking Felice Picano a distinguished novelist who had founded the SeaHorse Press in 1979, and Gay Presses of New York in 1980. Felice published the works of other gay writers at a time when mainstream publishers refused gay manuscripts.

The New Joy of Gay Sex was published by HarperCollins in November 1992.

In 1994, a Japanese publisher decided to publish *New Joy* in Japan. But the book would be text only. "No pictures of organs allowed in Japan," they said. Felice and I thought that ironic since Japanese pornography has been famous for centuries.

Neither Felice nor I had ever been to Japan and Felice was overjoyed at the prospect of an all-expense paid trip to Tokyo. I was ambivalent because I remembered neighborhood men who had died in World War Two fighting the Japanese. Felice chastised me, saying, "It's been forty-seven years since the end of the war. Give it up!"

The Japanese publishers arranged for a long series of meetings with Japanese newspapers, magazines and what there were of gay liberation organizations. I was most interested in the gay organizations, one of which had just done something considered unthinkable in Japan; they had sued the City of Tokyo. The group had arranged for a large meeting in a public hall owned by the city. When government officials learned that homosexuals were to meet there, they canceled the event. Suing the city was considered a slap in the face of traditional Japanese authority. It did not make the local papers because such disrespect is not publicized. The gay group refused to back down. I never learned how the suit fared in the courts.

Felice and I had a number of interesting discussions with gay liberationists in Tokyo who complained about the effectiveness of the Japanese system in repressing homosexual activism. No one ever said anything bad about homosexuality. They described it like trying to punch a window curtain; your hand goes through it and you have gained nothing.

Ni-Chome (nee-show-may) is the name of Tokyo's gay ghetto to which we went on our first night—and virtually every other night thereafter. The streets are even narrower than in Greenwich Village, the place blazes with neon lights and they are crowded with gay men of every nationality and the gay Japanese boys who prefer them. "Are you rice queens," a wide-eyed young Japanese man asked us. "I'm a potato queen," he announced. "I'll show you the bars in Ni-Chome. Come on."

There are literally hundreds of gay bars in Tokyo, but at the time only three or four allow non-Japanese to enter. The bars prohibited to us are tiny, some holding no more than six people. "You wouldn't feel comfortable in them," they explain, denying the obvious discrimination. The other bars are large, perfect meeting grounds for Western Rice Queens, and Japanese Potato Queens. Tokyo is filled with gay Americans attracted to Japanese men. They learn the language, get jobs with multinational firms and settle down with Japanese lovers. We made the rounds, meeting Westerners and their lovers.

The publishers arranged to take over "Yellow," a straight discotheque in the Roppongi District for one evening to publicize our book. The house was packed, filled with straight young Japanese girls and their gay boyfriends. A panel discussion about homosexuality featured Picano-san and Silverstein-san with translators provided. The invited press listened respectfully as panel members talked about our book and about sexuality in Japan. Only two reporters asked questions, both of them exceedingly polite since they consider probing questions rude. Then one of the straight girls stood up and asked if I had met a Japanese boy yet, by which she meant had I gotten laid. I had not. "Would you like to?" she asked. "Of course," I responded to the giggles of the crowd.

After the panel the music came on and two men dressed as condoms started to dance, advertising our message of safe sex. Then everyone else danced for the rest of the evening. And these Japanese kids were fabulous, the vanguard of a new generation with a great capacity for fun. Felice and I also danced, but not with each other. An American grabbed him and they eventually left together. (I forever teased Felice about flying halfway around the world to have sex with another American.) The Japanese girl who had asked me whether I had met a Japanese boy ran over and pulled me to the center of the dance floor. Waiting there was her gay boyfriend who could not have been more than eighteen years old. He was very beautiful, wearing tight-fitting clothes that showed off a perfectly proportioned body. We stared at each other awkwardly. In the United States I might have represented his father, but in Japan I looked like a sumo wrestler and they are held in great esteem. The girl pushed us together and when we did not immediately start dancing, she put our hands together and motioned for us to begin. Her boyfriend and I danced for a few minutes, but he was far too young for my taste, and without a language in common I thought it best to thank him and move on. Wherever I danced, gay boys were pushed into me by their straight girlfriends, some of whom even walked the boys over and pressed our bodies together. I loved the attention.

I was told that Japanese gay baths refuse to admit Westerners, particularly Americans, because of their fear of AIDS. I found this ironic since the Japanese frequently fly to Thailand to have sex with the attractive Thai boys and carry the virus (and lots of other diseases) back with them. I have an American friend in Tokyo who looks Japanese and speaks the language fluently. "I can get you into one of the baths," he said. That was an opportunity I was not going to pass up.

"The Japanese do not cruise the way we do," said Bob as we entered the bathhouse. "No eye contact or grabbing someone's dick. They'll run away. You have to use indirection to make contact."

"Indirection? I'll never get laid," I replied.

We put on kimonos and walked down to the basement to bathe, a requirement in Japan where cleanliness and personal hygiene has been raised to a fine art. The bathhouse had two rooms for bathing. The first contained a set of Western style showers and it was there that I bathed. As I walked out, I noticed the traditional style of bathing next door where naked men sat on small stools in front of a water faucet. One filled up a pot of water from the faucet and spilled it over one's head, wetting the body, then soaping, followed by rinsing the body with many pots of water. Sitting on one of those small stools was a gorgeous man, beautifully built, with well-defined muscles and a cock that would put most Americans to shame. I have never been attracted to the Japanese in the United States, but I found them adorable in Japan.

"I think I'll try the Japanese style of bathing," I said to Bob as I wandered over to the empty stool next to the young man. I had to do something quick or he might finish and leave. I wracked my brain for an *indirect* idea, no small dilemma for this New Yorker. I filled my pot with water and made sure that some of it landed on my neighbor as I ostensibly poured it over myself. Nothing. My next pot of water landed squarely on his body. When he turned toward me, I bowed slightly as he did the same. Nothing. He stood up, put on his kimono and left the room. A minute later I put mine on and went exploring, my first attempt at indirection an abysmal failure.

Japanese bathhouses have the usual dark orgy rooms, men wrapped in kimonos and covered by white sheets. All the action takes place under the sheets because of their shyness about exposing the body (bathing excepted), although from time to time one could see feet rising in the air looking like a tipsy Halloween ghost.

I stood near the door to each of the three or four orgy rooms trying to figure out how to get laid by being indirect. It seemed daunting. But every time I walked to a new room a certain attractive young man walked into it and sat down on a mat not far from the door, looking straight ahead at the wall. That's it, I thought. That's indirection! He wants me. I decided to test the hypothesis by walking into the room and sitting next to him. His gaze never wavered from the blank wall. I put my hand on top of his and caressed it softly. He did not move his hand. Then I dived under the sheet and he dived in after me. It was fun but this man was averse to kissing, a real turn-on in my sexual repertoire and he fled the room after we both came.

When I was dressing to leave the bathhouse, another Japanese man came over and patted me on the ass. I ignored it. He patted my ass a bit harder, then made a circle with two fingers of his left hand and pushed his right forefinger through it. "Fuckee, fuckee?" he asked. So much for indirection!

The bold display of pictures in *New Joy* made the book susceptible to censorship in a number of libraries around the United States. In June 1998 two nutty women walked into the Belmont, California public library and removed the book from the shelves, informing the librarian that they were holding it for "ransom." According to newspaper accounts, they placed the book in a locker for safekeeping and demanded that it be kept away from children. Newspapers had a field day with the story and it was even satirized on TV by *Comedy Central*. People in the community contributed replacement copies of the book to the library, so that where there had been only one copy before, there are now three. Apparently the women who removed the book had their library privileges revoked.

In 1980, I began work on my third book *Man to Man: Gay Couples in America*, a clinical study about the strengths and problems of gay male love relationships. I wanted to get out of New York City and learn how gay couples fared in other states and in rural areas, so much quieter and low key by comparison.

I spent much of my time indoors interviewing couples. In St. Louis I interviewed a man who had just broken up with his hustler lover. He himself was running a gay escort service in the city and the former lover still worked for him. "Do you stay here all day in this motel room?" he asked, then offered to send me a young man to keep me company. "No charge. Let's just call it Southern hospitality. What kind of boy turns you on?"

I did not want to seem rude. I was in the South surrounded by corn fed farm boys with lithe, tight bodies oozing testosterone, speaking in mesmerizing Southern accents. That's who I wanted.

"No problem," he said. "How's 8:15 tonight?"

"That will be just fine."

At eight-fifteen there was a knock on the door. Walking through it was a charming young man exactly what I had described. "I read *The Joy of Gay Sex* and I always wanted to meet you," he said, putting his arms around me and giving me a warm kiss. Mickey was a delight, affectionate, highly aroused sexually and accommodating to my every wish. After we had both come and ever the interviewer, I asked him about the kinkiest sex scene he had ever participated in. He had once been hired by a man to get fucked by a Great Dane while the man watched and jerked off. "I'd never do that again," Mickey said as he described how mittens were tied around the dog's feet and a muzzle placed over his mouth. "He was really into me and he kept drooling onto my face. And when he came, you wouldn't believe how hard he pulled out."

Mickey spent the night cuddled up next to me and we had sex again in the morning. I offered him money during breakfast but he refused, saying that it was one of the best nights he had spent with a man in a long time. That's Southern charm for you. I gave him a big hug, said goodbye, packed my bags and went on to the next city.

I have always had a soft spot in my heart for Southern sissies. I met Jimmy in a gay bar in Houston. His heavy Southern drawl hooked me immediately and we went back to my motel room, undressed and started kissing. He was very attractive, but a bit morose. Within minutes he started to cry. I cupped his head in my arms and said, "I may not be the greatest lay in the world, but I didn't think I was that bad." He explained that the police had arrested his boyfriend that day and Jimmy did not have the money to bail him out of jail. He was not even sure how much money he needed, but hoped that I would provide at least some of it.

I did not mind giving him money but it is very difficult to have sex with someone who is crying. I called a gay friend who was well connected with the Houston police. Within half an hour the boyfriend was released without bail and we arranged for Jimmy to talk to him over the phone. His boyfriend safe, Jimmy, gushing with appreciation was all over me. "Anything you want," he said while licking my ear, "but I always cross myself before I get fucked." He stayed the night and in the morning (after crossing himself again) we had breakfast and said good-bye.

There is a myth that gay relationships never last. In my research for *Man to Man*, I found many couples that had been together for decades. More discreet than young gay men in the ghettos of large cities, they kept low profiles and weren't seen at late-night dance clubs. I found many couples that had been living together for at least twenty-five years.

The oldest couple I interviewed had just celebrated their fifty-first year together and I devoted a whole chapter to them in my book *Man to Man: Gay Couples in America.*

More important, I learned about the crucial relationship between a gay man and his father. The prevailing psychiatric myth was that a gay boy was sexually attracted to his mother (Freud's Oedipus Complex). I found exactly the opposite to be true. The erotic attraction is between the gay boy and his father. During my interviews some gay men told me about the sexual fantasies they had toward their fathers from the time of their adolescence. One teenaged boy in Boston masturbated while listening through the wall to his parents having sex, imagining that his father was fucking him instead of his mother. Another man from Chicago daydreamed that during supper his father would get up, walk behind him, play "horsy" and fuck him. Gay men told me stories about sneaking looks at their fathers' genitals or getting sexually aroused seeing them in a tight bathing suit at the beach, or just looking at his hairy chest. All were invariably attracted to their father's masculinity.

Some of my respondents had actually tried "to bag him," as one of them put it. One Texan, short and lightly built, had joined his high school football team not only to please his father, but also to provide the right environment in which to seduce him. Keeping his football uniform on until his father returned from work, he would lie on the couch and pull his pants down to his knees and his shirt up, exposing his jock in the hope that his father would initiate sex. (He never did.) Yet another teenaged boy in bed with his father in a motel room put his hand down his father's underwear and grabbed his genitals. (The father leaped out of bed.) After discussing the memory of wanting to have sex with his cruel and emotionless father, a New Yorker went home and masturbated to the fantasy. "I had the most powerful orgasm of my life," he told me the next day.

A few gay boys did have sex with their fathers. Most of the time they were raped by fathers who were probably psychotic and who raped their daughters as well. These gay boys grew up emotionally scarred from the rape, from the violence and from living in a home without love. It is instructive how often they kept the secret, even from siblings who were also being raped.

A few gay men had had consensual sex with their fathers claiming that the experiences were filled with affection and caring. "It was the only time I ever felt loved by him," one man from Missouri said while being interviewed with his lover. There is virtually no research about these men or how the sexual relationship with their fathers affected them in adulthood.

I put what I learned about the relationship between a gay boy and his father in the first chapter of *Man to Man* that I titled "Fathers, Sons and Lovers." Published in 1981, it was the first time any psychologist or psychiatrist wrote about the father's importance as a sexual and love object to his gay son. In 1991, gay psychoanalyst Richard Isay published the results of his analytic work with gay men, concluding that gay men have an erotic relationship to their fathers. He suggested that it was a normal part of gay male development. Our work was independent and I was pleased to learn that he had confirmed my earlier studies.

I had a lot of rewriting to do before the book was ready for publication. William and I accepted an invitation in the fall of 1979 from Ed White and Chris Cox who had rented a house in Key West, to stay with them for a week or so and work with Chris who was editing my book.

Three books were being written in the house. Ed had just begun *A Boy's Own Story*, Chris was working on *A Key West Companion*, while I was completing *Man to Man: Gay Couples in America*. We wrote only during daylight hours, saving the evenings for socializing. William therefore, spent much of his time sunning himself on the gay dock called the "Dick Dock" (alternately the "Queer Pier"). While sunbathing one day he spied an attractive man reading *The Joy of Gay Sex*. Hoping to lure him back to our house, William said that he was staying with both authors and asked if he would like to come home with him and meet them. The gay man obviously surmising a fraudulent come-on said only, "Humph," and turned his back on William.

"I know who you mean," said Ed. "I've seen him there many times, but he's very young, only twenty-one, I think."

"Ah! I enjoyed that age for many years," replied William.

One evening the four of us went over to Jimmy Merrill's house. Jimmy was out of town at the time and we socialized with his lover, David Jackson. They had a pool, but William was afraid of the water and refused to go in. I suggested that we return later that night when I could give him a swimming lesson. "Only if you arrange that *no one* is here to watch," he said.

"You want me to throw David Jackson out of his own house?" I replied. Needless to say we never returned to the pool.

In the evenings we went to dinner or cooked at home. We often played "Botticelli," a game requiring an encyclopedic knowledge of everything. William was in heaven playing a game that tapped into his vast reservoir of useless information. Both Ed and Chris gave him a run for his money. I was the dope of the group.

William Bory

Photo by Michael Leonard. Used by permission of the photographer.

Eleven

We May Share Many Queens, Said Garry, But Not The One You Mean

A darker side to William's life began on a summer day in 1972 the year we first met. While he sat in Central Park he was approached by a thin, attractive Hispanic boy, about the same age, with a jaunty swagger and hair like William's that draped over his shoulders. There was an instant simpatico between them. "Would you like to smoke some good weed?" said Mick who would become William's friend and adventurer for the next couple of years. They walked out of the park along an Upper West Side street and into a brownstone to Tom Flynn's apartment on the third floor.

Flynn was a bit of a curiosity among those who knew him at GAA. There were many apocryphal stories about him. He had an attractive face and one could easily see he must have been a beauty in his youth. Exactly when that youth was, was a matter of dispute. There were people who claimed to have known him for over twenty years and who swore that Tom looked exactly the same then as he did today. It was rumored that he had been a surgeon in the employ of some European power (some said Hungary, others Britain) during the First World War and that he had amassed so great a fortune that he never had to work again.

Tom's handwriting contributed to the illusion of foreign breeding. The script was well formed, a style of cursive writing born of obsessive training long since out of fashion in the United States. His speech was elegantly constructed if a bit frozen. His clothes on the other hand were drab, cheaply made, thoroughly undistinguished, which ironically proved his wealth all the more to his observers. It was as if underneath the threadbare clothes lay the raiment of gold. All these things were untrue.

He was as poor as a church mouse, not a seventy-year-old Hungarian physician who stumbled upon the fountain of youth. His greatest assets were these: the contents of a locked bedroom closet and like the Pied Piper an ability to attract young men to his apartment.

William often described the apartment as consisting of a bedroom in which Tom slept, a living room where everyone else bedded down helter-skelter, a small mostly unused kitchen and a bath. The furniture was torn, stained, and smelled—but one of the many odors that permeated every fabric, the rug, even the woodwork. Every window was covered with dark venetian blinds, over which were heavy dark material stapled to the wood frame, the better to keep out the slimmest rays of light that might have sneaked past the closed blinds. The window treatment was unchanged day and night, a permanent part of the apartment landscape so that light never invaded the boundary. The isolation from the sun had the effect of hermetically sealing the place, making day and night the same, obliterating any sense of orientation in time. The only uncovered window was a small one in the bathroom with filthy pebbled glass.

There were three people in the apartment when William and Mick arrived—Tom and two other boys sitting around in their underwear. All the boys were in the eighteen to twenty-year range, gay and friendly. They all smoked pot together that afternoon and afterward William lay on the floor and napped. When he awoke, he was offered more grass.

For supper Tom put out cheese sandwiches, potato chips and soda for himself and his guests. There were no plates or cups and they sat on the floor more or less in a circle, ate the sandwiches and passed the bottle of soda around. Tom asked William if he wanted to live there for a while to which William said "yes." He thought it a perfect hideout from home, school, and the outside world from which he felt completely alienated. The other boys had already whispered that Tom had an endless supply of drugs that he handed out after supper. A hideout and free drugs to anesthetize the pain, to put his brilliant mind to sleep was the quickest path to a passive denial of all responsibility and self-respect.

There were rules however, William continued. The boys were not allowed out of the apartment except for weekly shopping trips. The front door was locked from the inside and the keys kept on a chain around Tom's neck.

The boys were prohibited from washing or taking showers, or from washing their clothes, William said. This had the effect of concentrating the pheromones that lay so heavily in the room that they came close to forming a haze. Exceptions were permitted for shopping or if a boy was allowed out for a social event. It did not happen often and always at Tom's suffrage. He kept a lone bar of soap in the drug cabinet, protected by its lock against the possibility that one of the boys might sneak in a shower while Tom slept. Tom's own schedule was rigid; he woke at five a.m. every day and retired at nine every night. He warned the boys that his sleep was not to be disturbed under any circumstances. He spent most of his time reading and writing, occasionally talking on the phone (which was also locked). There was no radio or television.

Tom renamed William. He was called "Aldo Maria Bory" from then on. The name would stick and for years afterward William introduced himself as Aldo to whomever he met including me.

After Aldo (née William) and the other boys ate their sandwiches, Tom unlocked the drug cabinet and brought out a handful of pills of various shades and shapes. It was as if he were handing out after-dinner mints, the coda to a fine meal. He let the boys pick and choose among the drugs and they did so capriciously by shape, size or color. They had not the slightest idea what they were taking, how much, or whether the blue-colored pill for instance, might be harmful when swallowed together with the round white one. Nor did they care. They had long since given up any sense of personal responsibility and voluntarily wrapped themselves in the cloak of masochism. They were "white powder" drugs, a vast pharmacopoeia of prescription drugs, but not cocaine, heroin, or alcohol all of which Tom disapproved. Everyone smoked pot and popped the pills for the night.

William remained there for a couple of months and called it home. But one day Aldo and Mick wanted out. They put the contents of a sleeping pill into Tom's orange juice and when Tom drifted off they took the keys from his neck, opened the drug cabinet for the other boys (and themselves), unlocked the front door and charged into the street.

They were both so alienated from their families that it did not occur to them to go home. They went to Central Park instead and when night came fell asleep under a tree. Cops standing over them asking for identification, which neither of them could supply, awakened them. Through stupidity, self-destructiveness or a drug-induced fog, they told the cops where they had been living. The cops marched them back to Tom's apartment. Tom was furious, made a number of phone calls, then told Aldo and Mick that they would have to go to London where they would be taken care of by Lord Walter Radson with all expenses paid. They were given airline tickets that afternoon and shuttled off to JFK Airport for the evening flight. They were still prohibited from showering or cleaning their clothes, so that they emitted so foul an odor that other passengers kept a wide berth from them. In later years William expressed the greatest compassion for those sitting in close proximity on the plane.

One can just picture the sight these young men presented to the immigration officers when they arrived at Heathrow Airport. "Filthy hippies" would have been the most lenient description. Their dress was slovenly, the odor extraordinary, long hair which in those days symbolized drug-taking youth, bandannas around their foreheads, hostile postures and terse responses to the questions asked by her Majesty's Immigration Service—and not a penny in their collective pockets. They were detained immediately, placed in a holding room with a number of Pakistanis (who avoided them because of the odor) and searched for drugs. Immigration did not find the drugs Aldo had secreted in one of his shoes. When asked why they were in London, the boys handed the officer the piece of paper with Radson's name and phone number. There was a short conference between the officers, then one of them made a phone call. The boys were told to sit and wait.

Lord Walter Radson was a wealthy, English aristocrat who although married, was openly gay and had served a brief period of time in prison for gay related activities. William always told people that Walter was arrested for molesting Boy Scouts in his sauna, but the story sounded apocryphal.

In about an hour their passports were stamped for entry and they were shuttled outside to a waiting limousine. They were driven to Radson's London townhouse and put up in one of its apartments. They obviously made showering the first order of business. In the evening, Aldo and Mick, wearing new clothes (bought by Radson) accompanied him to an elegant restaurant. They were thrilled with the arrangements. Only twenty-four hours before they were sleeping on the grass in Central Park, filthy, smelly, with not a clue as to how to find their next meal. Now they were sitting in an expensive British restaurant, catered to by its solicitous staff, eating course after course of expensive food after which they would leave, money from Walter in their pockets to their own London apartment. They knew there was a price to be paid for Walter's largess. He wanted sex with them. That was just a matter of using their bodies and they were quite experienced at that. They had both had sex hundreds of times before in couples, three-somes, and orgies at Tom's house (while Tom slept). Satisfying Radson was a small price to pay for their English adventure. They even looked forward to it since it would be their "insurance policy" for remaining in London and so they agreed to make sure that Walter had a good time. After dinner they all went back to the townhouse where Walter sampled his investment. He must have liked what they had to offer because he invited them to stay for the summer. Neither of them had ever been outside the United States before and everything about the future looked promising.

Upper-class British society, or at least the homosexual side of it dazzled Aldo and Mick, children of New York working class families. Aldo's favorite dish at home was pork chops and sauerkraut while Mick's was black beans and rice. Night after night in London they were served food with foreign names on plates of delicate china. Mick was distinctly uncomfortable with it, looking down at the white linen tablecloth, the sparkling glasses and more sterling silver than he had ever seen. He had not the slightest idea which fork to use with which course and felt profoundly stupid and inadequate. Aldo on the other hand, although just as uninformed, felt as if he belonged. As each course arrived at the table he started talking, waiting until Walter or another guest started to eat—with the correct utensil. Only then did Aldo begin. When a dish arrived with its contents completely unknown, Mick stared at it, upset that he could not identify it or know therefore, if he liked it. One evening for instance, a fish was placed in front of him including the head and tail. Poor Mick was terrified because he did not know whether he was supposed to eat the head, a prospect that revolted him. Aldo, on the other hand, in just one evening, had picked up proper upper class British dining behavior. He ignored whatever dish lay in front of him, as if it were a servant, something invisible. No matter how offensive the food seemed to him, he ate it in perfect haughty upper class style. He also never ate everything on the plate whether tasty or not. He considered it poor manners. To do so would have expressed an excitement about food.

Radson's homosexuality was a public secret and taking young men to elegant restaurants as a prelude to sex an old habit. His friends were also upper class English gay men, some like himself members of The House of Lords or the royal family. Others were wealthy businessmen. Most were married as he was, had families to which they did or did not pay attention. They had sired their heirs, the fortune therefore preserved in the family name. They used their money to satisfy their carnal needs with an ever-changing stable of gay boys from around the world. If any of them actually had lovers with whom they established long-lasting relationships, Aldo was unaware of it.

William said that Lord Radson treated them well. Most nights they slept in the London townhouse. There were also occasional nights at Salisbury, Walter's huge twelfth-century estate. What quaint dinners there must have been, Walter, his wife Maggie and the two kept boys from America. Aldo, Mick, and Maggie spent many hours together chatting and if she objected to her husband's dalliances, she kept it to herself. Walter also owned a large motorboat and Aldo was thrilled to ride with him along the British waterways, his long hair lifted by the breeze.

William returned to New York at the end of the summer 1972. It was months later that I met him on Halloween night at the Ninth Circle and months later yet when we began our life-long relationship.

I finally met Lord Radson in New York City a few years later. For reasons I never understood he was the darling of a group of gay New York psychiatrists who always threw a party for him when he came to New York on business. Their admiration for him perplexed me. He did nothing to help the cause of gay liberation, used his money only for his own pleasure and could not have cared less about these doctors who gave no support to our struggle for gay rights. William still felt charmed by Lord Radson and I was naturally curious to meet this man I had heard so much about.

I remember feeling competitive and jealous, predisposed to dislike him. I did not own thousands of acres of land, a multi-million dollar business, a large estate in which to live and I was aware that William missed all the elegant British things he had experienced that London summer. I also anticipated not a little hostility toward me from the psychiatrists who resented my participation in the Gay Liberation Movement. They wanted things kept quiet, to stay in the professional closet while I and other gay professionals were stirring the mud.

Walter was delighted to see William again, although he insisted on calling him "Aldo."

"This is my lover, Charles," William said, introducing me to Walter who proceeded to ignore me completely and to carry him away to another part of the room. I sat down on a couch. I admit feeling angry, jealous as hell, not wanting to be there but respectful of William's desire to see Walter again.

Shortly afterward William and Walter strolled over to the couch and stood right in front of me, although Radson still acted as if I were invisible. Walter was facing me, William's back to me. Then Walter placed his hand across William's butt, his fingers pushing hard toward William's rectum almost lifting him off the floor. And he kept his hand there even when William gracefully tried to free himself.

I was livid. The arrogance of this bastard, I thought. I took my cigarette and pushed it into the back of Radson's hand. His hand burned, Radson pulled it away from William's ass, said nothing and walked away a minute later. William chastised me for being rude. "Rude? You mean it's not rude for that bastard to ignore your lover and then try to push his fingers up your ass in full view of me and everyone else at the party?" William said that he hoped I would never do that again at any other party with Radson, to which I replied that I was bringing a blowtorch to the next one.

Years later, Garry Henderson, a young Irishman moved in with us as a roommate for about a year. Garry had been given an upper-class education in an Irish boarding school, a place he hated. But it gave him a proper British speech pattern and the bearing that goes with it. While in New York, he was invited to a party where he met Lord Radson. Overhearing Garry talking Radson said, "Ah! A fellow Englishman." Hating the English as the Irish do, Garry said, "I'm not English, I'm Irish."

"At least we share the same queen," said Radson.

"We may share many queens," said Garry, "but not the one you mean!"

Twelve

Keep Your Mouth Shut, Your Dick Hard, And I'll Do The Talking

After we had lived together for over a decade William asked if I had made plans for retirement. Given that he was fifteen years my junior I said, "Yes, I thought it would be you," a reference to the fact that he had not worked for all the years we had lived together. A few days later he walked into Fordham University and applied for admission. That was not an easy act for someone who hated educational institutions as passionately as he. He completed an undergraduate degree in art history with honors. Then he took the LSAT in order to apply to the Rutgers University School of Law. William was the only person I ever met without test anxiety. He had not the slightest doubt about his knowledge or his ability to convey it. Oddly he did not score in the top ten percent in the LSAT and that mystified me. A copy of the exam was returned together with both the correct answers and those given by the candidate and I scoured it to learn how William missed getting the high grade necessary to gain admission to a first rate law school. He scored in the eighty-eighth percentile and only a few more correct answers would have put him over the ninetieth.

It did not take long to find the problem. It was vintage William. He purposely left out all the answers to one set of questions and I knew why. "William, if you had answered these questions you would have scored in the top ten percent."

"What?" he shouted. "You want me to answer some stupid questions about baseball? How dare they ask questions about baseball on a law exam? If they wanted someone to answer them they should have called on some stupid, fucking jock." He had left the answers out because the questions offended him!

William started at the Rutgers University Law School in Newark that fall. Knowing his finicky food habits, I prepared sandwiches of his favorite cold cuts from Zabar's and a thermos of good coffee to take with him every day for the next two years. He studied very hard the first semester, and then realizing that law was a snap for him, he relaxed.

William had a strong aversion to all things mechanical. He was offended, for instance, by typewriters and years before when I brought a used IBM Selectric typewriter into the house, burst into tears, as if I had betrayed him. He refused to enter the room in which the offending object was placed. Law school forced him to come into contact with hated mechanical things—typewriters, telephones, computers. He went ballistic over the even newer electronic devices. An answering machine, for instance. He had his own phone, but when he was away at school the phone rang incessantly disturbing my sessions with patients on the other side of the wall. I insisted he buy an answering machine. He refused. (His compromise with modernity was to allow it acceptable for people to write on common paper with fountain pens, instead of papyrus and quills.) I bought one for him, the easiest operating machine I could find. I had forgotten that I could not win on the battlefield of passive-aggressive behavior. He listened politely to my instructions on how to operate the machine and thanked me for my help. He even turned on the machine each morning before leaving for school. His phone continued to ring unabated because he refrained from putting an outgoing message on the damn thing. I recorded the message and made sure the machine was turned on when he left for school. My message was, "Hello, William will return your call when the sun rises over the Heel Stone." The reference was to the stone at Stonehenge, England above which the sun rises perfectly just once a year marking the summer solstice. William gave me a knowing grin when he heard it and kept it on the machine.

Each day when he returned home and noticed that he had messages, he erased the tape, rewound it and turned the machine off! A few months later he learned that some of his professors were trying to contact him by phone, so he started listening to his messages—every Friday afternoon.

My computer represented an even more serious invasion of his existential world. He stared at it as if it were the anti-Christ, the epicenter from which all goodness in the world would be destroyed.

On those occasions when he asked me to type some law notes, he gave me the hand-written copy, then stood at least five feet away from the blasphemous machine, as if any nearer would fatally infect him with contemporary society. Yet by the end of his first semester of law school he came to accept its use as a word processor and learned to do his term papers on it. To balance his compromise with modernity, William refused to learn any of the commands by which computers work. Instead he asked me each and every time how to turn on the machine, turn it off, bring up a file, erase a word, print the documents and so on. It drove me out of my mind until I finally typed a one page set of instructions on how to use simple, often used commands and taped it to the machine.

William's computer phobia was not yet over. The evening of a speaking engagement in Connecticut, I received a frantic phone call from him. I could hardly get him to calm down and tell me what was wrong. "I've done something awful," he said and began to cry. I feared that someone's life was in danger. He finally told me that when using the spelling checker, he must have done something bad (it was definitely tinged with the feeling of *mea culpa*) because the words in very large type appeared across the screen—"FATAL ERROR." This was an unfortunate choice of words for someone who still believed that Zeus threw lightning bolts down from Mount Olympus. I assured him that no one was going to die (unless I killed him for not learning how to use the computer) and explained how to fix the error. Those were the days of 64K memory, more tiresome to use than today's brainy computers.

William was made an editor of *Law Review* at Rutgers, although not the coveted Editor-in-Chief and after graduation accepted a job with the Legal Aid Society of New York defending poor and underprivileged people in the criminal court system. It was the perfect job and it gave him almost limitless license to vent his hostility toward the police by cross-examining them on the witness stand. He was very skilled in the courtroom, but I was a bit nonplussed that through his wits drug dealers, muggers and other low-lifes were being released back onto the streets. "Have a nice day in court," I would say as he was leaving, "and I hope your client is sentenced to twenty years of breaking rocks." He understood.

He hated the routine stuff and the paper work but he loved getting his guilty clients off. One day he was defending a man accused of dealing drugs. He and his client appeared before the judge for pleading. "Take your hands out of your pants," he said to his client and as the drug dealer did so, a small packet of drugs fell onto the floor. The schmuck brought it into court! Without missing a beat William stepped on the packet throughout the whole proceedings and no one saw it. His client got off.

On another occasion he was defending a young, cute, straight man accused of some petty crime and they were scheduled to appear before a gay judge later in the day. The young man was about to discuss his involvement in the crime when William said, "Shut up and do as you're told." He instructed the accused to call home and have someone bring down a pair of his tightest pants. When they arrived, William ordered him to put them on ("Nice ass," William said). Then, "Before we walk into the courtroom, you are going to play with yourself. I want to see a stiff hard-on in those pants, and I don't want to see it go down. Just remember if it goes down, you go to jail. And when you're standing in front of the judge with me, make sure you rub it every minute, nice and slow, so the tip of your dick is pushing against your pants all the time. Keep your mouth shut, your dick hard, and I'll do the talking."

"Case dismissed," said the judge.

Thirteen

This is a Letter from Ramses the Great

When most people talk about going for "R & R" they mean "rest and recreation." In our case it meant "rocks and ruins." William spent the first ten years of our relationship reading from the time he woke up in the morning, to the time he retired at night. He read extensively about ancient civilizations and extant archeological sites. His extraordinary knowledge of archeology and culture provided the foundation for our travels around the world. I would plan an itinerary, book the air and hotels, while he quietly set to work refreshing his amazing memory about places to visit. However, it was in the nature of his personality that he confined the list in his head and never divulged them to me beforehand.

He was implacable with respect to exercising absolute control over where, when and to whom he would divulge his encyclopedic knowledge. One humorous example of this quirk occurred in the British Museum in London. We went straight for the Egyptian collection where he walked over to a stone tablet containing hieroglyphics. His face lit up and he called to me. With uncommon excitement he said, "This is a letter from Ramses the Great." Then he started reading the hieroglyphics, but after a minute stopped in mid-sentence and turned around. All the people in the room had inched toward us, huddled together listening to his explanation—and why not since they had found someone who could explain what the hell they were looking at?

Nothing could better illustrate the differences in our personalities than this event. If it had been me, I would have looked at the group of eaves-droppers and said, "Come closer, please," then pretended to read the letter making it up as I went along. "Now if you follow me to the next exhibit" I would have continued and gone on to explain the significance of the other artifacts in the room, ad libbing everything, a perfect venue for my exhibitionistic personality. William's reaction was consistent with his. Furious that the onlookers were violating our privacy, he walked out of the museum and refused to return until the next day. But one can just imagine the richness of our trip when we later spent three weeks traveling in Egypt. He brought the sand, the stones and the lives of the pharaohs to life.

One year we traveled for two weeks in Portugal with my cousin Marilyn. Toward the middle of the trip we stayed for a few days in the Bussaco Palace, the former hunting lodge of the King and Queen of Portugal. I had reserved the royal suite for us. It was time to do our laundry and what could have been more appropriate than to wash our clothes in the royal bathtub? We threw the clothes and the soap into the tub, stripped and got in. We washed the clothes, sometimes like children threw them at one another (it was a very large tub) and ended up on the floor of the wet and soapy bathroom having sex. There is something to be said about slipping and sliding during sex.

The next morning we left the hotel. "Take this road," he said.

"Why?" I asked.

"Just do as I say." I knew from experience that he had something special in store for us.

After thirty minutes of driving on a narrow, winding mountain road we arrived in Lorvao, a small town that claims to be the toothpick capitol of the world. "Drive in there," William ordered, pointing to a large open gate. "Now park." Our car was instantly surrounded by a group of very shabby looking people who walked like rejects from "The Night of the Living Dead." I instinctively understood where we were.

"You took me to a lunatic asylum?" I roared at him.

Ignoring me he said, "Get out of the car." (Marilyn refused.) The psychotic patients from the sanitarium surrounded us and mumbled among themselves. "We're waiting for the caretaker," William said and sure enough in a few minutes he arrived and knew why we had come—even if Marilyn and I did not. He unlocked the door to the adjoining church and turned on the lights and we were greeted by an extraordinary interior, the altar made of silver, beautiful frescoes on the walls and stained glass in the windows. It was all in perfect taste. It had not been used for decades and the richness of the hues had been preserved by the absence of light. The caretaker spoke only Portuguese, but by this time William understood the language, and translated for us. (In another week, he was able to speak it.)

Neither of us could understand how anyone might prefer an escorted bus tour, here today and gone tomorrow, instead of traveling independently. But there were a couple of times when daylong bus tours were the most efficient way to get to and from a site. For instance there are beautiful Etruscan tombs in Tarquinia, just north of Rome but you must join a tour group in order to see them. One follows the tour escort who speaks only Italian, down long flights of dark stairs in order to enter the tomb. Once inside, he turns on the lights. In the first tomb the light fell upon a magnificent fresco of a man (presumably whose tomb it was) fucking a woman from the rear. By chance standing directly in front of the fresco was an Italian mother and her ten-year-old son. Shocked by the fresco she grabbed his head and quickly turned it to the left. On that wall was another fresco of the same man fucking a man in the butt. She tried to cover the boy's eyes but he wiggled out for a good look. William wrung his hands in satisfaction.

We also took an escorted day tour of Pompeii. (On another trip we spent two days there.) Of course William had already studied the layout of the city for months. He knew it so well he could have been its mailman. He was incensed that the guide was not up to William's archeological standards and could not discuss the city's economic and historical importance. In retaliation (he took all these things personally) every time the guide pointed to a royal house, William pointed to a whorehouse— and there were many of them in Pompeii.

We took long vacations in two Arab countries, Egypt and Morocco. A camera is always at my side as I wander through such enchanted places. The most memorable picture I ever took of William occurred just after dawn in Giza outside of Cairo. I wanted the best pictures I could get of the Pyramids, especially wanted to avoid the huge crowds of people who invade the place from the moment the gates open. I therefore arranged for a cab driver to drive us before dawn to a small hill overlooking the Pyramids. ("Bakshesh" got us through the closed gates.) The picture shows him from the back sitting on a nearby ledge studying the three kings and three queens Pyramids. It is a wonderful shot.

When we had finished the driver could not start his car. We tried to push it but failed to budge it. An elderly man walking his donkey came over to help and the four of us were then able to push it down the hill and the car started. I said to William that that's the picture I should have taken—a donkey watching four jackasses push a car!

Morocco is very exotic and where we had many zany moments. In 1987 we were staying in Marrakech and decided to visit a "souk" not far from town. A souk is a country market held once a week. One can buy fresh vegetables, meat, spices, or get a haircut for yourself or new shoes for your donkey. It is colorful, exotic, and very charming. We arrived at the souk in the company of two young Moroccan men who were acting as our guides.

At the souk I was pursued by a man who wanted to buy William's jeans. They were a rare commodity in 1987 Morocco. "No," I said, he could not. He offered *all* of his merchandise for William's jeans. I ignored him. William, walking twenty feet ahead, was unaware that someone was trying to buy his pants.

Suddenly the man offered more dollars than the jeans were worth.

"Sold!" Did I say that? Yes, I had. What was I to do?

The gleeful man and my guide (together with an eavesdropping crowd) were already at William's side. The man tugged at William's pants clearly indicating that he wanted them taken off right there and then. "What's he saying?" William asked. Our big mouth guide explained.

"You WHAT?"

"Take your hands off my pants," William said crossly threatening the new owner of the jeans with the point of a "solid silver brooch" he had just bought for one dollar and seventy-five cents. Still surrounded by the crowd I paid off the disappointed Moroccan, giving him enough money to buy a pair of jeans for himself. William berated me continually for the next two hours as we waited for the bus back to Marrakech, interrupted only to help catch a chicken that had jumped out of the arms of a man who had bought it for his family's supper.

These foreign trips were not without occasional problems between us. There were times especially in our first ten years together, when William acted like a hermit and refused to leave our hotel room. It was like a case of agoraphobia and I thought him a pain in the ass because of it. In Bath, England, he loved our hotel room and refused to budge from our bed, which, after a few minutes was covered with books. (One suitcase was always filled with books.) He only ventured out the next day to have tea in the famous Pump Room that he adored because of its quaint atmosphere. He was much worse in Amsterdam where except for meals, he did not leave the room for three days and I was forced to go sightseeing by myself. I had no idea what he was afraid of and any attempt I made to discuss the problem was met by a stony, rage full stare.

William also exhibited his masochistic streak of self-denial on these trips. The best example of this occurred in Palermo. Sicily is one of my favorite places and I made my first trip in January 1971 when I was a graduate student at Rutgers University. William heard me tell stories of the trip many times. For instance one sunny day on the Isle of Ortygia, in Syracuse, I stood together with a crowd of people listening to the local band playing excerpts from Rossini and Puccini. They all wore tattered, ill-fitting uniforms and torn caps on their heads. They were awful, yet the people stood respectfully and applauded as the band finished each number, even the adolescents who in the United States would have used the time to spray paint parked cars. For a few hours I thought about leaving school, living and working in Syracuse, but fortunately I woke up from this dream. He also heard stories about the fabled, and expensive San Domenico Palace Hotel in Taormina.

William wanted to see it all. Sicily is filled with archeological ruins including the finest Greek sites in the world and Goethe called the view from the Roman Theater in Taormina the single most beautiful sight on Earth. In Palermo we did the usual tourist stuff including the Cathedral in Monreale, in which all the stories of *The Bible* are painted on the walls in gold leaf. (If one tipped the priest he turned on all the lights and the gold sparkled in every direction.)

The next year we toured Southern Italy and in Reggio Calabria spent hours studying the Warriors of Riace, the most magnificent Greek statues in the world. We also toured Apulia where we ate the two most amazing meals in Italy, but William also wanted to spend a few more days in Palermo. When there, he said that the city housed some of the last works of Giacomo Serpotta, who lived during the sixteenth century. He was the finest stucco artist that ever lived and while many of his works have been destroyed over the centuries, they can still be seen in some of the private oratorios in Palermo. William said, "All my life I dreamed of seeing them."

"But why didn't you tell me about them when we were in Palermo last year? You could have spent as much time viewing them as you wanted." My question was met with one of his usual brush-offs. "You can't do everything at one time." For the next two days we looked at every oratory that housed the work of Serpotta. These chapels are seldom visited and we had to search for whoever was in charge of the keys. He was right, the plasterwork was incredible. I took pictures of everything that William wanted and bought him a fabulous book of the man's work. The book not available in the United States, cost a great deal of money and William cherished it as if it were made of gold. When we arrived back home, he placed my photographs in the book.

Our trips were more than mere vacations; they were our contact with history. We shared the conviction that all of us are the product of thousands of years of culture, which included the beauty of the arts and literature, as well as the desolation of war and the genocidal attempts of one religious group to kill off another. In Spain we visited the sites of "auto-de-fes," places where the Marranos (which means "swine"), converted Jews and Moors were burned after *The Inquisition* sentenced them to death for heresy. In Luxor Egypt, William insisted on hiring a Coptic taxi driver for the week because Islamic terrorists were murdering them. These trips fed our souls, made us feel that we understood ourselves and our place on Earth much better than we ever had before. And they deepened the love between us.

Fourteen

I Just Want to Sit There and Watch Him Sleeping

It was the winter of 1984. We were vacationing in a gay guesthouse in San Juan. I would dunk in the pool, compare notes with other guests about places to eat while William lounged in a beach chair reading, wearing his light green revealing Lycra bathing suit to taunt the boys. The suit never got wet.

One afternoon he closed his book, looked at me for a few seconds, and said, "Look." He pointed to his left leg. There were two small, round, purple spots as bright as a child's purple crayon. The spots popped out at me like fingers reaching to the sky, an illusion founded on their meaning.

We knew what they were and what they meant. We were on vacation and in a few days we would be home. There was time enough. William said nothing more. Neither did I. We kissed. Then he opened his book again and I returned to the pool.

Until that day I had been able to armor myself against the raging AIDS epidemic killing gay men all over America. A couple of patients were ill and the health of some friends was deteriorating, but I kept a professional detachment from them, even as I knew that things were going to get worse not better. What I did not know was how many of the ill would die in the next ten years.

I have nothing to say that has not been said a thousand times before, no insight into caring for a dying loved one. I have lived to see so many deaths: father, mother and any number of close friends, colleagues, and patients. I witnessed the disease since the beginning, watched Kaposi Sarcoma lesions spread across the skin of so many people, visited during the repetitive hospitalizations, listened to tales of pounding headaches from taxoplasmosis, the stabbing poker-hot pain of peripheral neuropathy, the constant diarrhea of criptosporidium. I watched men, some I barely knew, many who were friends—-the handful whom I loved whose deaths pained me like flesh torn from my body. Their faces visit me periodically, sometimes on my white pad as I write, sometimes on the dark ceiling of my bedroom or sometimes as I innocently walk past a grocery store and notice a food that a dead friend had a special yen to eat.

When I see for instance, a large hero sandwich, I remember that fall day in 1979 that Chris Cox the writer and editor, took me to a bodega in Key West to order "The Heartburn Special" (as he called it), a hero sandwich stuffed with every cheap processed meat and cheese imaginable and drenched with spicy oils. How we wolfed down our Heartburn Specials. We sat like sisters on the porch swing and Chris, who had been an actor, put on his best Tennessee drawl and imitated a good Catholic boy who always crossed himself before getting fucked. "Why darlin," Chris drawled, "We Southern chillin' always thank God when she gets us a good pluggin."

A decade later I visited Chris in a New York hospital. He was recovering from a bad bout of PCP. His lover had died the year before and Chris told me, "I took care of him until the end, but now there's no one left to take care of me."

Six months later I visited him in his apartment and found him near death. Chris lay on a mattress on the floor. His eyes were buried deep in their sockets, the cheeks hollowed, his facial expression frozen into a death mask. He did not respond to my words or to my touch. I struggled with the competing desires to hold him in my arms and to flee. Although I wanted to bolt from the room I knew I would never have this chance again. I bent down, put an arm underneath his shoulders, and hugged him. "I love you," I said. I did not believe he could hear me or even know who I was, but with his face still frozen he replied, "I love you too."

Chris died a few hours later. I felt so glad that the last words he heard were about being loved.

And I want to tell Jason's story, at least the few days of it we shared. He was John Preston's lover. Preston was the author of *Mr. Benson,* arguably the most famous S & M novel ever published and a man of great charm who befriended many younger writers. William and I visited John soon after he moved from New York City to Portland Maine in 1979. Jason was a recent émigré from San Francisco's leather scene, a slave and a devotee of kinky scenes. By chance we arrived a couple of days before his birthday. "Will you go dancing with me?" he pleaded. "John refuses to dance." So we went dancing that night, Jason dressed in leather, a dog collar and leash around his neck ("You don't have to hold it if you don't want to") and worn out, scuffled black boots that flopped around as he walked. How out of place he looked on the streets of Portland and how out of place he felt.

As a birthday present he asked John to strip him naked, handcuff his hands, tie his legs, urinate on and beat him periodically during the day. "You think it's easy being an 'S,'" John complained as he walked up the stairs to the third floor torture chamber and down he came a few minutes later to drink the next six-pack.

William and I decided that our present would be to cook lobster for Jason's birthday dinner. It was his favorite dish. In the late afternoon I called up the stairs to the torture chamber, "Jason, after you take a shower and get dressed, we'll start cooking the lobster."

And he called down the stairs, "I'm not taking a shower and I'm not getting dressed, so start cooking." John shrugged his shoulders as if to say, "I'm not getting involved." William and I agreed that water sports should be confined to the torture chamber, nor did we look forward to the aroma of urine in the dining room. A stronger approach was required.

"If you don't take a shower and get dressed before dinner, we won't cook the lobster," I yelled up the stairs.

My threat was greeted by silence for a long minute, then, "I'll take a shower and put something on." We heard the ambiguity but by this time we were all famished, so we agreed and threw the lobsters in the pot.

Jason was a man of his word. He ambled into the dining room showered, shaved, hair combed, a contagious smile on his face—which was all he wore, except for the dog collar. "This is the best birthday I ever had in my life," he said his eyes teary, as he kissed the three of us. It was a wonderful dinner, the lobsters, the birthday candles, the wine and Jason's few hours of joy in John's house that night, an island of safety surrounded by conservative, straight New Englanders and discrete homosexuals. I loved Jason even though there was a vast, unbridgeable chasm between our sexual worlds. I loved him the night we danced, the night stark naked (except for the dog collar) he cracked open his lobster, the day later in the week when we drove to John's cabin in the woods. There Jason told me that he could not remain in Portland anymore, that he loved John but felt so isolated, so much a fish out of water, that he had to return to San Francisco. How I loved Jason for his warmth and kindness, but most of all for his childlike vulnerability. I think I envied it.

AIDS did not kill Jason. He left Portland and moved back to San Francisco. A year later during an eroticized hanging, an unusual form of masturbation, he died of asphyxiation unable to loosen the knot that choked the life out of him.

I told you that I had nothing new to say, nothing you have not read before in at least a dozen books or have not heard on TV, some maudlin special about how one fag helps his fag lover "let go," or on New York's Broadway stage where at least half the actors are playing characters who eventually die of AIDS—the other half actually dying. Yes, movies too, although maybe not in your town, not cock on the screen, certainly not a fag cock that somehow looks different than a butch one—maybe because of where it's been. I will not ignore those of you that were caretakers for friends and lovers who lived all these stories as I did, experienced the ambivalence of love and hate, the conflicting desires of wanting to save and wanting to kill, the facade of strength containing an interior of Jell-O—and for a few, the pretense of God in order to shield you from the truth—your helplessness in the face of disease and death.

I am telling stories about the illnesses and deaths of people I loved. Perhaps you have stories of your own. Your parents may be dead, from cancer after a long illness or suddenly in an automobile accident. You have friends who died, lovers or spouses, perhaps even children. The only time you and I can stop people in our lives from dying is when *we* die. That is what I mean when I say that the death of loved ones is so banal, so commonplace.

So why do these deaths still hurt so much?

I know what I am going to write in the following chapters. I hear the words clearly like the sound of a huge church bell ringing in the distance.

These stories I tell like Chris and his hero sandwich, like Jason and his dog collar—like Ken, whose life and death I have not yet opened in these pages, like the stories about William and me after we returned from San Juan—they are all stories of hurt, loss, and abandonment.

Some gay men faced their infection gallantly, searching for whatever new medicine was touted to make a difference. The road they traveled toward cure or a palliative was littered with devastating illnesses and hospitalizations. There were a few who demanded that they exert control over how they died, not the HIV. They committed suicide. William could not accept the disease and his personality changed dramatically.

One winter morning in 1991, John Preston, William, and I had breakfast together on Miami Beach. John was in town for a reading at a Miami book convention; William was in residence for the winter after going on disability and I had come down for a long weekend. We were dining at the News Café in South Beach. The weather was pleasantly warm, a breeze running through the fronds of the palm trees. John had almost died the year before from a number of opportunistic infections. He had been given up for lost but had somehow bounced back. The two of them started trading stories about diseases, hospitals, doctors, and keeping track of medications—and about dying.

I felt a wave of sadness rush over me, even as they chatted amiably. It was the irony. The background of waving palms, the sun, the people scurrying past us—the gym boys pumped up by weights and steroids, the models walking to a shoot—people walking, running, whizzing by on skate boards or roller blades all part of the vibrant, youthful South Beach scene. But in the foreground were my lover and my friend suffering from the same disease and though animated at the moment, both destined to die. I see that memory and feel again what I did; there was nothing I could do to stave off the future.

And now to introduce Ken. Six feet two inches tall, dark hair, flat, well-defined abdominal muscles, and powerful legs. He had a beautiful butt. His eyes were blue/gray and they changed hue depending upon the light. His face was as handsome as his body, the proportions just right, not rugged masculinity, or merely strikingly handsome as some gay men are, but the kind of men gay fashion designers have in mind when they design underwear. Any gay New Yorker knows the type, one of a thousand faceless and at once beautiful men who wait on us at restaurants while waiting for their acting/modeling ships to come in. Ken, too, was an actor, a vocation he took very seriously, but he worked a humdrum nine-to-five job and lived cheaply in "Alphabet City."

He was a man of extraordinary energy. Nothing pleased him more than getting up early and visiting the lobby of a grand New York City public building such as the Trump Tower. He just wanted to look. He would beam with delight at how beautiful it was (at least to him). Ken felt just as passionately about people. When attracted to another man he fell completely in love without qualification or ambivalence, consumed by an idyllic fantasy of the other person. His world narrowed to only himself and the object of his affection, toward whom he gave every sign of love he could muster: all his time, passionate sex, small but meaningful gifts, acquiescence to the other's preferences and enough affirmation and caring to please a dozen men. He was indefatigable, loved everything about living and his warmth and charm, his helpfulness was as genuine as I have ever met. He never as far as I know, had a mean thing to say about anyone else.

The object of all this passion was William. They picked each other up at a bar one night, went over to Ken's apartment, opened the sofa bed and fucked. From that moment on Ken was obsessed with William, whom he called "Billy." Every star he saw in the sky was Billy; the beauty of every public lobby was Billy, every painting of a beautiful man, Billy. Ken attributed to Billy all the characteristics he cherished: warmth, public affection, kindness, empathy, compassion, and most of all reciprocity in love. They were all true of Ken, his characteristics projected upon the latest object of his passion, who, just incidentally happened to be my lover.

William and I had long since rejected monogamy in our relationship. To him the desire for outside sex was only "an itch that needed to be scratched." It took me a long time to accept that men were constantly falling in love with him and phoning him repeatedly (on his answering machine which continued to be erased each Friday afternoon). He exhibited not the slightest jealousy toward guys I bedded as long as my time with them was fueled only by lust. "I'll scratch his eyes out," he said if I formed an attachment to another sexual partner. But Ken became far more important than an "itch."

Ken came to our apartment often. He sat on the couch, face pointed downward like a forlorn child, sheltered by the light of his guiding star, William. He would drink coffee or tea, the cup held close to his mouth, covering the lower half of his face, which served to accent his gorgeous eyes that "mooed" at William. The "moo face" was the sign for me to leave them alone. I would walk into my adjoining office and read from a pile of psychological journals scattered on my desk. Within an hour or so I could hear their footsteps in the hallway. I allowed a few minutes for Ken to kiss and hold William, a minute more for him to plead to stay longer and the sound of the door closing and the lock click shut.

These manipulations were designed to convince William to dump me and move in with him. He showered "Billy" with unconditional love and fabulous sex. He told William that I was old, ugly, fat, and worse yet boring.

His strategies were doomed for failure. There was too much glitter in Ken's eyes for him to understand his beloved. William was not warm; he abhorred public displays of affection; he wasn't sweet, empathetic, compassionate nor did he believe in reciprocity in anything. He hated most public lobbies as grotesque and vulgar. Literature and the arts were foreign to Ken but at the center of William's intellectual life. He was however, a great lay and for a long time that, as well as his charm and energy provided the impetus for the relationship. William introduced Ken to our friend Michael Leonard. Michael had been using William as a model for years and welcomed Ken's participation. Posing nude together only increased the sexual tension between them.

A crescendo in this chorus of absurdity occurred one weekend at our country house in upstate New York. "Can I go with you?" asked Ken. William was about to give one of his evasive answers when out of a mean spirit I replied, "Yes, we'd be delighted to have you for the weekend." I relished the probability that they would get on each other's nerves, which appealed to the Machiavellian streak in my character. I also had a crush on Ken and I liked looking at his beautiful face and extraordinary body. I felt that I held all the trump cards that weekend and I was out for a grand slam in order to get even with both of them.

William was furious at my unilateral decision. He was feeling ill and wanted to spend the weekend recuperating quietly. He knew that I would leave him alone until he recovered, but Ken made insatiable demands because his ego required continual feeding.

When we arrived William still feeling under the weather, went directly to bed. I showed Ken to his bedroom on the second floor and then started tinkering around the kitchen preparing supper. Within a few minutes Ken bounded down the stairs and into our bedroom where William was trying to sleep. A minute later he came out. A minute later he went in again. Out again. In again. William begged me to keep Ken out so that he could recuperate. "You're not being kind to 'Ken Doll,'" I said using the name William called Ken, although not to his face. "All he wants is to show how much he loves you," I sarcastically remarked, cruelly savoring the moment.

"Please," begged William who returned to the bedroom, followed closely on *his* heels by Ken Doll, followed on his heels by me. William lay on the bed. Ken sat on the bed. I gently took Ken's arm and said, "We're leaving the room now." Without a murmur, Ken left the room (William crossed himself as we left) and returned to the kitchen with me. "William is ill and needs rest," I said. "He doesn't want anyone in the room with him. I'll call you when he gets up."

"But I won't disturb him," Ken said. "I just want to sit there and watch him sleeping."

"Absolutely not," I said.

The signs of rejection were all over Ken Doll's face and he ran upstairs to his bedroom. A few minutes later I heard the water running in the upstairs bathtub and over that the sound of crying. I felt sad for Ken because he was so needy, so demanding, so overpowering with his love and so vulnerable to the slightest signs of rejection. I went upstairs. Ken was sitting in the tub holding his head in his hands and crying. I tried to console him. At the same time, I felt profoundly guilty that my Machiavellian manipulations had worked so well. Out of envy toward Ken I had hurt him far beyond what I intended.

That was in 1981. There was not an epidemic yet, but the seeds were there. They were awake while William was sleeping in our country bedroom; they were inside Ken crying in the bathtub. At the time I thought of William and me as though we were George and Martha in

Who's Afraid of Virginia Wolf, catching a young minnow in our net, Ken Doll. But we did not know that anyone was going to die. I have often wondered what I would have done if I could have foreseen our future, if I could have looked into a crystal ball and seen that night in Houston so many years later when I held Ken, ill in my arms. Or if I could have seen the slow, progressive deterioration of the most brilliant mind I had ever met, so helpless in his last year of life that I would have to carry him to and from the bath in order to wash his frail body.

I am glad I did not know. We still had more than a decade together to come. William and I still had many more countries to see, places to visit, dinner parties to give, tricks to meet. William had yet to complete his undergraduate degree, attend law school, and then join the combat of criminal law. I had at least three more books to publish. Ken had yet to leave Manhattan, live in L.A., fail as an actor, get into and out of a relationship and finally become my friend.

Ken Neumeyer

Photo by Michael Leonard. Used by permission of the photographer.

Fifteen

Would You Like to Try Some of Mine?

A sero-positive diagnosis today is not what it meant when William and I returned from Puerto Rico. Newly diagnosed gay men today are given the "cocktail," a set of drugs including the new class of protease inhibitors that has changed the AIDS landscape from a sentence of death to one of hope. The gay community has watched this metamorphosis with wonder. Men whose flesh had evaporated leaving behind a skin-covered skeleton gained weight and muscle mass after taking the new drugs. Hollowed eye cavities filled out and cheeks regained the rose color lost years before. Energy surged through their bodies like electricity waking up a set of simple dormant pleasures like eating out, going to the movies or the gym. Their testicles swelled with hormones as lust popped out from its long-term hibernation and the infected man started to covet some cute guy down the street he had not noticed in years.

It is a picture of a body rejuvenated, alive once again, a person who for the first time in years thinks about the future. Only a few months earlier he might have been planning his memorial service or struggling to find the courage to end his life. He runs to the doctor to get the results of the latest blood test and rightly calls up lover, friends and family to announce that his T-cells have gone up as his viral load has declined.

It was different when we arrived back in New York from Puerto Rico. GRID, Gay Related Immune Deficiency had been renamed Acquired Immune Deficiency Syndrome (AIDS), partly because straight I.V. drug users were becoming infected, but also for political reasons. We did not want the word "gay" in the name of the disease; we did not want to give straight people another reason to hate us. We knew about T-cells but the ability to directly test for the presence of the virus, what we now call viral load was a decade in the future.

My observation is that every serious illness begins the same way. There are tests to be done, appointments to be made with specialists, questions to ask, fears to face, then back to the doctors again to learn the results of the blood tests, x-rays, bone scans—more questions to ask—and always the same answers; "We'll have to see," or, "Maybe this will help" or, for the doctor who is either a Pollyanna or terrified of telling the truth, "Don't worry, everything is going to be fine."

One could search the horizon of the AIDS landscape and see nothing there, no treatment whose efficacy was assured, only medications whose significance was that something was being done. Infected men went bi-weekly to their physician's office to sit before a vaporizing machine and inhale aerosol pentamidine, the contemporary prophylaxis for PCP, much as the elderly go to health spas to inhale gases from the ground to cure real or imaginary diseases. It was considered a medical advance when HIV positive men could buy their own aerosol machines and breathe pentamidine at home. AZT was the drug of choice to attack the virus, but it had significant side effects and no one knew its long-range hazards.

Not every symptomatic person was diagnosed with AIDS. Some suffered only from AIDS Related Complex (ARC), whose symptomatic illnesses were less severe. People with ARC had symptoms such as night sweats and thrush, debilitating but not deadly, whereas AIDS patients suffered from potentially terminal diseases such as Pneumocitis Carnii Pneumonia (PCP), Kaposis Sarcoma (KS), and lymphoma. Patients with ARC asked their doctors if their symptoms represented a different disease than AIDS and whether they would remain relatively benign, or were they a way station on the path to what was then called "full blown AIDS" and death. The obvious question had no obvious answer. No one knew, at least not then.

Some medical facilities were as hysterical about AIDS as the general population. Accounts of the mistreatment of gay men by hospitals, physicians and dentists made the rounds of infected men who desperately needed to know where they could be treated with dignity. It was customary for visitors to don full infectious disease gowns including hats, masks, and gloves when entering the room of an AIDS patient. This medical "drag" helped to create an environment of danger, although medical authorities collided in explaining why; some said to protect the patient, others to protect the visitors. AIDS organizations kept a list of funeral homes in the city willing to hold a service and burial of an AIDS patient because many others refused to do so.

I supervised a young psychologist who was hospitalized with PCP in 1990. One day his attending physician appeared in the doorway to his room wearing a large, brown paper shopping bag over his head with cutouts for his eyes and mouth. He proceeded to ask questions about his patient's condition. "Wouldn't it be easier to examine me?" said my supervisee.

"No, it's fine from here," said the terrified physician from the doorway. I was pleased to learn that the patient made a complaint against the doctor.

Another friend was in a hospital elevator when one of the hospital employees whispered "A," and everyone in the elevator fled at the next floor leaving the patient alone and feeling like a leper. These examples are from New York City hospitals where doctors had more experience with AIDS than almost everywhere else.

Probably the most egregious example of medical discrimination occurred in a southwestern city hospital when a man who was dying from AIDS related illnesses showed up in the emergency room. Not only did they refuse to admit him, but to get rid of him completely they put the dying man on a plane (at the hospital's expense) and flew him back to California where he died within a few days of his arrival.

The darkness of the landscape, medicine's ineffective treatments, the hysteria and fear in the gay community and the nation at large laid down the perfect soil for charlatans, crackpots, and quacks who emerged from the mud to prey upon desperate men. "Anything is better than nothing," some patients said. A Manhattan physician, Steve Ciazza, claimed that AIDS was caused by an advanced form of syphilis breaking through what is called the "blood/brain barrier." His cure was injections of huge amounts of penicillin. He was the darling of certain circles of gay men who left their own physicians to begin treatment with him. At least it was a theory for them to believe in. "See, I'm still alive," said a psychotherapy patient of mine who had been treated by this medically certified quack. And it was true; he was still alive, although his symptoms had not abated.

There were testimonials to Ciazza's genius by other men who also said, "See, I'm still alive." They all died. So did the genius doctor and from the same disease.

"Look at me, I'm still alive," said another of my patients and with the same enthusiasm that he brought to every other aspect of his life. He was eating blue and green seaweed, which, according to theory was a "natural" cure for an immune deficiency. The word "natural" was important, representing an antidote to the (unnatural?) man-made chemicals most physicians prescribed for their patients. So convinced was he about the effectiveness of seaweed if taken in the correct proportions and dosage that he became a salesmen for the company and sold them first to AIDS patients, then to others as a prophylaxis and broader yet to everyone for keeping healthy.

AIDS patients in their thirties and forties had their ears to the ground listening for any rumor of a new non-medical treatment to replace the previous non-effective ones. With the best of intentions friends alerted them to the latest "drug of the month," believing that by doing so their infected friends might get a leg up the ladder toward a cure.

Many gay men bought blenders for mixing a variety of ingredients said by someone to cure AIDS. Into it went the prescribed recipe, a variety of "natural" products that when properly mixed was drunk by the patient once, twice, three times a day according to instructions. A few of them remarked that they felt like medieval witches brewing potions from spiders and the wings of bats. "But I'm still alive," they said week after week until I visited them in the hospital just before they died.

Vegetarian activists had a field day pointing their protein-deficient fingers at seropositive meat eaters. It might not be too late for flesh-eaters to cure the disease if they would only begin a total vegetable diet—preferably from "organic" vegetables. If the vegetarians cured from one end the "high colonic" missionaries cured from the other. Patients were told to flush out the "poisons" that lined the bowels with toxins that were the residue of agricultural chemicals. But a conventional enema would not do; one had to use a long nozzle in order to reach far enough up the colon before opening the floodgate.

AL721 was a popular drug for curing the disease. It was egg lecithin manufactured in Israel it was claimed, which probably gave it an air of authority. After all everyone knows that Jews make the best doctors. Packets of the stuff were kept in the fridge or the freezer and after mixed with a fluid, drunk three times a day. It was ineffective but lucrative for the opportunists who sold it. There was also Hyperacum, actually St. John's Wort, an herb that was effective as an anti-depressant. And "Compound Q" had a spectacular rise as a cure for AIDS until it killed a few people. It was the root of the Chinese cucumber, which sounded harmless enough.

Yet even these totally ineffective drugs were not the worst exploitation. The epidemic let loose a group of psychopaths who moved in for a killing. My friend Mel went to California for "Ozone" treatment. Of course he got no better, just considerably poorer, but he looked for another alternative. He called me one day to say that he was leaving for Moscow that night to join a group of American AIDS patients to undergo a new treatment for the disease. There was a doctor there he said, an elderly scientist who had discovered a cure for cancer but the staid medical establishment refused to acknowledge his discovery. He was going to use the same treatment on them. He had invented a machine that transferred the electro-magnetic energy from the Earth into the body of the patient, which, the unappreciated doctor said led to a cure.

I faced that moment so many times over the years, listening to a friend or patient describe some crackpot scheme for beating the reaper and not knowing what to say. For so many years in the 1980s and 1990s medical science had nothing to offer. There was no cure, not even symptomatic relief so that witches' brews, vegetarian diets, herbs and enemas while useless as a treatment for the virus, gave a gay man the feeling that he was doing all that he could to combat the disease. At least they did no harm. But there were other treatments, like Russian electro-magnetic machines that stepped over the line by encouraging gay men to leave their physicians and to replace them with psychopathic opportunists who promised survival for a price. It was one thing for a gay man to eat benign herbs, another to join a treatment that would hasten his death. Physicians and psychologists like me tacitly approved of the former but warned against the latter. We were often accused of being part of the uptight "medical establishment" that denigrated "alternative" medicine.

"Don't say it," my friend Mel told me over the phone after a long pause in my response to his announcement about Moscow. "I'm not asking for your advice. I know what you think about this kind of stuff. I want you to tell me that you love me and that this is a good idea and that I'm coming back cured. And I'll give you the phone number of the hotel so you can reach me."

"I love you, Mel, and I'm glad you're doing everything you can to fight the disease. I'll call you in Moscow next week." We said our good-byes and hung up the phones. Desperation leads to actions that would otherwise be perceived as foolish and futile. While Mel forced himself to believe that he was traveling to Russia to be cured, I knew that they were going to kill him. I hated "them," the faceless charlatans who fed on the vulnerability of terminally ill gay men. I called Mel a couple of times during the next two weeks. He was not feeling well. When he returned to the United States he collapsed as he walked off the plane. The Russian geniuses did not notice that he had PCP. He died in September 1993.

Not all the stupid and potentially harmful treatments were promulgated by psychopaths. Some came from otherwise rational people in the gay community. Chuck Ortleb, my old dancing buddy from GAA, Editor of *Christopher Street* and the *New York Native* vehemently denied that HIV caused AIDS. He claimed it was a swine flu virus and attacked medical authorities for covering over the evidence. Gay conspiracy theorists published articles hypothesizing that the federal government had intentionally introduced the virus into the gay community to kill us off, probably via the new Hepatitis B vaccine. Slightly more benevolent paranoid thinkers suggested that the virus had been developed for germ warfare in a government lab and escaped into the population due to carelessness.

The enemies of medical research spawned people like John Lauritsen who published a number of attacks upon traditional medicine. He too claimed that HIV did not cause AIDS and that AZT was poison that killed gay men; he therefore admonished them not to take it. He said AIDS was a "psychosocial disease." His encouragement to gay men to stop taking AZT, I thought bordered on the criminal.

Ian Young is an old friend, a Canadian poet of much talent and an early publisher of the works of other gay poets at a time when no mainstream press would publish them. He is exceptionally bright, well read, an early leader in gay liberation and a sensitive man. But he too did not believe that the HIV causes AIDS and like Lauritsen, argued that AZT causes the symptoms that lead to death.

Ian was dining with us one night when William complained about all the medications that he had to take in the course of a day. Talking about the disease always sounded like an alphabet soup. There was AIDS, ARC, AZT, CMV, DDI, DDL, DHPG, EBV, KS, PCP. The two of them talked privately as I prepared dinner. After Ian left William said that they talked about "natural" alternatives for AIDS.

"Ian said that some people drink their own piss," William said looking for my reaction to this idiotic idea. I refused to step into the trap for if I had, he would have parroted all the usual arguments about my being part of the uptight, conservative medical establishment, which I am.

"If you want to try it, go ahead," I said nonchalantly. William stood up and walked to the bathroom. He returned a minute later with the most awful expression on his face.

"I'll never do that again," he said.

"Maybe yours isn't the right kind," I replied. "Would you like to try some of mine?"

The failure of home brews brought the infected into the arms of psychological healers. It began benignly enough. It was "stress" that caused the deterioration of the body and seropositive people were told they could extend their lives by removing it. Just how stress decreased T-cells was unclear to say the least, nor was there the slightest shred of evidence that decreased stress led to better health. Physicians and therapists told their patients that reducing stress would increase T-cells. I do not know how many of them believed it. I did not.

AIDS patients became "survivors," the new ubiquitous identity of twelve-step groups, the offspring of Alcoholics Anonymous. Like other survivors, rape victims, incest victims, and child abuse victims, AIDS patients dressed in "survivor" drag proclaiming their infection as a sign of empowerment, a public statement that they were victims no longer. The gurus of the survivor/empowerment movement claimed they were healed of the scars of rape or incest or child abuse. Many AIDS patients joined the list of survivors in the hope that they too might join the ranks of the healed.

There were a few special healers. Foremost among them was a compassionate woman whose seminars were attended by hundreds of gay men at a time. There was something of the charismatic about her, an ability to touch the emotions of many gay men who were either infected or were among what was then called the "worried well." She had her followers speak to the disease in their bodies and confide their fears to the group and for many of them it was the first time that they had done so. She gave people hope; she helped men regain the psychological strength to face the coming ordeal. She was a nurturing Earth Mother with unconditional love for all.

She went on however, to claim that our health is a mirror of what we believe about ourselves. Illness was, therefore, a sign of self-hatred. Cure the self-hatred of the soul and one cures the illness in the body. Men gave tearful testimonials at weekend-long seminars that they had been cured of AIDS by her philosophy, that the virus had been banished by self-love. "See, I'm still alive," was again the message but this time with the added, "And I'm not going to die." But they did.

It sounded like a new theory of homophobia to me. We gays were born a despised class and suffer a deep sense of shame because of it. Then the HIV infected some of us and we were told that it was our fault, the result of sexual promiscuity. Then healers took frightened sick men and made them feel guiltier still because they could not cure the illness in their bodies. It was our fault again: for being gay, for getting sick, for not curing ourselves.

Self-hatred does not cause disease, and self-love does not cure it.

*

William's attitude toward his illness was to ignore it. He hated doctors, hated medications, and hated the idea that he was not in full control of his body. Underneath was a deep-seated fear and vulnerability. He was not "strong" in the sense we usually use the word to imply the capacity to face danger or an inner fortitude and he denied his vulnerability by refusing to divulge his recent diagnosis to anyone.

For years his symptoms were mild ones. There were a few night sweats, thrush, and occasional night chills in bed when William would tuck himself underneath me for warmth. KS we were told, augured a good prognosis in the sense that early Kaposi's Sarcoma (KS) had shown itself a predictor of longevity.

His physician Ira was an old friend, generally competent in medicine with a good sense of humor, but very slow in his thinking processes, his talking and most of all in his examinations which could take as long as two hours. We later learned his pace was the result of ingesting sleeping pills and other drugs that he self-prescribed. On more than one occasion his secretary heard a thud from his examination room and found him on the floor unconscious. It was drugs, not illness that caused the collapse. He was also HIV positive although we only learned that after his symptoms could no longer be hidden.

William liked Ira as his personal physician for any number of reasons, all of them irrational. For one, Ira was Jewish. This may not be a conventional way to choose one's physician, but it made great sense to William who saw in every person the sum total of the history of his race, religion, and nationality.

But there were other reasons for choosing Ira. William could and did boss him around. Ira also and quite ironically hated doctors and the two of them traded stories about the incompetence and stupidity of this or that doctor. At one point in his treatment, I objected to William's going to Ira's office bi-weekly for his aerosol pentamidine (that he called being "Pasteurized") because his T-cells were too high to catch PCP. "Ira needs the money," he responded and off he went, as if that were sufficient reason to justify a useless medical procedure.

Consistent with the roles we played in our relationship, William did everything possible to fight the significance of the disease, while I picked up the slack and mobilized resources for the future. We both avoided our feelings of terror this way. My first thoughts were about him. It seemed so unfair. He had finally learned how to use our computer to write law papers, completed his education, passed the bar exam and went to work each day in a white shirt, tie, and jacket. The diagnosis was an irony, a chuckle from "the Gods" (the Gods of ancient Greece), a punishment for making these positive changes in his life. "You should have stayed on the couch reading esoteric books," I could imagine them saying, implying that as a hermit he would have been spared.

It was right after the diagnosis, one of those little things, a very intimate form of communication that goes on between lovers, married couples, possibly any two people in a long-standing intimate relationship and almost always behind closed doors. I remember one man who talked to his wife's toes, telling them all the news of the day. I have worked with any number of couples that have named their genitals, "Peter and Patter," for instance. It is not erotic, merely the kind of tender, childlike things some couples do. My friend Mel (the one who went to Russia to be killed) had a large dick that he called "Thumper." Many couples speak in baby talk and bits of it sometimes slip out in the company of friends at dinner ("Please pass me the salt, Boopsie"), but others have no idea of its full extent when they are not around.

For us it made no difference if people were around or not because they would not have noticed its subtlety. William and I would extend the forefinger of a hand and lightly touch the tip of the other's forefinger. The tips of our fingers were joined for only a second, representing our union, our feelings of love and intimacy, our sharing the moment—a reaffirmation of everything we meant to one another. "Buzz" we both said at the moment of contact, the verbal representation of the voltage shared between us. We would often "buzz" when we made up after an argument and when we took the "animals" to dinner.

We had bought a couple of stuffed animals on a trip to Provincetown. One was a baby shark named "Whimpy," the other a red lobster hand-puppet called "Cranky." Whimpy was a timid shark. The story as William told it, was that Whimpy was a baby shark who refused to bite people. His parents were very upset about this, afraid he would grow up to be a sissy shark that could not feed himself. So they decided to send Whimpy to "Biting School" with the other young sharks and where he would learn how to take a good bite out of people swimming in the water. Whimpy refused to go. "I want to go to ballet school and learn to dance en point," he said to his horrified parents who locked him in his room. Cranky, incidentally, had no story. He was all attitude, tough, ready to confront anyone unfair to lobster-dom.

We often ate at the Bello, one of our favorite Italian restaurants on the Upper West Side with the puppets in hand. "Table for four, please," I would say to the maître d who knew the routine. When the waiter arrived, I would put Cranky on my hand and interview him. "Have you been cooking any of my friends here?" If he said no and they always said no, William, who had been sitting quietly with Whimpy, would say, "Don't believe him, get the chef." A minute later the chef would arrive and get into a conversation with Cranky about being kind to lobsters ("Even a lobster has a mother, you know") to the amusement of the other diners, one of whom one evening sent a beer over to our table for Cranky. Needless to say children surrounded us and talked to Cranky, who occasionally tried to bite off their noses ("We need it for the soup," he would say). After fun times like these, one or the other would extend a forefinger. "Buzz."

It must have been William who originated this unique and powerful sign of our relationship. He would never hold hands in public but "buzz" was perfect precisely because of its privacy. We might both be reading on the couch, when one or the other would extend a forefinger. The other would meet the touch and "buzz." Then we would go back to whatever we were doing, fed by the private symbolic act. The occasional buzz meant the world to me, a simple moment in time when the outside world was banished from my consciousness. Otherwise I was surrounded by the epidemic in friends, patients, and colleagues. It consumed a significant part of my professional practice and in time consumed part of me.

Ira, William's physician, became a serious problem. We had mutually referred patients to each other, but some of my patients came back to me with stories of Ira's irrational behavior. After having lunch with Ira one day, William returned, saying, " He's whacked out of his mind." Ira was making a number of bad medical decisions in his treatment. Steve, Ira's closest medical colleague believed that the effect of the virus was multiplied by his drug use, perhaps to the point of accelerating cerebral deterioration. Ira's patients were in potential jeopardy. We agreed to ask Ira to stop practicing medicine.

The three of us met for dinner. Steve took the lead. He was direct and to the point. "Ira, you have to stop practicing. You're making bad medical decisions, and I know you'll blame yourself if anything bad happens.

We want you to end your practice and start taking care of yourself." I expressed my agreement.

"So you guys are telling me that I'll kill my patients if I keep treating them." Neither Steve nor I responded. The next week Ira closed his practice, I think relieved; we remained good friends. That was in 1989. He died November 1990 at the age of thirty-eight.

Many of my own patients and supervisees were either seropositive or diagnosed with AIDS. There are a number that stand out, especially Lex. He was in his mid-twenties before he came out right into the center of the AIDS storm. He contracted the virus and had a number of hospitalizations. Lex was a member of a therapy group and group members visited him often in the hospital and aided him in every way they could. One day in April 1990 I received the news that Lex had died only an hour or so before the next group session. I announced it at the beginning of the group and obviously his death consumed our time. Toward the end of the group I asked each member to say good-bye and whatever other words he wanted Lex to hear. After the last group member did so, I started to say my good-bye and with it began to cry, feeling sad for someone whose experience in gay life and whose life had been so short. Two group members reacted to my tears. The first himself a bit teary said how much it meant to him to see me cry. He said, "Now I know that you really care about us." The other said, "I'm not going to be in a group where the leader can't control himself," and walked out of the group and never returned.

His memorial was strange and upsetting to the group. His mother hired a small theater and gave tickets to those whom she personally invited. At the start she welcomed the audience and introduced the quartet hired to play chamber music. At the end of their program she thanked everyone for coming—and the memorial was over. No one spoke. No one had said anything about Lex being gay or how he had died. None of his drag queen friends were invited. Nor was the disposition of his body announced. It was very quiet, uninformative, emotionless—and upsetting.

It was as if I stood upon a barren island surrounded on all sides by an inhospitable sea. There was AIDS at home, AIDS in my office, AIDS in my consultation work, AIDS in my writing and at some point

I started to think about the physical and psychological changes going on in William and to worry about what life would be like for me after he was gone.

The clock was ticking and each day felt like a minute closer to midnight.

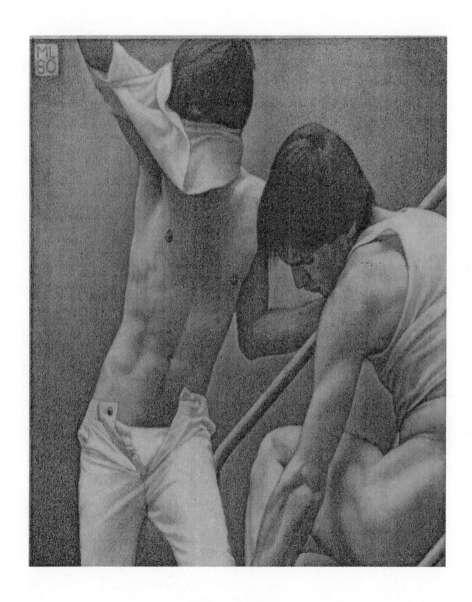

William and Ken

Drawing from *Changing* by Michael Leonard (Gay Men's Press, London, 1983). Used by permission of the artist.

Sixteen

It Looked Like a Coffin

Ken's postcards and letters continued unabated, even after 1983 when he left New York for Los Angeles and dreams of stardom. They were adolescent to the point of ludicrousness. One postcard had the word Billy written ninety times. Long letters describing what he had for lunch and filled with accounts of his daily activities, like the movies he saw and how he climbed up the "O" on the L.A. "Hollywood" sign and shouted "Billy."

So now the truth. Why did I allow Ken into my home knowing that he wanted to take William away from me? Why did I make him coffee, leave them alone in the living room, invite Ken to the country and on other occasions leave the two of them in New York while I went to the country? Why did I encourage William to introduce Ken to our friend Michael Leonard the artist, who used them as nude models?

I did everything possible to smooth the way for William to leave me. I wanted Ken to sweep William off his feet with his gorgeous face and body, his charm, his energy, his devoted worship —and plentiful passionate sex. I knew a relationship between them would never last. William would never accept Ken's constant demand for attention, his high energy that for another person would be immensely appealing. Ken would learn that underneath William's charming exterior was a reservoir of rage that exploded with all the unpredictability of a volcano, laying waste to everything and everyone around him. Ken would melt under the heat, feel deeply abandoned and go straight into a major depression. But why should I care? He made his own choices in life. I had only to sit back, move as many obstacles out of the way as I could and finally feign sadness when William moved downtown to Alphabet City.

What a cowardly way out of my dilemma. I wanted out because I was unwilling to continue to be responsible for William financially and emotionally, but I manipulated the circumstances so that William had to take the responsibility for leaving. While I said, "I won't stand in your way," I never said the truth, "I want you to leave." There were a couple of reasons why I lacked the courage to end the relationship. The prospect of being abandoned terrified me. On one of those weekends, Ken and William went walking in the woods. They were doing exactly what I wanted, taking a romantic walk through our pine forest. Yet I felt isolated and began to cry. I felt small, alone, and helpless to change my mood or to call out for help. As it was, William returned and finding me upset held me.

Getting William to go with Ken also relieved my feelings of guilt. He had no means of support, so I denied myself the right to throw him out on the street. But Ken would gladly support him financially.

There was a third reason. I still loved William. So there you have it. My turmoil consisted of abandonment, guilt, and love, with Ken the knight in shining armor to solve my ambivalence. I had become as passive-aggressive as William.

I had supported William for over ten years and never in that time did he feel the desire to contribute financially to our relationship. He was not a spender. In fact he was a miser about money often criticizing me for spending money for things no hermit would want in his home, like furniture to sit on, lamps to read by or food to eat. And what need would a hermit have for an electric typewriter, since he would not have electricity to begin with? I ultimately found myself in a trap of my own making, sprung that February night in 1973 when I took William from that filthy Brooklyn basement and brought him to my apartment in Manhattan.

There were other reasons why our relationship was sometimes mercurial. William's feelings toward me had always been divided, but never so strongly as they became as his disease progressed. He had the greatest admiration for my personal and professional integrity. Just occasionally in private moments when we would both be reading or watching television or dishing about a friend, at a moment when his comment would be non sequitor to the subject, he would say something short and to the point about his affectionate feelings for me.

There was an evening for instance while he was reading Nietzsche when he turned and said, "There are only two men in the world I respect, Nietzsche and you," and went on with his reading. I hardly knew what to say in response, but he meant only to convey his feeling, not to initiate a conversation. On another occasion when our friend Daniel came to dinner, the discussion turned to the ancient Hebrews a subject dear to William's heart. In the midst of the conversation William said to Daniel, "I love Charles because he is one of the wise men of ancient Israel." The sum of these two statements convey the deep sense of respect William had for me above everyone else in his life.

We had known each other since our meeting in 1971 at the Gay Activists Alliance's Firehouse. He lay in my bed only a few feet away the night I wrote my presentation to the American Psychiatric Association's Nomenclature Committee requesting that they remove homosexuality as a mental illness. That was February 7, 1973, only six days after he moved in with me. He was there at the founding of the Institute for Human Identity and the *Journal of Homosexuality*. He critiqued and corrected every book, every paper I wrote, sat with me at every professional conference I attended and helped me organize gay caucuses. He traveled with me on book tours and critiqued my presentations; he watched me on radio and television and sat in the audience during my lectures. He was my constant companion at home and witness to my every professional activity. William saw me at my best and my worst; he saw every mistake I made, every person I hurt unintentionally; he watched as I refused to compromise my professional integrity and in my role fighting for gay rights. It took him a long time to tell me how much he admired me professionally. He also had a high regard for my intelligence, my ability as a therapist and as a role model for younger gay men.

There was also the day in Napanoch that he phoned me. With uncharacteristic excitement in his voice he said that he had made an important decision. "I've decided to stay with you and not go to L.A. with Ken Doll. I want to be with you this weekend. I love you, Charles. I'm taking the bus to Napanoch now."

I cannot remember how I felt, whether I was pleased or disappointed. I suppose pleased that he loved me, but I am far from sure that I wanted to spend the weekend with him. He never arrived on the bus anyway and hours later I called to find out why. "I missed the bus," he said. Characteristically he had just hung up the phone and run downtown to the bus station as if a bus would be waiting just for him.

"There was another one in two hours," I said, accurate enough but motivated by the desire to punish him. "Why did you decide to stay with me?" I asked.

"Because you're more of a man than Ken," he replied.

"What do you mean?"

"Never mind. Neither of you guys understands what I mean by being a man, so there's no point discussing it. Please come home early tomorrow. I love you so much."

I knew what he meant. It was about internal strength, about fortitude in the midst of adversity, about choosing to serve a higher morality than the arbitrary rules of society and perhaps most of all the willingness to suffer the consequences of doing so.

These things were deeply ingrained in me. The lessons started in Brooklyn when as a Jewish boy, I was taunted by and called a "Kike" by a few kids who attended the parochial school on our block. It was the time of the Holocaust and the previous centuries of killing between religious groups each claiming their murders in the name of God. And there was also the memory too of a ten-year old boy driving down south with his family for the summer, passing the chain gangs of men dressed in prison gray, surrounded by sadistic-looking guards holding large shotguns.

That's what William loved about me; that was the man he wanted. That is who I was.

Now the other shoe.

The disease and its deterioration of his body brought out all the terrors of William's childhood and all his resentments of dying young. He did not like working. Getting up at eight a.m. was not his idea of civilized living. He was also worried that contact with his clients at the Legal Aid Society would expose him to tuberculosis, a distinct possibility for someone with AIDS.

The "volcano" erupted constantly attacking whomever he wanted and wherever we were. Waiters were accused of being stupid and incompetent. He would turn to people who might have glanced our way and order them to turn around. We were sometimes asked to leave restaurants. He also attacked friends at dinner. Most of all, he attacked me. My friend, Al Sbordone, joined us for dinner one night, being almost the last friend who could forgive William's public hostility. When William went to the bathroom, I complained that he attacked me all the time. Al said, "No, only when you open your mouth." And it was true, he verbally attacked everything I said, day and night and with such vehemence that no rational person would respond. He was capable of escalating his fury at times continuing the harangue for well over an hour without stopping. Any interruption was cause for him to increase his ferocity and continue until he was finally exhausted into silence.

He attacked friends as well. Daniel was a good example. They had much in common, literary interests, singing Gilbert and Sullivan songs and discussing a variety of intellectual matters. After the AIDS diagnosis William began to attack Daniel unfairly, accusing him of trying to compete with William intellectually. The idea was absurd and Daniel was stung by the attacks. Throughout the illness Daniel never wavered as William's friend, never stopped visiting, trying to help him under the most hostile conditions. The kindness on Daniel's part was all the more amazing after one night when Daniel had written a proposal for publishing *The New Joy of Gay Sex*. He came over and we put the proposal on the computer. Uninvited William arrived and started to attack every idea, every word that Daniel had written. He screamed constantly at Daniel, yelled at me to make changes in the proposal. At no time did he allow anyone else to speak. Poor Daniel was shaken by the time William walked away from the computer since he had been humiliated and belittled. I brought Daniel into my office to console him.

The basic problem was that William was murderously envious of anyone who had published his or her work. One of the ironies of his life was that he was a master of the English language, but was unable to write a book of his own. Although he had outlined a couple of them, his writer's block prevented their completion. He was especially angry with me for being so well published, but the thought of Daniel and me together made him burn with envy—hence his attack upon us, but especially on Daniel.

These intense bouts of anger were episodic and random. There was no way of predicting them. The harangues became frequent and longer, up to two hours of continual fury. He broached no interruption for any reason and if I did his fury intensified. It was his mercurial personality that was driving me insane. I never knew when he was going to give me a "buzz," or assault me verbally, start kicking posters in the street or curse an innocent passer-by.

William applied for Disability Insurance in June 1990 and when it was approved, his mood changed for a while and he became less extreme. He adored receiving the income without having to work. He wanted to return to southern Italy. This trip took place in May 1991. Only in Italy did his appetite return. He also started a book of poetry there.

May in southern Italy is magnificent. Fields of wild flowers and bougainvillea bloom everywhere. William sat in the gardens of the Villa Igea in Palermo, wrote every afternoon and read to me in the evening what he had written. While we drove or walked, he studied the road signs, the people and the architecture; everything became seed that germinated in his fertile mind and was transformed into verse. The poetry soothed his pain in a way nothing else ever had. It was the medication of his soul that started to heal his fears and the terror of watching his body deteriorate. Death was the predominant theme of the poetry, though often hidden in symbols, like the beauty of falling autumn leaves. The other main themes were sex and religion, the former praised, the latter condemned. He desperately wanted to publish a book of his poetry but worried he would not complete it in time.

Disability insurance was as much a curse as a blessing. On the positive side it provided William with a steady tax-free income for the rest of his life, released him from the burden of working, freed him to write about the disease that was consuming his body, the friends who had already died and about feelings that he was better able to express in verse. The poems were new songs in his life and whether in New York, Europe or at our country house, he brought his spiral notebooks with him and wrote far into the night.

There were other songs, however, not so harmonic as verse. Like alcohol. He and I had come from such different kinds of families. Alcohol in my traditional Brooklyn Jewish family was virtually never a part of our consciousness, though we always had a bottle of "schnapps," rye whiskey kept on the top shelf of a kitchen cabinet, presumably placed so high the children could not get their hands on it. When my extended family came for dinner during a Jewish holiday for instance, the men gathered around in the kitchen to have a shot of schnapps. My father took the bottle and a bunch of shot glasses from the kitchen shelf. Invariably my mother complained about the dust on the bottle because it had not seen the light of day since the last holiday. She would wet a rag and wipe off the dust. Only then did my father pour the whiskey into the shot glasses and hand them out to the men. "L'Chaim," he said and in one gulp the men swallowed the liquor. Then the bottle was returned to the shelf where it would lay undisturbed, collecting dust until next year.

Alcohol on the other hand was a frequent guest in William's house. William's father was a beer drunk and much despised for that by the children, as much as for his general insensitivity to their needs. During family gatherings the alcohol flowed freely as people indulged according to their desires, although in the many years I attended Bory family gatherings, I never saw anyone drunk.

There was always a subtle clash between these two cultures in our relationship. I was the ever-vigilant watchdog, scowling if he ordered a second drink at a restaurant, refusing another one for myself as an example whether I wanted it or not. I never had to say a word, merely to pause in mid-sentence or look away for just a moment. The message was clear, don't. He usually didn't, but he resented my controlling behavior.

There were a number of reasons why I controlled William's drinking. The propensity toward alcoholism was in his character. We both consumed too much; I ate everything in the house (like a good Jew) and he drank everything in the house (like a good gentile). My hostile attitude toward drinking provided a brake upon his indulgence. I recognized that he had an alcoholic personality and I was determined to do everything I could to prevent him from going over the line.

There was an irony to his alcoholism. In all our years together William was never a more passionate and thoughtful lover than when he was drunk or stoned, or the combination thereof. Those were times like no other when he connected with me physically and emotionally, when his kisses came from the heart and his touch like a "buzz" of my whole body. His eyes were alive gazing into mine, then to other parts of my face, while his hands gently caressed me, magically transforming us in time and place as if we were making love on a flying carpet. Given this irony, my conflict about his drinking is obvious. When he came to bed tipsy from alcohol or too much "smoke," I was morally indignant, yet enthusiastic about the potential sex. If angry at him, I would discourage the sex, but if I ignored the indulgence, I would encourage the drinking. I did not know what to do, botching it up much of the time.

William had too much time on his hands after we returned from Italy. He spent much of it writing, putting his poetry on the formerly hated computer and talked about publishing a book of his verse. Then he started going out to bars late at night, returning many hours later, often drunk. He would sometimes wake me up and kiss me, but I did not respond kindly to his slurred words and shaky gait, hurting his feelings. He sometimes tricked with men he met in the bars, but that seemed secondary to anesthetizing his brain with alcohol.

In a while he started to write his poetry and to read in "my cave" as he called it, the small maid's room off the kitchen. It had a bed, a bare bulb overhead, a small useless desk with no chair and it was cluttered with a variety of household objects being stored there.

I was afraid of the cave. It was a reminder of the basement in Brooklyn from whence he had come in 1973. It represented the boundaries of his world drawing tighter around him, isolating him even more from friends and from me. We still slept together in the bedroom, but often only after he returned from a night of drinking and sensing my hostility when he would cuddle next to me, reach for my hand and touch my forefinger with his, saying the word, as I did and feeling renewed we forgave one another. William rationalized that alcohol and pot were the only things that relieved the physical pain of his disease, but it was quite obvious that the pain he wanted to relieve was also psychological.

There was nothing I could do to stop his excessive drinking. He absolutely refused to go to Alcoholics Anonymous, in fact expressed the most strident hostility toward them. Psychotherapy was rejected with equal vehemence. He also adamantly refused to talk about the disease in his body, his fears of physical and mental deterioration and the probable death that lay sometime in the future and this was the most hurtful thing he did to himself and to me. I was helpless to instigate any changes and I knew it.

But what about me? Who was I during the period that began with William's disability? Perhaps there is someone out there who under these circumstances can attend to his own feelings, be able to take care of himself as he cares for his dying lover. I could not. Caretakers do not have time for themselves. I mean "caretaker" in both its literal meaning of caring for someone who is physically ill and the psychological one of taking care of someone else. I remembered when William had to take his pills, make appointments with doctors, get there on time and pay outstanding bills. I shopped, cooked, and cleaned up. My nose sniffed the air in order to anticipate his needs. I had not the slightest idea of my own needs or my feelings about him. They were obscured by the conflicting feelings of resentment, guilt and love.

I felt like a man under siege as if I were made of thick stone protecting a medieval tower from foreign invaders. The illness was dreadful enough in the late 1980s, a virtual sentence of death. Though I might come to terms with William's physical disease, the alcoholism created the greatest turmoil for me. It was such a waste of his mind and his talent and it only alienated us further.

I condemned myself for my Puritanism. Why not let William drink to excess and greet him with love instead of hostility? I wondered whether changing my behavior would make a positive change in our drifting relationship. Even though I loved the man, I was continually furious at him and I condemned myself for that too.

So why not join him, I thought? My plan was to join him at bars at least on those nights that my schedule allowed me to stay out late. I hoped that these night owl activities would bring us closer together and that our renewed relationship would help him come to terms with his illness and thereby reduce his need for alcohol. William seemed amused by the idea and welcomed me on the journey.

The theory was impeccable; the practice a disaster. I had ignored what a terrible bar personality I am, how frozen I act in those places, how inadequate I feel, how quickly I want to flee from those dens in order to avoid the conviction that I stand out by being socially inept. "Have a drink, you'll loosen up," William said one night, observing (yet again) what a basket-case I was in the bar. One or two drinks merely make me a tipsy basket-case which, from my point of view was even worse. Around me people were socializing and seemed to be having fun. They knew what to talk about, enjoyed being there and every once in a while made a connection with someone who looked sexually inviting. I listened to their conversation hoping to learn from them, only to conclude that their talk was idiocy, chit-chat of the lowest form. I was incapable of maintaining such inane conversations; yet at the same time I rebuked myself for judging them so harshly, aware that underneath my condemnation was envy that they could chit-chat about nothing and I could not and that in the end they would make new friends and I would not. To make things worse, William was superb at the chit-chat language of the bar, so I could not claim it just the province of the dull-witted.

Whether I was sitting or standing, you would have concluded that my feet were nailed to the floor. All the terrors of coming out returned to me, especially the dreadful belief that I was unattractive. I heard again my father's words, "Why are you so ugly, Charlie?" and believed it still, even as I believed it as a child. I was fine on a one-to-one basis or speaking in front of a group, but bar society was my Achilles heel. The well-intentioned experiment was an abysmal failure.

William never liked New York's winter cold. He preferred the warm sun of a beach resort, so it was no surprise that he decided to spend the winter of 1990-1991 in the gay boy's camp of South Beach, Florida, the historic art deco section of Miami Beach. South Beach, often called "SoBe," is self-contained. One does not need a car to get around since you can walk its whole length in a matter of minutes. With his reliable disability income, he could afford to get a place for the entire winter season. I encouraged him for a number of reasons. We both needed relief, he from the frigid New York winter and the relentless face of AIDS mirrored in our friends, and I from the difficulties of taking care of him and his alcoholism. His going to South Beach would be my vacation. William was too fearful to choose a winter apartment by himself and so we spent a very pleasant, long weekend there in November 1990, inspecting available housing for the winter season. We settled on a suite with two beds in a Collins Avenue hotel on Eleventh Street only a block from the beach. It was perfectly sited, had a full kitchen (not that he cooked much) and its own telephone.

We delayed our departure from New York until January 4, 1991 because William wanted to attend our traditional New Year's Day party. The South Beach week was consumed by taking drives, visiting friends and sampling the new restaurants that had sprouted up after SoBe became fashionable. On Saturday night he went to the "Wausau," a SoBe gay dance club while I drove to Fort Lauderdale to drop dollar bills into the G-strings of go-go boys. It was "underwear night" at the Wausau. At one point the emcee asked all the "tops" to go to one side of the dance floor and the "bottoms" to the other. If they were on a ship, it would have capsized. Virtually the whole dance-floor hurried over to the side for bottoms. William said everyone—unless one was a top—was severely depressed for the rest of the night.

William's mood was level, thoughtful, that of a good companion and lover and the week conflict-free. He appreciated my presence during the transition, we said our tearful good-byes and I returned to New York. It was the first time in his life that he lived alone, although one might say that he brought a companion with him, AIDS, that never left his side. I admired his courage in making the trip and understood how frightened he was to live in a city where he had no friends.

The first few days in South Beach were difficult. Except for buying food to cook he did not leave the apartment. He read, watched TV, wrote his poetry and called me. The calls were very sad. He missed me greatly and he was afraid of the new gay scene, far more frivolous than in New York. Gay conversations in SoBe were limited to talking about bathing suits, tanning oil, models, and steroids. He was shocked to learn that few gay men practiced safe sex even in Miami which had one of the highest infection rates in the country. His characteristic way of dealing with these fears was to isolate himself and for a while he became a hermit in South Beach.

William had sensibly arranged for a number of friends to visit. That was one of the reasons that we had taken an apartment with two beds. His friend Jim Spinks, a collector of kitsch, spent a week with him. So did David Varas, who kept losing his Prince Albert in the apartment and William's description of two naked men crawling on the floor looking for it and after finding it David's joy in putting it on (not unlike a bride placing a wedding ring on her finger) kept me in stitches. I was pleased that he had made these arrangements with friends, equally happy that the burden had been taken off my shoulders. I deposited his monthly disability check in the bank and he withdrew money as he needed it from an ATM machine.

The Gulf War began in January 1991 and it provided William with an excuse to remain in his apartment and watch it on television for much of the day. One night he met an Israeli soldier on holiday in one of the gay bars and they began a short affair. The Israeli had a lover serving in the Israeli Defense Force. One morning the news showed a picture of a collapsed apartment house in Jerusalem and the head and shoulders of a man, partially buried in the ruins. Soldiers were trying to get him out. "That's him," the Israeli shouted. It was his lover still alive. He returned to Israel the next day.

William also continued to drink to excess and his words were slurred in some of his late night calls. I enjoyed the peace at home, my professional work and knew that things would change soon enough when he returned. During one phone call I asked if he wanted to remain in Florida until the spring, but he would not hear of it. He said that he missed me too much to stay that long. He returned to New York exactly two months after he left. The rest of 1991 was more of the same, excessive drinking and tricking in the bars and in the park.

William and I made our last trip to Italy in May 1991. Not once in those three weeks did he drink to excess, probably because he was so happy to be in a country that he loved, to have food that he could ate and to be with me. I drove the car as he sat with our maps on his lap, checking road signs and pointing out turns. He was the navigator on all these long Italian drives, a role he performed with astonishing accuracy. William never knew his right from his left and we joked about that frequently. Instead he navigated by the sun and the stars, as an ancient mariner might, and said, "Turn here," pointing in one direction or the other. He never got us lost in the mountain roads of the heel and toe of southern Italy, even when the roads were signless as they frequently were.

We stopped for a few days in Positano on the Amalfi coast where he began writing poetry again. There were beautiful gardens in our hotel that overlooked the water far below. He sat at table writing surrounded by flowers as I shopped in town. Then we drove to places tourists rarely visit, to the real southern Italy where secondary roads are the best the region has to offer. We stopped at the house where Carlo Levy wrote *Christ Stopped at Eboli*. Mussolini had exiled him there for political reasons before World War Two began. Then to Matera, an important town not far away, which stood on top of a high ravine and joined the *passengiata*, walking arm in arm as Italian men do. We felt self-conscious, perhaps even a bit naughty; two homosexuals walking arm in arm in the crowded streets unnoticed by young mothers and their baby carriages, children skipping and hopping with their friends and middle-aged men also arm in arm.

But Matera was crowded and so we drove to the Adriatic coast, taking almost an hour to drive eight kilometers up a one lane mountain road with a precarious cliff to one side and arrived in the deserted, small central square of Bombile, where no one spoke English and which probably has not had seen another American tourist since that day. That was our kind of town. We knocked on the door of the church and the priest gave us the keys to the "Sanctuary of the Madonna of the Cave," a long walk from the square. Excavated in the sandstone mountain was a cave containing a marble Madonna and child and pilgrims from southern Italy come by the thousands during holidays to pray here.

We drove across the mountains to Tropea, a resort on the Tyrrhenian Sea where William roared with laughter as I taught a band of local pre-teen-aged boys how to make fart sounds with your arm and mouth. After my lesson they showed us where to buy the best French fries in town and we all sat on the steps of a nearby church eating the French fries and simulating farts.

We always ordered "vino locale," the locally produced wine. It was absurdly cheap, highly alcoholic and we judged it a classy vintage if the bottle had a label glued to it. Most of the time it had neither label nor cork and we joked about the bouquet being a blend of the grapes in the backyard and the proprietor's children's feet. We were both at peace driving along the sea coasts, up and down hairy mountain roads, trying to buy ex-votos, but most of all never wanting further company than each other.

The glow from our southern Italian trip lasted for quite a while and the rest of 1991 was fairly uneventful. In July I did two workshops at the National Gay and Lesbian Health Conference in New Orleans.

For William's birthday, August 18, I gave him a plate of Blue Willow exactly like the plate he had used as a child, the one with separate compartments that kept foods apart from each other. He was touched by my thoughtfulness and put it away in a safe place in the china closet. He used it only once or twice, mostly for its memories.

In November we went down to South Beach again to choose an apartment for the 1991-1992 winter. William finally decided on the same hotel as the year before. Once again he left after our annual New Year's Day party but by train this time. We had secured a berth for the twenty-eight-hour ride to Miami. He packed a large duffel bag, a box of books and with his spiral notebooks under his arm we took a taxi to Penn Station. I brought a Zabar's shopping bag filled with some of his favorite foods, strudel, rugelach and candied fruits.

The sight of the "berth" let an indelible mark in my memory. We knew that it was small but we never gave a thought as to how it might be designed. We stood in shock as we opened the door, hesitating to enter, both having exactly the same fantasy, but finding it unnecessary to verbalize. It was a horizontal space, composed of a long bed, a shelf on which to hold baggage, a lamp and a ceiling so low that you could not stand. You entered through the door and crawled onto the bed and out the same way. There was no chair on which to sit so one was forced to lie prone for the whole trip.

It looked like a coffin; it looked like William's coffin as I passed him the luggage, the Zabar's bag and the thermos of coffee that would last him the first few hours of the trip. My fantasy was that I was providing enough food so that he would not starve to death before "they" opened the coffin a day later in Miami. The fantasy terrified me because it represented an omen of the future, as well as a reminder of my responsibility to keep him alive with food, a symbol of nurturance and love.

We said good-bye by shaking hands because the car was filled with other people and William never kissed in public. He closed the door (the lid?) and I left the train, watched as it gathered speed and left the station. Then I went home, partly relieved, but also more worried about the coming months than I had been the year before. There was something different this year but I could not feel the pulse of it.

William never left his berth until the train arrived in Miami. Then he went straight to his hotel and called me to let me know that he had arrived safely.

The phone calls from Miami were very disturbing. William had made many friends the year before, people who lived and worked in South Beach. They were all overjoyed to see him return especially those who liked to drink since William was a generous host with alcohol. He bought a battery powered electric mixer and an ice chest and he brought them, the liquor and a blanket to the beach each day. It did not take long before his alcoholic buddies arrived on the blanket and joined him in drinking Manhattans or martinis, or whatever he was mixing that day. He was often drunk long before nightfall when he went to the bars or clubs, drinking more and bringing home whoever tickled his fancy for the night. He would often call late (as alcoholics often do) and with slurred words tell me about the day's activities.

One night William called to report a bizarre event. He had met a fabulously wealthy man with a magnificent home on one of the chic islands off the causeway and he accepted an invitation to trick with him. First they had sex, then the man asked William to beat him up. I do not mean an S & M scene; just beat him enough to draw blood. He wanted to be punched in the face and body and kicked hard in the groin. William said that he did as he was asked and was paid three hundred dollars.

I hardly knew how to react to this grotesque account. Should I respond to the idea of its being a commercial transaction, to the fear that William's rage would get the best of him and he would hurt this dangerous masochist badly? I also wondered why William was chosen for the role. I knew that such men existed in the world and taking the moral, if not the practical high ground I begged William not to see him again. He tepidly agreed.

A few nights later he called again to tell me that he had met the wealthy man again in another bar and once again had gone home with him. This time however, after sex the masochist repeated his request to be beaten bloody with a fire iron near his fireplace. "I'll give you five thousand dollars if you kill me with it," he said.

How would you respond to a call like that? Tell him not to take a check? I had no way to ascertain the truth. He agreed not to see the man again, although Mr. Kill Me, real or imagined, called often at least according to William's reports. At the time I wondered whether the story was a metaphor, his way of trying to convey that his anger about his illness had reached a state in which he wanted to kill someone—or himself.

About a week later I got a call from his physician. "William slipped through the cracks," was the way his doctor put it. For over a year the doctor had overlooked the fact that William's T-cells had dropped below three hundred, the point at which a prophylaxis for PCP was medically necessary. He prescribed Bactrim and insisted that William begin talking the medication as soon as possible. I sent the pills to Miami and William started taking them even though he suspected he was allergic to the drug. We both believed that his physician, one of the most experienced AIDS doctors in New York knew what he was doing. We were wrong. Just as he had not noticed that William's T-cells had dropped, he had also missed reading the place in his chart that noted the allergy. William had an adverse reaction to the drug and the physician agreed for him to stop, but never apologized for his error.

Then the doctor called William and demanded that he immediately go for pentamidine treatment in North Miami and if William refused, he would drop him as a patient. The doctor confirmed his threat to me over the phone. William's point of view was that his doctor had made both errors and was a little late and hysterical in requiring treatment. He wanted to wait until he returned to New York in a few weeks, especially since he had no way of getting to North Miami without a car. I agreed with him. We also decided that it was time to change doctors.

Jim Spinks, William's kitsch-collecting friend called me from South Beach. He said that William's alcoholism and drug taking was completely out of control. He said that William was very depressed, looked ill all the time and that I should bring him back to New York. He refused to divulge what drugs William was taking, but I suspected they were the usual "white powders," recreational drugs used by gay men, particularly when dancing in clubs. I knew that Jim would not have called me capriciously and I took his alert seriously.

I called William to say that I was coming for the weekend but nothing about Jim's call. He greeted me warmly and immediately said that he was coming home with me. He had had enough of Florida. He was quite relaxed with me for the next couple of days and on Sunday February 9th, just a month after he had arrived, William packed his duffel bag, his books and spiral notebooks and we left the hotel. As we passed through the lobby, the desk clerk asked where he was going. William responded, "Home."

"Are you coming back?" the desk clerk asked, to which William replied, "Never."

Back home William sat on the couch, opened one of his spiral notebooks and read some of the poetry he had written in South Beach. It was less perceptive and more rambling than before. I also noticed that his handwriting was shaky like that of a person with poor manual dexterity. I wondered whether it was the beginning of peripheral neuropathy or even worse, cerebral damage due to the virus and his excessive drinking.

The drinking stopped after we returned from Florida. It took me awhile to realize this since he often left the house after I retired for the night. Occasionally I would wake up late and find that he was not in bed and I would look around the apartment for him. On a few nights I found him asleep in the cave. It was a significant change in his behavior. I interpreted the change as an expression of his anger at me for my disapproval of his alcoholism. I was wrong. It had nothing to do with me. It was only that he had changed his drug of choice. I was soon to accept Proust's dictum, "We pick out in love only those who are capable of satisfying our senses and agonizing our hearts."

William Bory

Photo by Michael Leonard. Used by permission of the photographer.

Seventeen

Buzz Was All We Needed To Say

Michael Leonard called to say he was coming to town for a show at a Fifty-seventh Street gallery. He invited us to the March 5, 1992 opening that featured a number of paintings and drawings of Ken. Quite naturally he invited Ken as well. William and I thought that the nine years since we last saw him sufficient time to forget the past and renew the friendship by asking Ken to stay with us. Ken was overjoyed by the invitation. In the intervening years he had had a relationship with a man who became a cocaine addict and Ken finally threw him out. He had also given up acting and begun working for a company that produced videotapes for corporations. When the company had moved to Houston, he decided to join them.

We talked on the phone for an hour, filling in the blank spaces of our lives, only toward the end of the conversation venturing into the territory of HIV. He was not defensive.

"I'd like to go on disability," Ken said, "but it doesn't pay enough money for me to support myself." His disability allowance would pay for little more than his rent in Houston.

"Perhaps we can talk about it when you come up to New York," I suggested.

The plan was already hatching in my mind. I knew that Ken and I would get along well. Our temperaments were similar, high-energy, a capacity for fun, and an iconoclastic attitude toward society's rules. The truth was that in many ways he was more like me than he was like William. Even before we said good-by, I knew that I was going to invite him to live with us. He could have the spare bedroom rent-free and keep his disability income to pay for his personal expenses. The arrangement was perfect because it would give him a place to stay and someone to take care of him when he got ill. In return I would have someone else to talk with and to balance out William's capricious and moody behavior. I kept the idea to myself for the moment knowing that his visit to New York would be crucial to the plan. I told Ken that we would pick him up at the airport.

William anxiously waited for Ken's plane to land. He was not pleased that Ken was to spend a week with us, but would not tell me why. Ken walked out of the gate and waved to us. I embraced him but William hung back. William only shook his hand, then stepped back again and remained silent during the whole drive home.

The opening took place that evening. The three of us stuck together as we were surrounded by the wealthy patrons of the art world. A huge nude of Ken with a watermelon half at his side was given the place of honor. Even though Michael had put a beard on the subject and Ken is hairless, he felt embarrassed watching so many people stare at his nude body on the canvas. We teased him saying that if he dropped his pants, everyone in the room would recognize him. Another nude painting pictured him lying down, one arm covering his face and a skull, draped with a cloth around it at his side. It was Michael's image of the plague, representing models who had already died and Ken and William, both so ill that they could no longer sit for him. The watermelon painting sold but not the one with the skull.

The next day William and Ken took a walk through the park. "I can't stand him anymore," Ken said when he returned. "I cannot stand his constant harangues." I understood exactly what he meant. William had spent the morning criticizing Ken for leaving his acting career, moving to Houston and for things that made no sense at all. Ken refused to go anywhere with William for the rest of the week, which was fine with William who told me that he never wanted to see Ken again. My plan had come completely unglued.

"I can't come back here," Ken said as we walked through Central Park one day. "He's impossible to live with," he added. "And I know that he's taking some heavy drugs. I lived through that once and I'm not doing it again."

"I thought you might go on disability and live here," I said. "You know I'll take care of you, and there's no one in Houston that will."

"I was thinking the same thing and I thought that this week would give me an idea if it could work. But I can't live in the same house with William."

Ken and I spent hours each day going to shows and exhibits. We talked about the nature of our relationship almost a decade before and confided in each other about living with a drug addict. I had been infatuated with him before, but by week's end we became friends. At the airport we said our good-byes, uncertain whether we would ever see each other again. He asked me to visit him in Houston.

Ian Young arrived in May. He read William's poetry and said that he was willing to publish the book privately. Ian had produced many books of poetry and literary criticism over the past twenty years and he knew how to get the job done right. William was delighted that other people would read his work and I knew that Ian would do a good job.

Ian took copies of William's verse and started reading it in order to make selections for the book. He also formed a small team of friends to computerize the poems, design the book and the cover and take pictures of William for the back book cover. William was incapable of helping with the task both because of his deteriorating thinking processes and his drug use. He knew that Ian and his crew were the last chance he had to see his work in print before he died. William's mother paid for most of the cost of printing the book, the rest of the funds came from William and me. It was a very kind act on her part and I assured her that I would be responsible for paying the bills so that none of the money would go for drugs.

Ian is a take-charge kind of guy and insisted on working directly with William, purposely leaving me out of the loop. I was delighted with his plan although I knew that he was not aware of the extent of William's drug use. During the next six months, William and Ian made all the decisions about editing the work and the order of the poems, until one day William printed out the final version of the book (on the now beloved computer).

In May we made our last foreign trip: Three weeks in Turkey. Too much time was consumed by harangues against the Turks and me. (Fortunately I was number two on his list.) They abated only when we traveled to Cappadocia in Central Turkey, the area containing the "fairy chimneys" and early Christian communities that carved huge homes and churches into the soft rock. Many of these massive rocks had stairways that led up one or two flights into multi-room apartments. Thousands of people lived in these pre-Turkic rock towns, hiding from invaders who would have slaughtered them.

Our days driving around the countryside, climbing in and out of the "houses," were the most satisfying part of our Anatolian adventure. "It's my cave," he said, as William walked up the stone stairway and into a small room, surrounded on all sides by solid stone and bare walls. He sat down all smiles and said, "I can just live here." He sat in the room for at least thirty minutes and the smile remained on his face for the rest of the day. Smiling or otherwise his face was drawn, the lines deepening further into the flesh like hollows in the Ozark Mountains.

*

The nightmare began in July.

You cannot catch hold of an addicted person. Walk away and never come back you say to yourself. But how do you do that after he has been a warm companion, a tender lover and perhaps ultimately most of all your best friend? Your emotions are tangled as your desire to protect is equally balanced with your wish to kill. You are caught on a treadmill, cannot keep up, and cannot jump off. Nothing will ever change, but love or hate or guilt keeps you there so that in time you end up just as much a victim as the victim you want to save.

Drug addiction was never a moral issue for me. That is the province of society, of the police who arrest drug addicts, of the courts who prosecute them and of the treatment programs that face the Sisyphusian task of "curing" the addiction. For a member of an addict's family the problem is solely that of survival. Just as addicts often find themselves drowning from their own destructive behavior, so too their families while trying to save the addicted person, learn only too late that they too are drowning in the same swampy water. Working with addicts and their families might have prepared me for what was to be my participation in William's addiction, but I had had little professional experience working with drug addiction.

William was smoking crack.

He used to make occasional late-night forays into Central Park in order to have anonymous sex. There is an entry in his business calendar in which he wrote short notes about his tricking, that one night in October 1990—months before his first winter in Miami—he'd had sex with an eighteen-year-old crack addict.

Crack use may have been the reason Jim Spinks called from Miami asking me to bring William home on February 15. A week after we returned, Daniel joined us on a long weekend in D.C., and William never relented in his unfair attacks upon him. His impatience was palpable the next month, March, during Michael Leonard's show, when Ken visited us for a week. During our May trip to Turkey, his vengeance toward me (Cappadocia excepted) came roaring out. I now realized that our physical closeness interfered with his crack use and the temporary withdrawal of the drug on these trips led in part to his unreasonable rage.

At this time (July 1992), William smoked his crack at night leaving the house only after I went to sleep. It is at those late hours when men and women who work regular daytime jobs go to sleep, that a whole new set of people awaken to begin their day. From midnight to daylight the soft underbelly of New York comes alive as the denizens of the night make their rounds of the streets, the hustlers and the hustled, the aggressors and the victimized. White middle-class men and women from the city and the suburbs venture into ghetto neighborhoods at night to buy drugs from people they would otherwise never converse with even during the day. Drugs, alcohol, money, sex and violence are the touchstones of the night, fortunes made and lost, sexual fantasies acted out or frustrated. One can buy relief from whatever pain, physical or emotional may ail you.

This good Jewish boy from Brooklyn knew nothing about the drugs of the underworld. My professional work taught me the language of the popular gay middle-class "white powders"—ecstasy, special K, crystal and cocaine. Virtually everyone I knew over the past thirty years had smoked grass at one time or another. So did I for a brief period in the 1970s but tired of it long ago. William adored smoking pot either alone or with friends. I cannot remember his ever being angry when he was stoned and he was never so charming, witty, and kind as when under the influence of the drug.

We were on opposite schedules. When I was awake, he slept; when I went to sleep, he went out. It reduced our contact and therefore, our conflict over his drug taking. Still, the tension in the house infected me with an awesome rage and my sleep was fitful and anxious. I worried about what was happening to William even as I slept. I wondered what I would do if a friend whose problems were an exact mirror of my own sought my advice. What would I tell him? I would suggest that he enter therapy.

I walked into a therapist's office, sat down and said, "You won't have anything to do except listen to me for a few weeks. That's all I want right now. Please don't interrupt." I spent the time ventilating all my frustrations, my rage, saying everything to her that I wanted to say to William and using exactly the words I wanted to use. I did not expect it to change my situation, only to take a bit of the pressure off. It worked quite well from that point of view. I remained in therapy with her for only a few months because we came to a crucial impasse; to remain in therapy would open the question of ending my relationship with William. That was unthinkable to me.

The evening of Sunday, August 2 started quietly enough. William was in our bed editing his poetry for the book, while I was in my adjacent office writing down some public relations ideas for the publication of *The New Joy of Gay Sex* (co-authored with Felice Picano) due to be released in November. From time to time William walked into my office to consult with me about the order of the poems or how many of his AIDS poems should be included. His mood was upbeat if not joyful since the book was sure to become a reality. For whatever reason the previous week seemed to be drug-free. The tone between us was close and intimate. I remember our talking in bed the night before about nothing in particular, our words a mask for the meta-message that a sense of trust was starting to build between us again.

My phone rang. It was William's mother. "I want to talk to Billy," she said. "I tried to call his number but no one answered. I want to tell him that Mr. Bory died tonight." I walked into the bedroom and asked William to pick up my extension. She repeated the message to him that his father had died of emphysema caused by decades of smoking. She said that she would call him in a couple of days concerning plans for the funeral. They both hung up their phones.

We were both in shock but for different reasons, William because of the death of his father and I because of the brevity of their conversation. It was as if after the news, William could go back to editing his verse and his mother to whatever she was doing before her husband had died. She could not contact her other son Gerard and her daughter Marie because they were away together for the weekend, but she was able to speak to her youngest daughter, Menakshe, née Margaret who lived and worked full-time in a yoga camp in the Catskill Mountains.

"William, she's all alone," I said. "Her husband just died and there's no one there. We have to go tonight." William was stunned by my suggestion and he reminded me that she said we did not have to visit her until the funeral.

"Call Menakshe," I said. William's sister agreed that someone had to go to her mother's house and that we were the closest. She would not get into town until the next day.

We drove to William's parents' house in Queens.

"What are you doing here?" Mrs. Bory asked, surprised at our arrival. "I said you didn't have to come over until I knew when the funeral was going to be."

"See, I told you," William said to me in a voice as if to say, "You're overreacting again."

I explained that we were concerned for her since we knew that she was alone and that none of the other three children could arrive until the next day at the earliest.

"I'm fine," she said. And she was. One could not tell that her husband of forty-five years had died only hours before. I could hardly miss the observation that neither mother nor son could be accused of wearing their emotions on their sleeves.

William and I drove to his father's wake a few days later. The family was sitting in the first row and they motioned for William to join them. The priest was about to deliver a small talk, a few words about the man lying in the coffin and they not unreasonably wanted William as the oldest son in his place before the priest began. William resisted going preferring to stay with me, but moved to the front after I pushed him down the aisle. The priest began his remarks, something to this effect:

"William Bory has been taken from us."

That was enough for William, my William to bolt out of his place as eldest son to the astonishment, if not the embarrassment of his family, and rush back to where I was sitting. There was the direst expression on his face and it was quite clear that his move was motivated by the need for safety.

The priest spoke for only a few minutes, mouthing the usual clichés expected in today's mass produced wakes. He often called out the name of the deceased, "William Bory." Both William Borys had the same body type, so that looking at the body in the coffin made my William think all the more that he was looking at himself.

"I want to go home," William said when the priest finished and the family got up and walked toward us. One could see from their faces that they thought his behavior outrageous, which it was, but they failed to hear the words that tore at William, that drove him first to leave the front row and finally the funeral home—his own name.

William Bory was dead and his son, William Bory was dying. "I kept seeing myself in the coffin and I kept hearing my name called," William said on the drive home. He hated his father, hated that as the first-born son he was given his name and now he saw himself in the coffin dead of AIDS at age forty-one.

The funeral was held a few days later. The four children and their mother were herded into the lead limousine. William was morose, uncommunicative and scared. More words were said at the burial site about the death of William Bory and with each word a bolt of electricity jolted William's body. It was as if he were dead, his family bidding him farewell.

The death of William's father dissolved whatever resistance he had to smoking crack. Good feelings about his book were washed away by waves of fear and depression. If William had denied his own imminent death up to that time, he no longer could and he was terrified by the prospect. Crack was the only thing that comforted him.

I am tempted to say that there is a straw that broke the camel's back, but with drug addiction, it usually takes repeated straws. In between them are discussions, arguments, promises—lots of bullshit on both sides—and finally either resignation or self-delusion. We "caretakers" choose to put off the inevitable because the temporary truce is less painful than the emotional tearing of one's soul that comes from feelings of betrayal and abandonment.

The straw that broke this camel's back occurred late one night a week after the funeral. I awoke sensing that something was wrong in the house because William was not beside me. I got up, walked into the hallway where I could see light seeping from under the living room door. I walked in. William and a stranger in his mid-twenties both sat on the couch smoking crack. I had not ever before seen William smoking the drug. They were obviously shocked at my entrance and the stranger seemed frightened that I would assault him. They were both fully clothed, their companionship for the drug, not sex. I would have much preferred to find them in each other's arms than in the embrace of crack.

"You, get out!" I said to the stranger.

"He's my friend and if he goes, I go," said William.

"So go," I angrily responded. William stood up, collected the drug paraphernalia and ran after his crack-smoking friend. In retrospect I see how naive I was to be enraged that my lover, who had helped to buy things of value that covered our walls, trinkets bought from years of travel, would bring a drug addict from the street into our house. For a few moments standing in the center of the living room after this conflict, I exempted William from the category of *stealing* drug addict, but my denial did not last long. It suddenly dawned on me that William and his "friend," had probably smoked together before. Were there others whom he had brought into the house to take drugs? How many? How often? By habit I always left my wallet and cash in my office desk and I went quickly to search for them. Cash and credit cards were safe—at least for the moment.

"What do I do now?" I thought. It was then after three a.m. and William would have to return home. Would he return in an hour or after daybreak, alone or with one or more crack-smoking friends? I was not physically afraid because crack addicts do not have a reputation for violence, but I worried that if I slept some unknown thing would happen, some greater tragedy than before. The adrenaline was still rushing through my body and the beat of my heart, my heavy breathing, the tension in my muscles all cried out "Alarm." I returned to bed in a heightened sense of arousal, with my ears listening for the telltale sounds of William's steps.

Daylight returned before he did, walking past our bedroom, through the kitchen and into his cave where he slept until sometime in the afternoon. He was furious that I had made a scene the night before and wanted to go into one of his harangues, but he did not have the energy.

"You must go to a residential treatment program to stop your drug use," I said. "You cannot stay here if you're smoking crack. I won't put up with it anymore. It's not only killing you psychologically, but physically too. And it's destroying our relationship. I want you to go as soon as possible."

To my surprise he agreed. I spent the afternoon making inquiries about treatment programs, while William used this time to smoke as much crack as he could until he left for the treatment program. We agreed that only a gay treatment program would do, so I made arrangements for William to be accepted at Pride Institute, a gay and lesbian program in Eden Prairie, Minnesota. I knew some of the staff because of my professional work. I had also been a guest speaker at one of their professional seminars. I thought the program sound and I knew that if William had any chance to defeat the troika of problems hounding him, AIDS, drugs, and depression, that only by being surrounded by other gay people might he succeed. The admission's office made arrangements for William's arrival the next day.

William knew that he and his baggage would be searched for drugs when he arrived at Pride and so he spent the night smoking up whatever reserves he had hidden in the house. He may also have bought more in the morning before I awoke. He was therefore, zonked out of his mind as we packed his duffel bag in the morning, but that had the advantage of tranquilizing him in preparation for the trip. I could not be sure whether or not he actually understood that he was about to fly to Minneapolis where a car would pick him up and deposit him in a residential program where he would be without drugs and alcohol for a month. When he dressed, he put his "Buddy" cap on his head. It was a red and white cap with the word "Buddy" written in front. "Buddy" meant his body that was failing due to AIDS. It was the stigmata he wore on his head but understood only by the two of us.

When the drugs wore off completely within a couple of days, William found himself over a thousand miles away in a place with rules and responsibilities. There were group meetings and individual counseling. He wanted none of it and if he could, he would have walked out and taken the next plane back to New York. But people addicted to drugs are not known for their sense of responsibility or planning for the future. He had left his credit, ATM cards and his keys at home. He did not have a nickel in his pocket.

When he called and asked me to mail his credit card and ATM card, it took a great deal of willpower on my part to refuse. His return would only put us right back where we were a few days before. In retaliation he said that he was going to leave and get home anyway he could.

"If you leave Pride," I said, "I will not let you into the house. You aren't welcome back here until after you complete the program." This was not easy for me, the people-pleaser to say. My knees were shaking and I felt weak even though I was sitting at my desk.

"You have all the power now and you're using it, aren't you?" William said defiantly at my standing up to him. "You're happy that you sent me to prison, aren't you? "

"Yes, I am quite pleased that you're in prison, so cut out the guilt bullshit. I'll spend a weekend visiting you but you're not coming home now and that's that."

I flew to Minneapolis two weeks later to spend a long weekend with William. Those days were interesting from a number of points of view. Because of my professional reputation and my previous contact with Pride, I was given considerable freedom by the Pride staff. I even ran a therapy group for the residents. The other patients were delighted by my presence since many of them had read my books and William had obviously talked about me during private conversations and at group sessions.

There were stories to tell. One of the first I heard was about the consulting physician who examined each new resident. The doctor had a propensity for taking an excessive amount of time doing rectal examinations. One of William's new friend's jokingly remarked that the doctor kept his finger up his ass even while asking questions about health and writing with his other hand. They dubbed him, "Dr. Finger." Even though they all resented the obvious exploitation, no one reported it to the medical director. I encouraged them to do so since any professional institution would want to know about the problem. They did and Dr. Finger was gone the next day.

"My husband came," William wrote in his Pride journal on September 11, 1992. "I was scared, but he immediately saw the difference in me, my angel character. He was deeply pleased." William latched onto the literary trope of the battle between the devil and an angel. The devil was his tyrannical self, his rage, his accusations and resentment against me, everything dark in his personality. The angel was the good side, his charm and sense of humor, his warmth and love that had been so deeply repressed, especially since the day in Puerto Rico when he first noticed the purple spots. It was the angel character who greeted me the whole weekend. His mood was calm and even, not accusative. He was openly affectionate, walking hand in hand with me in the halls, something he would never do in New York. We ate a few meals together in the dining room surrounded by other residents who gossiped with me openly about each other and about the institution's attempt (partially successful) to prevent sex between them. The cook joked about William's peculiar eating habits, how he ate exactly the same meals each day.

With his mind clear of the effects of the drugs, William spent much of his time writing and after breakfast on Saturday read to me for almost an hour. The poetry was all about death, a subject always in the foreground of his mind.

In the afternoon I attended his group therapy meeting and we got into a ripping argument about his alcohol and drug use (my concern) and my controlling personality (his concern). It was actually a good start in opening up negotiations for the future. All of the other group members, none of whom had ever been in a long-lasting relationship were intimidated by our expressions of anger. Not one of them said a word for the entire hour. Later in the afternoon we agreed to work out a contract for the future.

William had made friends with Dan Kopka, a tall, good-looking twenty-something boy from New York who was addicted to heroin. He worked as a master piercer, making holes in other people's bodies and plugging the holes with loops, bars, studs or whatever his clients desired. He himself was a walking advertisement for his work, which put some of the boys off but not William or I. It was very important to Dan that William and I patch up our differences and he did everything he could to support us. It was touching at times. He physically pushed us outside the back door to the deck, where it was quite cold and brought out fresh, hot cups of coffee every fifteen minutes and stood at the door barring anyone else from interfering with our privacy. His immediate affection for me was surprising and I wondered whether I had quickly become his "good father."

Outside on the deck William and I came to a number of agreements about the future. Most of them were about his taking responsibility for things like paying bills and so on.

"I want a retreat of my own," he said. William wanted to rent a small cheap apartment somewhere where he could be alone at times. It was not that he wanted to separate from me, he explained; he just wanted it so that he would not feel trapped. I was suspicious of what use William would make of the "retreat," but if he wanted it, then I had to be supportive of him. He was surprised when I immediately agreed to the arrangement.

In the evening I participated in a ping-pong tournament with the residents. William had never seen me play before and he never played himself, giving his usual excuse, "I'm not an athlete." But he was very proud when in the course of the evening, I reached the semi-finals only to be defeated by one of the resident lesbians who beat me rather badly.

It was time for me to leave. Dan came over, hugged and kissed me and said that he wanted the three of us to get together in New York. I promised to do so. William walked me to the door where we said our good-byes. We hugged and kissed; our forefingers came together and touched. "Buzz" was all we needed to say.

I left for New York early the next day. All in all, I felt it a good beginning. William was in better health physically and mentally than I had seen him for the past two years. I was particularly encouraged by our discussion about after care. William had accepted the need for psychotherapy in order to deal with his feelings about the disease and his depression. He decided to consult with April Martin, a psychologist

colleague, whom William trusted. I was delighted with his choice because
I respected her both personally and professionally. He called her that
weekend from Pride to ask if she would accept him as a new patient
and she readily agreed. I knew he would be in good hands. William also
agreed to join one or more gay A.A. or N.A. groups as a support system
to help prevent his going back to alcohol and drugs. We each felt that
the other was listening and responding well. I looked forward to a better
future, but I am not a Pollyanna type of guy. I knew that abstinence is
a bumpy road, with lapses along the way. I was not, however, prepared
for the phone call from him a week later, a call that changed our lives
forever.

Eighteen

Everything I Loved Was Destroyed

With uncharacteristic excitement William told me that he finally understood what happened that made him so anxious and depressed in life. He could hardly get the words out fast enough. "This man came into one of our group sessions. He's an expert on sexual abuse and he had us fill out a questionnaire about our experiences with sex. When I finished, I found that I checked every single item that indicated sexual abuse. It was the highest score you could get."

Then William started to cry. "Listen Charlie, " he said. "Many things started to come back to me, things I've repressed all my life. There were terrible things that people did to me sexually. That's why I became a sexual compulsive and went out so much to have sex. I was reliving all the terrible things that people did to me sexually."

I wondered whether he was going to tell me that his father had sexually abused him. In the early years of our relationship he had maintained that the education of our youth would be better if, like in the ancient Greek system, teachers had sex with their students. This was not an idea in vogue in our contemporary educational system and I interpreted it as an unconscious desire to have sex with his father, the gay version of Freud's Oedipus Complex. Then on a couple of occasions and without a shred of evidence, he suggested that his father might be a repressed gay. These ideas suggested that William's hatred toward his father was more ambivalent than he wanted to admit. I learned not to make interpretations like these to him because he would become furious at the suggestion, proving that they were right on the money. I expected therefore, that he would follow-up his statement about sexual abuse by identifying his father as the culprit. I was wrong.

"Terrible things happened at Tom's house. You don't know what he did to me. It all came back to me after I filled out the questionnaire. And even worse things happened in England that summer. They raped me. Mick too. Now I understand why I always became so anxious traveling. Remember how I always used to stay in our hotel room and wouldn't come out, and you always got so angry with me? I remember now! I know why I was afraid to go out. Remember when I wouldn't leave our room in Marrakech? It's because of what happened to me in Morocco years before."

"But you weren't in Morocco before we met," I said.

"Yes, I was, but I never told you about it because I repressed it." He started crying again and barely got out the next words. "They did terrible things to me. They almost killed me."

"When were you there, William?"

"I can't talk now," he said. "I'm going to group now and I want to talk about this stuff in there. I want to remember more about what happened. Call me tomorrow night. Good-bye. Charlie, I love you."

Stunned is hardly the word for how I felt at the end of the conversation. I knew what had happened at Tom's house or at least I thought I did. He had told me about London, too—but Morocco? I had no idea what he was talking about, but I heard the urgency in his voice, his excitement about recovering the past. He was certainly right about one thing; William's anxiety when traveling. His travel anxiety depended upon where we were. I remembered how difficult it was to get him out of our room in Bath and in Marrakech he refused to leave the room after dark. He was a mess in Amsterdam. On the other hand he was as happy as a clam in Italy. And if he had been sexually abused in London, wouldn't he have been visibly upset when we stayed there? It was in London that we first visited Michael Leonard and spent hours at the British Museum and roared with laughter at the antics of people at Speaker's Corner. William appeared to be particularly happy there. It was very confusing.

I had not the slightest idea how these new memories were going to play out in time and felt frustrated that we could not sit down and talk about them. We were connected by phone each day only when our respective schedules allowed, usually at night after I finished seeing patients and he was free after the evening activity. I felt that I had to encourage his search for whatever helped him recover from drug addiction and if supporting his "repressed memories" did that then I would do so. The idea of repressed memories was very popular at the time, particularly when connected to sexual abuse. I thought it was nonsense and William knew about my belief that they were therapist-induced, what in the jargon is called an iatrogenic disorder.

The phone calls continued as William remembered more events, particularly in London where he was sexually abused. He was also given special privileges at Pride, such as a room to himself and he was permitted to skip group sessions. He stopped writing his poetry and substituted written accounts of his sexual abuse.

Our phone conversations were once again monologues, William telling me in minute detail how horribly he had been abused here and abroad. Trying to be the good psychologist, I believed that he needed time to ventilate his feelings about the abuse after which we might be able to regain some equilibrium in our relationship.

What follows are some of William's written accounts of sexual abuse from his Pride journal.

I was a very peculiar child and clearly identifiable as a future queer. My father didn't like it one bit. His extermination campaign was not physical, but psychological. Everything I loved was destroyed. My teddy bear, when he thought I was too old for it, was torn apart before my eyes, my blocks which constituted my fantasy world, went into the furnace. He eventually gave up, too drunk probably to pay too much attention. I survived silent and withdrawn.

I never had too much trouble about the homo thing. I said to myself, this is me and that's that. I was seventeen with hair to my waist. I was bored with school, and cut a lot. I would hangout, looking for someone with a joint. I was pretty immature. I had had crushes on boys, boys had crushes on me, but we were too shy for anything to come of it.

(William tells the story of meeting Mick in 1967 while sitting in Central Park. Mick takes him to Tom's house.)

Tom took my hand and led me into another room. He said "Would you take your clothes off for me?" I said "sure" because I was very high. Then he asked "Can I tie you up?" I said "sure." He bound my hands and feet and then tied them together. Then he said "Tell a story about a boy being whipped and raped." This makes me a little sick, but I figured it was just a story, and the other boys were in the next room. I did my best, wrecked as I was with pot, to tell the story. When he had heard enough, he untied me.

(William tells about the rules of not washing or going near the windows. He writes about a bizarre masturbation scene in which Tom sits on the floor with the boys in a circle around him and he has them taking turns telling a story about torturing a young man. William and Mick escape into the park, and after being picked up by the police they are sent to London by Tom.

This was my introduction into the wonderful world of homosexuality.

Now, I have to talk about the villain of the piece, and I'm going to use real names. Radson of Salisbury is the grandson of a duke, a multimillionaire, owner of thousands of acres, a castle, a luxury flat in London. He's married with children, and a monster.

(William describes how Radson raped them after which they are taken on a clothes-shopping spree. The next day they were taken to a party attended by a number of upper-class British men, some of whom had sex with them. Afterward William protested, but an endless supply of drugs and expensive clothes and dinners restrained him from leaving.)

So much for my virginity.

There was a constant stream of boys from around the world. Runaways, boys in trouble with the law, addicts, professional prostitutes, etc. Some stayed a few weeks, some a few months. We weren't allowed to touch each other. I was caught in bed with Giorgio, a blond Italian boy. We were beaten.

There was a lot of bizarre stuff I endured. One night there was this rich man who was watching me and Mick. We were being seen as a pair a lot at this time. We went to his house on Sloane Square. We walked in. The table was covered with coke. There were 3 big black bucks there. We did the coke and had drinks. The blacks were smirking and whispering to each other.

The man stood up and said "Okay, let's go to Paris." and we're still saying "sure." He had a private plane, of course. A ramp comes down, we drive into the plane, and we take off. We never get out of the car until we arrive at this big chateau in the middle of the country. It was late. He gave us downs and we went to sleep.

Next morning, after breakfast, he says "Let's make a movie." I say no way. I'm not being filmed doing these things. He says, you'll have to do it, pointing to the black guys, who were smiling. And they make me do it, beat me into it. They were at it all day and filmed it.

When we got back, he gave us a thousand pounds each. I complained to Radson. I said I wanted that film back, and I wanted it destroyed. He claimed he knew nothing about it, and that he would do what I asked. Of course, he lied.

This taught me that force rules.

One night this disgusting fat old guy with nine chins was watching me all night. "Such a skinny boy," he says. I moved away from him. Later Radson says "Somebody wants to take you to dinner." I go to the restaurant and the fat slob is waiting for me. He's already ordered the food. Course after course comes to the table. He keeps saying "Eat up, eat up. Clean your plate." Then he smokes a cigar.

We go back to his place. We have drinks in the living room. One of them tastes particularly horrible. He takes me into the other room. There's a table with a glass top and a chair covered with a white cloth facing it against the wall. He has me strip. He strips. His body is the most disgusting thing I have ever seen. He has me get up and squat on the table. He lies beneath it, his face directly below my asshole. "Take a shit," he says. The stuff comes pouring out of me, while he's jerking off furiously. The shit splatters all over my thighs as it comes out. He tells me to get off the table, and sit in the chair, holding my legs up. I do this, trying not to touch the stuff. He crawls over on all fours and starts to lick it off my thighs. When he's done with them, he cleans off my asshole with his tongue. Then he plants his mouth on it, mumbling "give me more, give me more, baby." I tell him there isn't any more. He makes a face.

I get up and run out of the room. In the bathroom I shower as quickly as possible, come out and get dressed. I just wanted to get out of there. He appears at the door. He has a roll of bills in his hand. He tries to hand it to me. I won't go near him. He shoves it in the pocket of my jacket. As I leave, he says "You didn't do it right." On the way back, I threw the money in a sewer.

Lord Radson sent me out to a "friend's" house one night. This guy wanted to tie me up. This had been done to me before several times. By this time, mid-November, I was completely submissive. Anyone could do whatever he wanted to me. He says my friend's waiting for you. I think it's another guy. He opens the door and a big German shepherd trots in. The dog is immediately licking my face. Then he says fuck him, tiger, fuck him. The dog is already excited. He's on me and in me in no time. His claws are in my sides. This was, up to now, the worst thing that had happened to me. "Fuck the dog-boy," he keeps on saying. I'm screaming "off me." The fuck is quick, but the dog's knob didn't go down for fifteen minutes. He keeps trying to pull out of me. This was really torture. The guy all through this, is laughing. He gives me money and pushes me out the door.

Radson again claimed ignorance, but let me keep the money. I hid it. One of the other boys stole it and disappeared. I was also allowed to spend the night with Giorgio. We wept in each other's arms.

William was sexually attracted to Giorgio, who according to William disappeared suddenly. "What happened to Giorgio?" William asked Radson.

"Shut the fuck up," Radson responded, "or the same thing will happen to you if you ever mention his name again." William never did until years later when he returned from Pride. Until that day, I had never heard the boy's name.

In Giorgio's memory, William wrote the following poem after he returned from Pride.

"You're the first person to hear this poem," he said to me.

Once, we lay together all night and wept,
The only time that ever happened there
For we were beyond tears in our despair,
Boy toys trapped in that hell
Now, I am dying a second death,
One not as bad as the first
And soon I shall weep upon your breast,
And you shall weep on mine.

William was shaking as he finished the poem and I held him as he continued to cry and talked about how much he missed his friend Giorgio.

There was one more sexual scene William described. He was asked to strip naked. His hands were tied together, raised and placed around a large hook attached to the ceiling, his feet lifted just off the floor.

"I never knew how horrible men could be," William said as he described what happened next.

He lit a cigarette, smoked it for a minute, then he walked in back of me and jabbed the lit end into my ass. I thought that was bad enough, but he kept burning the cheeks of my ass with it and I screamed in pain. I didn't know that my screaming was turning him on even more. He was standing in front of me with this weird look on his face. I tried to get off the hook, but I couldn't. He didn't try to stop me. He just let me get exhausted. Then he put the lit cigarette on my balls and he kept it there while I screamed. Then he put it on my cock. He kept burning my cock and balls until I fainted. When I woke up, I was lying naked on the floor. He threw my clothes at me, told me to get dressed and report back to Lord Radson. When I got back to the townhouse Radson said that I could take a week off to recover and I didn't have to go on any house calls.

William reported that he and Mick attended a couple of cocktail parties given by a certain titled lord. One can imagine these two boys raised in poor families, being dazzled by a rich British Lord. At the last of these, a Christmas party, he and Mick decided to each steal a souvenir. William purloined a small, gold, jewelry box and put it in his pocket.

The next day Radson accused them of the theft. The party-giving lord had missed the jewel box. Radson was infuriated and said, "I know what to do with boys who steal. Pack your bags."

The boys were put on a plane to Casablanca. They were met by a man who took their passports away and put the boys in a waiting car. They drove for over two hours into the barren Moroccan countryside until they arrived at a large walled enclosure. They were told to get out and two burly Moroccans ushered them through the gate. When they asked for their bags they were told they would be sent to their room. They never were. Although they had not yet figured where they had been sent, they sensed that this was going to be the worst experience of their lives, far more dangerous than anything that had happened in London.

They were stripped naked and given gallabahs, the native Moroccan dress to wear on their bodies and sandals for their feet. They were then shown to a dormitory containing about a dozen boys, a couple of whom had not yet reached puberty, a few more who were showing sparse patches of hair above their genitals and the rest in the fifteen-to-eighteen year-old range. By his own account, William was seventeen years old so that he and Mick were in the upper age range of the group.

It was a boy brothel. The enclosure sat on a small knoll in the countryside with no other building in sight. A guard stood at the gate twenty-four hours a day and other guards carried clubs to discourage any possibility of rebellion by the boys. The boys ate and slept in the dormitory, were allowed time to play in the courtyard each day and the guards escorted the boys to and from the rooms reserved to entertain the guests who came from around the world to have sex with them. "We were slaves," William said.

Men arrived each day. One or more boys were chosen by the men to entertain them. They ate meals together and afterward sat around the pool. Then they went to one of the rooms prepared with clean sheets on the bed. The men could do anything they wanted, although William reported that no one mistreated him or Mick the way they had been in Europe. Almost all of the men stayed overnight in guest rooms, some making a vacation out of it for as long as two weeks.

"We've got to get out of here," Mick said one night. They believed that if they were caught they might be killed, but they reasoned that it was only a matter of time before all the boys would die of one thing or another. The two of them had already spent two weeks in the brothel and they knew that none of the other boys had been there longer than six months. They came up with a plan.

William and Mick had developed a finely tuned sense of who lusted after them. One of the guards did, but they were not allowed to have sex with the boys. They propositioned him. They told him that he could have sex with them one night if he opened the gate right afterward. He agreed. They had no way of knowing if the guard would double-cross them but they had no other alternative. The deal was made; the guard was sexually sated and after running through the open gate and with the greatest stroke of luck (for once), the boys hitched a ride with a passing motorist driving into Casablanca. There the boys hustled day and night until they raised enough money to return to New York.

"You see, Charlie. All those things happened to me in just a couple of months. I started the summer being feted by royalty and I ended it as a slave. I pushed it all down so I didn't have to remember it, but all my fears were still there and my rage too, like you always said. And you remember how I used to admire everything English, especially the upper class and royalty? That was my cover-up for the truth, how I hated them for what they did to me."

And he cuddled and cried in my arms as I kissed and stroked him, feeling both compassionate and confused.

At the Gay Pride March, 1973.

Left to right: Michael Giovinco,
Charles Silverstein, David Marans, William Bory.

Photo courtesy of the author.

Nineteen

I Don't Want to Die Alone

William's counselor at Pride suggested that he be immediately sent to a residential treatment program that specialized in treating patients who had been physically and/or sexually tortured (the advanced course, so to speak). I inquired about the program and learned that they did not have any other gay residents at the time, sounded a bit hostile to the idea and I learned that patients were contained in a locked ward throughout the length of their stay. William nixed the idea immediately. He had had enough of institutions and wanted to come home. He had already made arrangements to begin psychotherapy and to join both Narcotics Anonymous (NA), and Sexual Compulsives Anonymous (SCA) groups. He was also mindful of getting his book of poetry published which he could not do in an institution far from home. Since he was building a new foundation for himself, I welcomed his return. I said that I would cancel my patients for the day and pick him up at the airport.

But I was still perplexed about the stories of sexual abuse. They were so extreme that I found myself wondering whether they were flights of fancy. Obvious inconsistencies and errors cried out for explanation. For instance: William was not seventeen years old when he went to London. He was twenty-two. He may have looked younger but one's age is a matter of fact.

William had had a string of lovers in his late teen years in the United States so that his experience with Tom was not his "introduction into the world of homosexuality." And his original description of being at Tom's had none of the torture and violence he now claimed. He had not been a virgin. He had been sexually active for years before having sex with Radson in London if that happened at all. There were at least two lovers before me and I had met both of them.

The "dog story" is said to have occurred in "mid-November," but William was in London only during the summer. Nor could he have attended a "Christmas party" at a British lord's house for the same reason. He also knew about my experience in Missouri with the hustler who had been sent to my room as a gift who told the story of being hired to have sex with a Great Dane. I wondered whether my story was the seed for William's elaboration. And how could Mick and William have returned from Morocco without their passports or raised enough money to pay for a one-way fare back to New York?

Thinking about these questions got me nowhere. They were inconsistencies of fact in a man who was suffering from depression and who had gone through the most sexually traumatic experiences that I had ever heard in my entire professional practice. He was obviously suffering from Post Traumatic Stress Disorder (PTSD) and not for a second did I think that any other professional would diagnose him otherwise. Such a man I reasoned might confuse some of the facts without throwing suspicion on their core truthfulness.

The effect of the HIV was also part of the equation. The day we saw the first KS lesions in Puerto Rico meant that he was already symptomatic and therefore, could have been infected as long as ten years beforehand. I knew and I suspect that he knew that the virus was making its way into his brain, causing mischief with his reasoning processes. For instance William always used to check the bill in a restaurant for errors. Long before he left for Pride he stopped doing so saying that he could no longer count columns of numbers. It disturbed him greatly. There was no medication at the time that could slow up, much less stop dementia, so we left it alone, kept it on the back burners of our minds should any treatment appear on the horizon. William adamantly refused a CAT scan and given the absence of treatment, I saw no reason to push him into it. The deterioration of brain cells by the disease had to diminish his cognitive functioning such as memory for facts, names, and dates. It could also conflate two memories into one, combining elements so that the memory that emerges is wholly different than the two "true" ones now destroyed by the confabulation.

The quandary was very painful to me for a number of reasons. There was first the question of whether to believe the stories. I saw the inconsistencies but reasoned that PTSD, depression and dementia could more than excuse some lapses of dates and events. In fact as I was to learn, his reporting the stories to other people proved the reliability of his details over time; he never changed the facts. Colleagues who worked with PTSD patients assured me that his occasional errors were consistent with their experience working with such patients. They all believed him.

The second question was how to respond to William about my conflicted feelings. I knew what I had to do. I reasoned that my goal in sending him to Pride was to conquer his crack addiction and that I would support him in any way in order to help him reach that goal. Therefore, I expressed the greatest empathy toward his uncovering traumatic events. When friends asked if I believed him, I said, "Yes," but as I continued to say so, came more and more to alternately believe them and think them conscious fabrications.

The tales of William's sexual abuse often put off people because they believed that such horrors could not happen. They were wrong. There are a number of men whose sexuality is light years away from that of the rest of us. For instance I have come across any number of men who have sex with dogs. During an international sex conference in Montreal one year, we met a strange gay man who invited us to his house. The walls were covered with pictures of German Shepherds and a real one was lying on the floor. "He's my lover," said our guest. "Would you like to watch him fuck me?" our host inquired with as much emotion as whether we would like a glass of tea. We politely declined and fled.

Jeffrey Dahmer was not an invention. Nor was John Wayne Gacey who murdered teenaged boys and buried their bodies in his cellar. There are well-documented cases of men who combined lust with sexual sadism. Most people are familiar with the Marquis de Sade whose books describing sexual sadism are classics. But few people know about Giles de Rais who lived in the thirteenth century. He was a Marshall of France, equivalent to a five star general in the United States and one of Joan of Arc's most important commanders. After the war he returned home where he killed scores of boys and young men by disemboweling them while masturbating and mixing his semen with their blood.

Another example less known in the United States was Andrei

Chikatilo, sometimes called "the Butcher of Rostov" who killed and mutilated at least fifty women during the 1970s and 1980s. While he clearly searched for girls and women in which to practice his specific forms of mutilation, he admitted, "in a pinch a boy would do." There is enough evidence that monsters like these men are in greater abundance than most people would feel comfortable to know.

Morocco sounds like the most implausible story of all. How could such a thing be possible? But I already knew that the brothel existed, although it is no longer there, swept away by the broom of moral hypocrisy. William had not made it up. I learned about it from Eddie, the Swiss man I met at the Hotel Victoria in Santo Domingo years before. At dinner one night Eddie told me about spending a week each year at a boy brothel outside Casablanca. The place was in the desert countryside, with no other buildings in sight. One could not take the boys out of the building but you could meet with them around the pool and spend as much time with them as you wanted. He said that the boys ranged in age from about twelve to the early twenties and that they were sexually experienced. He had not been there for a few years and did not know whether it was still around. He did not, however, describe the setting as slave-like. I remembered the description of the Moroccan gay whorehouse after William recounted what happened to him there. The similarities of their descriptions gave considerable veracity to William's story. But I remember telling him about Eddie's experience after I returned from Santo Domingo. Could that have been the germ of truth that William embellished?

There was finally the question that bothered me most of all. How could I not have known? Granted all the traumas of sexual abuse occurred before William had moved in with me. Granted too, I knew about his experiences with Tom and that he and Mick had lots of sex with the British upper crust while in London in the summer of 1972. What deviled me was that we had already lived together for eighteen years. We were our mutual best friends, shared all of our most intimate thoughts and feelings. There were no secrets between us. The question framed itself clearly in my mind. *What kind of relationship could we have had for William to hide these traumas from me all these years?* The theory of "repressed memory" notwithstanding (a theory I believe deeply flawed), his lack of trust in me shook the foundation of our relationship.

Practical matters dominated when William returned home on September 24th. He began psychotherapy with April and joined NA and SCA groups at the Lesbian and Gay Community Center. His attendance at SCA was short-lived. At his first meeting William insisted on commenting upon whatever anyone said, a violation of the rule against "cross-talk," refused to extinguish a cigarette during the meeting and refused to stop talking after he reached his time limit. He gave the coup de grace to the group at the second meeting when William announced that he intended to have more, not less anonymous sex in the future but not with anyone in the room because "You're all a bunch of wimps." He is the only person I know who was expelled from a twelve-step group.

Talking about sexual abuse continued unabated. He told everyone he met the details of his summer in England whether they wanted to hear about it or not. The longer he talked, the more he included minute descriptions of the sexual acts. The words gushed out of him like a torrent flooding his listener until he or she drowned in his emotions. He cried when recounting the stories just as he did on our couch after returning from Pride. He repeated the stories to friends who had already heard them before, but who did not have the heart to tell him to stop because of the pain in his voice and the tears in his eyes. Everyone had the greatest compassion for him, but one by one they started to avoid our company. I could hardly blame them.

William kept reliving these experiences even with total strangers. For instance in October 1992, Jay Asher asked me to appear at a fund raising affair in Houston for their gay teen group and to speak at one of their meetings. One of the reasons I accepted the invitation was to spend time with Ken. We were picked up at the airport by Jay and while driving William spilled out the whole story of his sexual abuse to him, who understandably felt embarrassed to be the recipient of so much personal information from a man he had just met. At the fund raising dinner, he started telling the stories again until Ken pulled him to the side and prevented his telling more donors about his sexual abuse.

Radio Pacifica had asked to interview me in Houston and it turned out that my radio host had attended Pride at the same time as William. After the interview I left with Ken to deliver my talk to the Houston gay teenagers, while William visited his friend at the station. After my talk Ken drove me back to the B & B where we were staying hoping to find William and then go dancing together at one of Houston's clubs. He was not there.

"There's no point sitting around and waiting for him," said Ken. "Let's go, I want to show you some of Houston's night life." We penned a note for William and left. A few minutes later we were standing in front of a dance club watching the passing parade.

"Are you thinking what I'm thinking?" asked Ken.

"Yes," I said. "He found a connection."

William's friend at the radio station had cocaine and they used it up within minutes of their meeting. Then William bought more and they consumed that. It had been about a month since he returned from Pride and when he came back that night I confronted him about the lapse in what I believed to be a drug free month. Wrong again. He finally told me the truth.

William had started drinking at the airport before he returned home from Pride. The taste for alcohol however, was not there and so in New York he started to indulge in other drugs with his new friend Dan.

There was much affection between them. Dan unfortunately returned to the streets of New York only to take up heroin again but this time with his new friend, William. They mainlined together in our living room while I slept and in the small apartment on the Lower East Side, the "retreat" that William rented after he came home. He rarely went there, much less spent the night. When he did as I later learned, it was for the purpose of meeting Dan and others to mainline heroin. Dan even joined us for a weekend in Napanoch and while I was cooking in the kitchen, they were cooking in the guesthouse. I remember walking into the living room and finding them asleep on the couch wondering why they needed so much sleep at eleven a.m. How dumb can you get?

It was not until a couple of weeks later in New York when, one night I found a hypodermic syringe sitting on the couch did I realize that William was using heroin. He was reading in bed when I confronted him but he protested that it was not his, a rather stupid and unimaginative response from someone who usually excelled in creative excuses. He ignored me and went back to reading his book.

I was bombarded by an overpowering set of emotions as I watched William in bed calmly reading his book as if I had caught him eating an orange, rather than shooting heroin. I stood frozen to the floor, muscles locked into place, my fists clenched, my heart pounding so hard that I could hear the blood pulsing through my ears. I saw the color black, the rage in me and red, the blood vessels in my eyes enlarging as if I were about to cry—then black again as the two emotions joined into one, a heavy veil of depression and hopelessness descending upon me. I wanted to leap on the bed and beat him with my fists and bloody his face. I wanted to call him every cruel and hurtful name I knew, to hurt him as much emotionally as physically. I wanted to get rid of him, throw him out of the house, banish him to the streets to die—order him to return to his "retreat," change the locks on the door when he did and never let him back in.

I do not know how long I stood there, probably less than a minute, my feeling of helplessness cutting into my body like a knife. William never glanced up at me during the silence and I felt that he was mocking me, complacent in his power to do as he pleased and justify his actions because of his AIDS and sexual abuse.

I said nothing more and walked back into the living room, stood there for a few minutes emotionless, lightheaded and dissociated from everything that happened that night, from William, from myself, from the implications of William's new drug addiction in our lives.

Then panic set in. Adrenaline pumped through my blood, waking me from my stupor and mobilizing my thoughts. I thought only about protecting myself and my home from impending disaster and I set about making a list of things that had to be done. Our bank accounts for instance. We each had savings and checking accounts. Both our names were on all of the accounts. We had arranged this years ago just in case one of us had to write checks on the other's account in an emergency. There was never a question of trust. But it was different now. There is no such thing as enough money for narcotics.

There was also emergency cash in the house tucked away in a book. I removed it and searched for a new hiding place. "What else?" I asked myself. The apartment was so vulnerable to theft. I thought it unlikely that William or the other addicts he might bring into the house would be interested in our folk art collection, but we had the usual electronic equipment so highly negotiable on the streets.

The feelings of rage and futility were gone, depression too replaced by an emotionless functionality. I felt again that it is all just a play on the stage, that I am only an actor saying my lines but denied knowledge of the rest of the script. I was dissociating, the same psychological process victims of PTSD experience in the face of trauma. The mind clamps down on one's emotional pain and substitutes an eerie out-of-body levitation as one becomes a distant witness to oneself.

"Heroin is a death drug," he said to me a week later. William gave up the drug completely as well as his retreat on the Lower East Side. He went back to crack. By this time he also stopped psychotherapy and going to NA groups. He terminated every means of support in his life including what friends were still left and placed himself in the hands of crack cocaine.

Of immediate concern was a book tour scheduled for November and December. *The New Joy of Gay Sex* was published in November 1992 and Felice Picano and I were scheduled to appear for media coverage in a dozen cities around the country. I suggested that Felice cover the West Coast where he was better known and because the tour there would take the greatest amount of time. I took some of the eastern cities and all of Texas, while we appeared jointly in the mid-West. The tour took me away from New York for a few days a week for most of November and December of 1992. That meant leaving William alone. I was conflicted at first uncertain whether to leave but in the end reasoned that William's drug habit would continue no matter where I was. I went on the tour.

William joined me on the Texas tour of Houston, Dallas, and Austin. Ken had just left his job and started on disability and so we three ate almost every meal together. Only once did William and Ken dine together without me because I was at a book-signing event. William remained in Houston when I flew off to Dallas and Austin and we agreed to meet at the Houston airport for the flight back to New York. We spoke by phone and I could hear the slightly slurred telltale speech of drugs in his voice. "I have no idea where he is or what he's doing," said Ken, "and I'm not going to try to find him either." I envied Ken's firmness and his mature judgment, wishing that I could be as decisive and I appreciated his not damning me for my incompetence in handling William's addiction.

William barely made it to the plane on time. He looked terrible. He had not washed in days, his face was tired and drawn, his eyes red from lack of sleep. He was uncommunicative during the flight and when we arrived home went immediately to his cave where he slept for the rest of the day and through the night. By this time he was devoted to his drug, obsessed with getting it, smoking it, getting more, defining his world by it only occasionally to me. Under the influence of crack his rage and harangues toward me vanished in the smoke. At least I was grateful for that.

I was awaked one night in December by the incessant ringing of my doorbell. It was three a.m. I immediately assumed that William was outside without his keys. In actuality it was a neighbor informing me that William had been injured in a knife fight that had just taken place in our building lobby and that he was taken by ambulance to the hospital but she did not know which one. He could have been taken to any one of four hospitals on the Upper West Side. I called the Emergency Room of them all, only to be told that no one by his name had been brought in. Obviously one of them was wrong. I searched for him at each of them. Finally the guard at the Emergency Room of St. Luke's Hospital checked his list and said that William was not there, but when he saw the look of desperation on my face allowed me to enter the Emergency Room and search for him. William was sitting in one of the cubicles. There was so much dried blood on his face that I could not tell where the knife wounds were.

He said that he had gone out to buy cigarettes and was attacked by three guys who tried to steal his money. He denied that drugs were the reason for the attack. Fortunately he was able to get into the inner lobby of our building and lock the door behind his attackers. The story was an obvious fabrication. He had gone downstairs to buy crack and when the drug dealers saw his physical weakness, they tried to steal his money, to "beat" him as it is called.

It was dawn by the time the doctor stitched William's wounds. A light snow covered the streets when our taxi arrived back home. I could see how much trouble he had walking and he nearly collapsed as we walked up the steps to the front door of our building. It was only as we approached the lobby that I saw the blood on the glass door. It was smeared both inside and out and the sight gave vivid testimony to the fierceness of the battle. William did not own a knife, know how to use one, nor had he ever been in a physical fight and I realized how close he had come to getting killed. I helped him up the stairs and put him to bed in the cave. He thanked me for taking care of him and for bringing him home safely and kissed me. I went downstairs, cleaned the blood from the glass doors and went to sleep in the bedroom.

The doorbell again awakened me. This time it was just after nine a.m. When I opened the door a neighbor was holding on to William. After I went to sleep William, bandages and all with an uncertain gait, had left the apartment to find more crack. "He was wobbling on his feet in the middle of the street," said my neighbor. "He would have gotten hit by a car skidding in the snow." William was furious at our neighbor, but by this time he was simply too tired to protest and fell asleep quickly. I hadn't a clue what to do next.

Most of William's money was gone by the end of the year. His health was deteriorating as much from the drug as the disease. Neighbors reported to me that William was borrowing small amounts of money from them. His appearance was so poor that I decided to call off our 1993 annual New Year's Day party. Invitations were already out and I had to call everyone on the list to tell them that the party was off. Most of them concluded that the cancellation was due to AIDS but the real reason was that his addicted state would be too painful for our friends to see. Only a few close friends knew the truth.

By the middle of January 1993 I noticed small amounts of money missing from my desk. I searched my hiding place only to find the money gone. His stealing meant that his savings were completely gone. The only other money left was mine.

It is not easy to live with a crack addict in the house, all the more difficult when you work at home with patients coming and going. Alcoholism and drug addiction are all too prevalent in New York's gay community and gay men are sophisticated about the signs of addiction. There was no way that I could explain why a drug addict was living in my house and his bumping into them would throw a pall over our rapport.

I came to the conclusion that I had to get rid of him. Perhaps that is not the most charitable way to put it but charity is not what I felt. I could cope with the disease, felt prepared to minister to his illness with whatever might be required. I did not bargain however, for his theft of my money, the crack parties that he held in our apartment after I went to sleep and the potential disruption to my practice. But I could not banish him to the streets. Some people might see my reluctance to do so as a sign of my weakness, others, my strength. Whatever it is, I could not do it.

Therefore I decided to ship William to Miami. It was winter and while New York was covered with a blanket of snow, the weather was balmy there. Besides he had a friend in South Beach who agreed to let him stay for a few weeks. I did not present the idea as an option. I forced him to pack a duffel, paid for a one-way ticket to Miami and gave him spending money for a week. After that his monthly disability would arrive, which he could withdraw from an ATM machine. I drove him to the airport, followed him down the boarding gate and watched as the gate closed behind him. He was sad; he stopped and glanced at me before he walked through the door, his "Buddy" cap on his head, the expression on his face one of betrayal. But I felt free and I started to breathe again.

How did I feel about William as he boarded the plane? I had not a clue. I thought only of myself, that I could relax for an unknown number of days and that a measure of stability would return to the house. I would no longer have to listen while working with patients for the sounds of William rustling through the apartment or slamming doors as he walked in and out of the bedroom or the living room. But I also asked myself —and this is difficult to confess—whether I wanted him to return at all. "What does this question mean?" I asked myself. Out of the need for my own security I had forced out of the house my lover of almost two decades suffering from signs of dementia, depression, AIDS and drug addiction. Lurking in the back of my mind was the idea that he would never come back to New York and I felt profoundly guilty about the thought, unwilling to confess it as much a wish as a fear. I shamed myself, called myself bad, cruel, unfeeling for envisioning the potential scenarios that might lead to his not returning. I did not want him to return; that much was obvious. But more damning was my recognition that his death would be the only thing to free me from a burden I could no longer carry. My love for William, my belief in life-long commitment, my dedication to taking care of him through the plague all shriveled to a lonely dried-out spot in my soul. Whether the drug addiction caused my love to hibernate or killed it completely, I did not know. But in the next week or so I maintained a front of being resolute that I would not allow William to return to New York, while punishing myself in my private thoughts for doing so.

The phone calls from Miami came at least twice a day. I ignored his complaints, adamantly refused to allow him back unless he agreed to enter another residential treatment program anywhere in the country but not New York City. He would have none of it. His stubbornness went unabated even in the midst of his dire situation. It was during one of these phone calls that I remembered that he never carried a wallet or any other form of identification. I fantasized his being murdered by hard-nosed Miami drug dealers or killed by a car driven by the hordes of drunken adolescents on South Beach. Perhaps by an overdose.

Sitting by my desk after a phone call I thought about all the ways he might die in Miami. I realized that his body would be labeled a "John Doe," buried and that no one would know to call me. William would just disappear from the face of the earth leaving me alone to contemplate the silence. These worries remained in the foreground of my mind and although I remained resolute in not allowing him home when he called, surly though he might be, at least I knew that he was still alive.

"Okay, you win," William said one day. "Let me come home and I'll go for treatment."

I was not going to be manipulated this time. "No, you can't come home," I replied firmly. "First you have to go to a treatment program and when you complete it, you can come home." We argued fiercely on the phone and in the end we compromised. I agreed to pay for an airline ticket back to La Guardia Airport where I would pick him up. He agreed to go to his mother's house nearby and remain there for the day or two needed to arrange for residential treatment. After our talk I called his mother who agreed to the plan. I made the reservation and William was scheduled to return the next evening.

After the phone call I sat wondering about bringing William back to New York. I thought about a similarity between us. We were both men with strong passions in our lives. For me it may have started the day my family drove south and witnessed the inhuman chain gangs on the road and a year later when we were forced to abandon L.A. because of anti-Semitism. I brought this passion with me, this energy, working for the gay liberation movement, a lesson learned so many years ago fighting the schoolyard bully. Surely it was passion, a sense of having a mission, the belief perhaps the grandiosity that I could change the world that made me a leader in changing my profession's perception of homosexuality from perversity to normalcy.

William had his passions as well. For him it was books, knowledge and education in the purest sense of the word without a thought of external rewards such as college degrees or publishing, the gold stars of academic life. Knowledge was its own reward and no one I knew had a better grasp of the historical, religious, and cultural place of man in the world than he.

Our relationship therefore, was the nexus of our respective passions, the embodiment of our powerfully held emotions, our commitment to ideas and ideologies—and to our respective moralities. The moral sense was finely tuned in us both, William sometimes crying while recounting the massacres of small ethnic groups by large ones over the centuries, while I acted the role of a homosexual David out to slay the prejudiced psychiatric Goliath. While his feelings carried him back to centuries of prejudice, I was (and am) a champion of the present. We respected these passions in each other and it was an important component of the glue that kept us together over the years. We both loved and hated deeply, eschewing the wishy-washy middle ground. We both fiercely attacked any theory whose only grace was its fashionableness and those colleagues of mine who espoused it for no better reason than their impulse to run with the herd. Now William had found a new passion, crack, while I lost all of mine. He called the dance, choreographed the steps as he moved far away from me on the floor, leaving me alone, static, unable to mobilize the creativity that had always been a part of my character.

These were some of the thoughts that ran through my mind as I drove to La Guardia Airport. There were others. I did not believe him and distrusted his intention to go for treatment. I imagined him leaving his mother's house as soon as he could and living on the streets of New

York with his drugs. "Why then are you bringing him back?" I asked myself. The obvious answer is that I wanted to delude myself that things would turn out all right because I could no longer suffer the guilt of William's dying on the streets of Miami Beach as a "John Doe." I could not accept responsibility for the day when the phone calls would stop. Everything would work out better if the plane crashes and kills him. That is what I hoped for as I entered the parking lot and as I stood in the waiting room.

William walked slowly up the ramp into the waiting room dragging his duffel bag behind him, the Buddy cap still on his head, at least a week's growth of hair on his face. He stood in front of me for a few seconds, his head bowed, his hands energized as if he wanted to touch me, but did not as he correctly sensed that the gesture would be rejected.

"It was awful," he murmured and I instinctively sensed that his words were a mere statement of fact, not an attempt to manipulate me. "Let's go to my mother's house," he said confirming by metamessage that escaping treatment was not on his agenda.

Mrs. Bory prepared a bed for William in the room that had previously been her husband's bedroom. "What an irony," he said as she left to give us our privacy. "I'm being taken care of in my father's room. I hated him all my life. Maybe this is an omen that things will change, that I'll change." Then he talked a bit about living on the streets of South Beach after his friend threw him out for stealing. He peddled for drugs, begged for money on the beach eating whatever left over foods he found in garbage cans thrown away by tourists who had eaten enough fast food for the day. The cops whacked the hell out of him from time to time, trying to keep the sight of this new vagrant from the eyes of tourists who came to Miami for the green palms and the clean sand.

"Remember when you used to talk about 'bottoming out.' Well, I did and there isn't anything about it to recommend. Please try to get me in tomorrow. I want to live."

Until that moment we sat apart from each other on the bed. He knew that I would not accept an embrace or a kiss. There was too much ambivalence in the air for such insincere *pro forma* displays of affection.

"Charles," he said and moved a forefinger ever so slightly toward me.

"I don't want to die alone." I touched his forefinger but refused to say the word as we lingered together in the symbolic embrace until I said, "I'll call you first thing in the morning."

During the drive home I wondered about all the ironies in our respective lives, wondered whether this new one, sleeping in his father's bed, might work in our favor—for once.

Ken Neumeyer

Photo by Michael Leonard. Used by permission of the photographer.

Twenty

This is My Home

I have just written about how complimentary our passions were until drugs became an impervious barrier between us. I wrote such a compelling story about our meeting at the airport, driving to his mother's house and the sensitive moments we had sitting on his father's bed. It was a charming metaphor, his dead father's bedroom, a glimmer of hope for coming to terms with his drug addiction with the father who was dead and the symbolic one sitting a foot away. And ironies. How they "might work in our favor—for once."

Compelling or not, the story is a scene I invented as a substitute for the vile one that actually took place, one that fills me with dread even as I write these words. I substituted a "Hollywood" ending for the truth rather than reveal the dark side of what really happened that night and for many months to come. I hesitate to tell the truth, to stand so exposed before the world. The truth is that we did not meet at the airport that night, did not drive over to his mother's house, did not enter his dead father's bedroom and that he did not go for treatment.

I arrived at the airport long before the plane landed, paced back and forth in the waiting area in a state of agitation. Yes I was still mistrustful of him, yet at the same time I punished myself for bringing William back, convinced that it was for naught, that he would continue to use the safety of our home as a crack den. I feared that William might attempt to evade me and therefore, inquired exactly which ramp passengers would use as they entered the lobby and stationed myself there.

The plane landed and deplaning passengers started walking up the ramp and into the lobby, but William was nowhere in sight. I walked down the ramp searching for him, and then back again to look for other routes he might take to flee. No matter where I looked, no matter who I talked to, William had disappeared. It was inconceivable that he might have missed the plane since it was his only opportunity to get back to New York. The only other possibility was that even in his poor state of physical and mental health he had eluded me. I called his mother's house. He had not called there. There was nothing more to be done and so I drove back home.

I had only to walk through the door to know that William was already there because lights that should have been off were turned on. He had somehow escaped detection at the airport, arrived home before me and gotten into the building and our apartment even though he had no keys. I walked into the empty bedroom and living room. He was obviously in the cave. Its door was closed. I called to him but there was no response. Then I tried to open the door but it was barricaded from the inside.

"Don't come in," yelled William. "Leave me alone."

I cannot remember my response for the next minute or so. I remember only that through the barricade William said that he would never go to another treatment center, never go back to NA and that he was going to continue using drugs. "It's the only thing that mutes my pain," he yelled through the door.

A rumble started its journey from my bowels, amplifying in volume as it sped upward toward my lungs that expanded to hold the memories of a thousand resentments. The roar that fired from my mouth sounded inhuman, a noise more awesome than had ever come from within me. It was not a word or series of words, only a scream of such power that its force might shatter the door barring me from the room. The scream released all the bound energy in me that had burrowed its way into my muscles, locking them up—locking me up for months—damming the rage in me.

I threw myself at the door with the weight of my body while aiming the scream toward William. The bookcase moved under the onslaught and after slamming myself against the door again it fell away, the top shelf shattered by the force of the blow. William was sitting on the bed, the odor of crack in the air.

I said every hurtful mean thing to him that had ever crossed my mind in the almost two decades of our relationship. My only desire was to hurt him. I know that I wanted my words to kill and I told him at the top of my lungs how much I hated him, how much I wanted him to die, how I had hoped that his plane would crash and kill him, what a monster he was, a liar, a thief, the most selfish person on the face of the earth. I kept saying these things over and over again, my muscles like batteries releasing their energy all at once, hoping that my every insult might have the effect of shooting an arrow into him and with enough of them, that he would die of his wounds.

"Don't come near me!" he yelled and in that moment I saw him, not the person that infuriated me, but the one actually before me, sitting frightened on the bed. "I'll use this on you if you attack me," he said. On his lap was the prized, oversized Giacomo Serpotta book we bought in Italy, one of the two books upon which he cut his crack. In his hand and pointed at me, was the knife part, all two inches of it of a wine bottle opener. William had never hurt anyone physically in his life and I doubted his ability to stab me (or anyone else), no matter how hurt and this "knife" of his, a duller blade you could not find.

"Get out!" I demanded.

"This is my home. I'm not going to leave it until I die. I'll stay in the cave if you want me too, and I'll never come out, but I'm not going to let you throw me out of my house."

I question whether I can adequately convey my feelings seeing William's pathetic appearance and its contrast to his powerful words whose impact upon me was profound. I stood there my rage not yet abated, ready to let fly more arrows from my quiver, yet while I still yearned for the freedom of his death at the same time I felt proud of him, his words, his sentiment toward his home, and for his wish to die there. It is not that I melted under his defense, rather that all these feelings coexisted in me as I stood in the doorway, my eyes narrowly focused upon him, the book still in his lap, the "knife" still in his hand.

"I'm not going to attack you," I finally said. I did not feel guilty venting my rage, even about breaking down the door, but I did not want him to fear that I would kill him and I could understand how the force of my attack convinced him that I might. He closed the wine opener and put it down.

He was obdurate in his desire to continue smoking crack. Then he begged me to leave him alone in the cave until he came out the next day. I asked him to leave the door open probably because of its symbolic value since my request had no practical meaning. He said that from then on he would keep the door closed when he was using and open when he was not. I walked away resigned to the fact that William was back and that he would never leave again. But now after all that I had not the slightest idea how to integrate the feelings that predominated in my heart: love, hate and compassion.

While walking back to the bedroom, I reflected upon the Gods of ancient Greece who had been so assiduously studied and talked about in our house for so many years. The Oracles foretold the future of kings and foreign conquerors with breath-taking accuracy. No matter how hard or ingeniously a mortal might try to change his future, the Gods would not be satisfied by anything but their predestined announcement. I saw the filthy basement in which I found William, cold, grimy, its bare bulb overhead. And now he was in its mirror image the cave, an isolated room another bare bulb overhead. I could not have tried harder to defeat the Gods, but I could not change what seemed to me his destiny to die in that shabby room. I felt mocked by the Gods for defying them, punished for taking him home with me so many years before. I could see them watching me from above, smirking since they long ago knew what would transpire this night.

While in bed I thought about all the political battles I had fought in my life standing up to the bullies of society or to the institution of homophobia. I was always a fearless fighter, a champion for the rights of the underdog whether Jew, gay or black. They were easy; I was fighting an external enemy grown fat with power with companions at my side for inspiration and support. But things were different now; the real battle I fought was not with William—the enemy was within and I was ill prepared to do battle with myself. I knew that I would never have peace again until the end and I wondered whether beneath my desire to save myself, I might still love him. I knew that a long night was to come although I could not have known about the darkest corners yet to emerge.

"I don't feel guilty about what I did," I said to myself as I lay down in bed. Then I said it again. With my mind's eye I visualized the scene that just ended, breaking open the door, hurting William with words as he had so often done to me during his harangues and the vision of his frightened face and the "knife" pointed at me. His words echoed in my head, "This is my home" and once again I refused to feel guilty about my rage. I said it so many times and in so short a period of time that I could no longer continue the charade and finally admitted to myself that I felt profoundly ashamed of my conduct.

The fallout began the next morning when I walked into the kitchen. In the garbage were a number of large photographs of us taken in Napanoch by Michael Leonard. There was the picture of us laughing while climbing the apple tree and the one of us playing coyly together near the car. They were pictures of better times. William had obviously kept them in the cave to have them as a reminder of those days and now they were torn to pieces. Only one of the pictures could be saved. Then I spied pieces of ceramic below the torn photos. I recognized them as the birthday present I gave William two years before, the plate of "Blue Willow. The shattering of the plate and the tearing of the photos sent a clear message about his feelings toward me for hurting him so deeply the night before.

The next few months were dreadful, without question the worst in our lives. The days and weeks merge together so that I have no sense when a particular event occurred. William was faithful about only smoking crack in the cave at least during the day and with the door closed. After I retired for the night he would come out to smoke crack and cigarettes and watch TV in the living room. I was terrified that in a stuporous state his lit cigarette would start a fire. He also continued to invite other crack addicts home to smoke with him and I am quite sure that he played the part of the rich uncle who paid for the drugs just as he paid for alcohol when he mixed drinks on the beach of SoBe. The cigarette burns in our upholstered furniture gave concrete evidence of these parties. On a couple of occasions noise woke me up and I found three or four "guests" in the living room smoking with him. William was complacent when I threw them out and he walked away to the cave. I have no idea however, how many of these parties were held in my home in the next few months.

I desperately tried to keep his addiction from the notice of my patients. While William might have used my practice as a wedge against me, it was never in his character to do so. As time went on however, he started leaving doors open that were always kept closed during my working hours, especially the bedroom and living room. This was not maliciousness on his part, rather the effect of dementia; he simply forgot to close them. He also forgot to lock the front door when he went out at night to buy drugs. There was no point arguing with him about his neglect so I bought and installed spring operated door closures. For the front door I installed a mechanism that locked once the door was shut.

It was not as easy to deal with William's constant searching day and night for cash. Almost daily I could hear him rummaging through our bedroom looking for money, particularly the closet that shared a common wall with my office. There were times when I was trying to listen to a patient but tuned instead to the sounds of William moving things around in the closet. There were drawers and closet doors opening and closing. I had no idea what my patients thought of the noise. On one of these expeditions he found my collection of coins and I could hear the sounds of wrappers being torn apart and coins falling on the floor. In response I carried the rest of the coins to safety by depositing them with a gay neighbor, the artist Miles Parker who knew the full story and who would be very helpful in caring for William when things got worse.

I also brought down the two books William cherished most. The Giacomo Serpotta book was one. The other was another oversized book, *Nijinsky Dancing.* The Nijinsky book was beautiful, out of print and very expensive. It was written by Lincoln Kirstein who had read William's poetry and encouraged its publication. The book had to be protected because William started selling his extensive book collection in order to pay for drugs and I knew that he would hate himself if he sold these books. "I'll never sell them," William said to me when I explained why they were put into safekeeping, but I knew that drug addicts are always trading their most cherished possessions to pay for the demon that drives their lives.

If you have lived with someone for as many years as we lived together, your home will be filled with both sentimental and valuable gifts collected over the years. These small treasures presented for birthdays, holidays and for gifts given for no better reason than to express one's love will be scattered throughout the house. I had given William many such gifts over the years. Sometimes they were just sentimental like the Blue Willow plate. The others, gifts with intrinsic value, started disappearing. Years before I bought him a beautiful birthday present, a "Gibson Girl" folding mirror. The Gibson Girls were beautiful women, dancers on the stage who were all the rage at the end of the last century. A Gibson girl was painted on one side, the mirror on the other. There were three paintings and three mirrors in a triptych with a gold colored chain on top. It was beautiful and it sat opened on one of our dressers. When it disappeared, I knew that it had been traded for drugs fetching only a minuscule sum of what it was worth. But what difference did it make I asked myself, if it were sold for ten dollars which is likely, or the hundreds of dollars it was worth if all the money would be turned into smoke? In time every gift I ever give William vanished. To his credit however, he never sold anything that belonged to me.

Next went his book collection. There were many first editions, valuable reference books, and whole shelves of out-of-print but important historical volumes and a fine collection of old Baedecker guides that we often used on our travels. As he needed money, he filled his duffel bag with as many books as he could carry and marched downstairs to the used bookstore a block away. William was not the kind of person who could bargain over price in the best of times and he accepted whatever sum they offered for the books, even as he knew that they were cheating him. He took the money knowing that the crack would last for the day. How I hated those people in the bookstore, how I wanted to burn their store to the ground as retribution for their avarice.

Each day I watched William pack the duffel and carry it out, another shelf gone up in smoke, as I was powerless to stop it. He would return after buying drugs and go to the cave, close the door and not come out for hours. As the weeks progressed, the duffel was packed twice a day and the bookcases, most of which we built ourselves looked naked and started collecting dust.

There were times when William attempted to talk with me even while zonked out on crack. I think he felt lonely in the cave and missed my company. He sat on the couch next to me talking, his lower jaw moving from side to side, a characteristic sign of crack at least for him. But he could not maintain a conversation for more than a couple of minutes, after which he fled back to the cave. Like being on a rubber band he would sit with me, then leave again. Sometimes when the door was open, I would enter the cave. The ashtrays were overflowing with cigarette butts and crack paraphernalia sitting on the wooden board that replaced his two cherished books.

One day when I joined him in the cave, William begged for the return of his Serpotta and Nijinsky books. He was particularly upset about the absence of the Nijinsky book because of the special significance it held for him. Years before he told me that when he was about eight, he asked his mother to take him for ballet lessons. She agreed but after a few, his father turned up at the ballet class and yanked William out making some comment about not wanting to have a "dancing fairy" for a son. It was this aborted attempt at ballet that provided the fertile soil that grew into his attachment to Nijinsky, himself a depressed man who lived the last decades of his life in a mental asylum. I think there was also a sexual attraction that William felt toward the extraordinary, but ill-fated Russian dancer. William's identification with Nijinsky became the representation of his own genius and ironically his failed life and impending death. He begged me to buy him ballet slippers claiming that his feet hurt when wearing sneakers or shoes. In actuality he was transforming himself into the embodiment of Nijinsky (he had long before called himself "Vasily") as if the cave were the mental institution and he Nijinsky, once the darling of the world now turned into a morose, mad, hopeless body.

"I will never sell that book," he said. I brought it back to his hugs and kisses. He sat in the living room to read through it again, telling me about events from the dancer's life and we looked through the photographs in the book. He was so happy to get it back, as if a piece of his life had been restored. I will not be coy about this. Day after day the book sat on his lap as he cut his crack on it. While he sold off his entire book collection over time, he never sold the Nijinsky or Serpotta books.

By April peripheral neuropathy had set into his legs and we saw a neurologist who ordered a CT scan of his head. When we returned for the results, the neurologist called me aside and showed me the x-rays. "There is severe, diffuse brain damage," he said. "He must be a very intelligent person to be able to function at all." William, who usually hated physicians, liked this neurologist, probably because he was a gentle gay man who did not threaten or cause him any pain. The doctor prescribed medication for the neuropathy.

I sat with the prescription in my hands, but I did not want to fill it. William was sitting on the couch watching an old movie on TV. He looked if not happy, at least peaceful. I could get the medication I reasoned, after which his legs might return to normal and he might go out and buy crack, or I can substitute a Tylenol in which case his legs would continue to pain him and being unable to walk, withdraw from the drug.

What is the morality of this dilemma? I questioned whether I had the right to decide what kind of pain my lover should and should not experience. I argued with myself that I had a say about my own pain, what I needed in order to survive and to take care of him. So after convincing myself that the only truly rational thing to do was to substitute the Tylenol—after absolving myself of guilt for my devious intentions, I gave William the true medication, only to strengthen his legs enough so that he could continue his daily quest for crack.

I am still defensive about what I did. It is true that in time I learned that his neuropathy like his severe headaches were as much psychological as physical, but I did not know that then. I eventually learned that a Tylenol had the same effect of diminishing his headaches and neuropathy, so that my actions could neither encourage nor discourage his crack use. But that was not my dilemma. The safest thing would have been to give him nothing at all and let him lie in pain. I could not do that. I believed that making William an invalid, taking away what little independence he had left was the more disrespectful alternative. Perhaps it is my rationalization, or more damning my cowardice. Giving William the prescribed medication was expressing my love for this man whose body was weakening before me, whose brilliant mind had deteriorated and who was coping the only way he knew. Yes, I still loved him and took care of him because of love not out of a sense of responsibility. I also realized how much I still needed to be loved by him.

For months I went through a nightly ritual. I hid my wallet and money in order to prevent William from turning my money into crack.

My wallet also held ATM and credit cards and even though I had already changed the PIN on the ATM card, he could easily misplace or lose them. Every night as I slept, William searched through all the books in my bookcases, the drawers in my desk and through the closets looking for money or anything else that could be traded for drugs. He still did not sell any of our artwork or any of the gifts he had given me over the years. I can hardly claim that I slept easily at night knowing that the search would begin after I fell asleep. At first I put the money and wallet in the drawer of a night table by my bed, pushing the drawer firmly against the bed. If he came in while I slept and moved the table, the noise woke me up and I ordered him out of the bedroom. Of course he returned to search the closets and dressers in the bedroom and so I rigged a metal contraption to the door that came crashing down when it was opened, waking me up and scaring him off.

In time I started hiding my wallet in different places each night, moving it around as if I were protecting a black slave escaping through the Underground Railroad. I finally settled on keeping it on my person during the day and in a box for a computer program at night, since anything connected to computers had almost the effect of a phobia upon him. He never found it. I cannot say that I adjusted to these secretive nightly rituals that went on for months, only that I needed to protect myself.

In the beginning of April we took our last trip, a week in New Mexico. William rebelled after a few days, made a scene everywhere, so we sped back home where he literally flew out of the house in order to secure drugs. In retrospect I see how foolish I was to believe that he could have done otherwise. I know that I was thinking of myself, that I needed a vacation badly and I pressured him to go since I could not leave him at home. But we did accomplish one thing on the trip; we videotaped William reading his poetry.

My graduate school buddy Floyd Turner had loaned me his video recorder in order to make a record of William reading his poetry. Sitting in our hotel room in Santa Fe he read as well as he could, wearing for its effect, a yellow t-shirt with three skulls printed on it. We finished the taping after we returned home. Although he was short-tempered from time to time, I am amazed at how well he sat through these long sessions and the record they left behind is obviously important to me. I planned to use them at his memorial service.

There were two other notable events in April 1993. The first was the publication of *Orpheus in His Underwear*, William's book of poetry. Ian Young did a splendid job producing the book. Our friends in publishing joined forces to publicize the book. Ed White gave a blurb that said "William Bory is the American Cavafy, and shares the Alexandrian poet's obsession with boys, beauty and death." Edward Lucie-Smith, a well-known British art critic wrote, "This is one of the most remarkable first books of poetry I have ever read." Ian, himself a prolific literary critic, wrote of William's "ability to enter the dark emotional landscape of our times and illuminate it—fitfully, movingly, with astonishing flares of eloquence and beauty." Jerry Roscoe, at the time a reviewer for a number of gay publications, gave it a glowing review. It was also nominated for the 1994 Lambda Book Award for poetry. Ian arranged for the book to be distributed by an American company, which sold many copies but went bankrupt and never paid for them.

I suggested a publishing party. At first William protested, but I knew that the idea thrilled him and that his denial was just a continuation of his life-long trait of minimizing excitement and showiness. He had already read his poetry at informal readings of young gay poets to great applause. For days before the party William was obsessed about his choice of poems. He wanted to strike a balance between sad poems about disease and death, with those about sex and others that reflected his feelings about religion. He also wanted to read one or two poems about individuals whose lives had touched him. Serpotta headed the list. Others included the Prince of Palagonia (the monster) and Pope Celestine V. He also read a poem that Ian did not include in the book, "A Poem That Threatened Not to Be." It was about a Boy Scout who was murdered. The incident had deeply affected him.

He was nervous for days before the publishing party and he practiced reading before me often. As people arrived and there must have been at least sixty, he played the role of the poet to perfection, even to wearing a beret on his head. It was his show—for once—and I kept as far away from the spotlight as I could, busying myself by preparing food and beverages. William sat on a chair in the living room while our guests surrounded him sitting on the furniture and the floors, unaware of how much of his brain had been eaten by dementia. I was amazed at his outward calm and the verbal facility with which he read his work, especially since he had been smoking crack right up to the time our first guests arrived. He beamed with pride as people applauded or made those little sounds that convey pleasure.

How wonderful that William finally felt proud of himself, felt that he had at last made a mark upon the world. He had so often witnessed my professional and literary accomplishments, knew so many gay writers, attended so many publishing parties, had had brunch with so many editors and agents, people who could rightfully claim to have left their marks, that he pushed himself to the periphery as they moved further toward the center. The publication of his book and the party changed all that. Though suffering from dementia, addicted to crack, his performance was magnificent. Afterward he thanked me profusely for everything that I had done to make the party a success.

Of course many of the guests bought copies of the book and that was a mixed blessing. Some people gave me the money, while others, not understanding the problem gave it to William. (William charged them more for the book than I did.) After collecting the money, he left the party.

"Where's William?" asked his sister Margaret. She felt sad when I explained that with money in his pocket, crack was inevitable. By the time he returned, Margaret was the only guest left and she watched as her brother sped to the cave to smoke. He brought back enough crack to last for days.

The second event was my birthday. Without funds William gave me the only thing he possessed, a new poem. It was titled, "For a Lover." It was about the two of us, "the caring therapist, and the tyrannical boy," and our country house in which we had so many years of joy, "then seven miles past summer, struggling and abandoned, up a winding road through the trees."

"I worked on it all night," he said, "but it's not very good," he added.

He no longer wrote anything. His handwriting was almost unintelligible due to the loss of manual dexterity, the inevitable consequences of neurological damage. But somehow he managed to form the ideas, the literary images and metaphors for the work, type it on the computer and print the copy. I knew that he had not used crack that night because his writings under the influence of the drug were gibberish.

Composing the poem had been a huge hurdle for him. More than anything else he ever said or did, those words disfigured by dementia though they may have been, symbolized the love that characterized our relationship for so many years. The poem brings our two decades to life, our talks about the power of ancient Gods, the travels in which we walked among the ruins of once noble cities, the tender moments in bed and climaxes by the hundreds. The poem reflected upon a time when we were the best of lovers and the best of friends.

But that morning I was incapable of understanding and appreciating how difficult a task he had accomplished. I read the gift but not very carefully. Emotionally I rejected the present. I was cold, too angry, too resentful to hold him in my arms and tell him how beautiful the poem was, how proud I was to have it, how much I still loved him. I could hardly have said these words to him because I was unaware of them myself. I mumbled a perfunctory "Thank you," he walked away and we never spoke of it again.

Charles Silverstein and William Bory

Photo by Michael Leonard. Used by permission of the photographer.
Photo resoration by Charles Seton.

Twenty-one

William, for the Ferryman, I Whispered

We went through yet another metamorphosis in July as the disease advanced. Because William could no longer walk without my help, he could not maintain his crack addiction. While saddened to see his deterioration, I was pleased that the drug addiction was over. William appeared to suffer no withdrawal signs whatsoever nor did he ever mention crack again. He also left the cave completely never to return. Instead he spent his days on the couch and sleeping with me in the bedroom, so that our home returned to some form of normality. Since he could no longer read, I read to him each day for about ten minutes, the upper limit of his attention span. Then we would talk about the author, his writing style or about some of his other works. While much of the brain that I admired so much had vanished, I was still dazzled by the pristine clarity of what remained.

His rage also abated leaving in its wake a mostly mellow mood that made life at home calm and livable. He still got angry with those who annoyed him—like visiting nurses or Daniel—but his anger toward me evaporated. I suspect that some of the mood change was because of his dementia; he quickly forgot at whom or what he was angry. For the first time he accepted being a patient and stopped fighting my help.

Now I could take care of him. We started on the doctor circuit to mend some of the physical infirmities ignored during the crack period. Like many other AIDS patients and the lovers taking care of them we traveled by cab, often carrying a wheel chair with us from one doctor to another or to a hospital and back home. The internist sent us to the dermatologist, the hematologist, the neurologist, then to the dentist and the orthodontist because of infections in his teeth and gums that were reaching dangerous proportions.

At one point William needed a blood transfusion. I brought him to the blood room at Roosevelt Hospital where they started him on the first of three bags of blood. The nurse said she would call me when the transfusion was finished. An hour later she called back. "Please pick him up," the nurse requested.

"He's already finished?" I asked.

"No," she said, "he only had one bag, but he's creating so much trouble that you better bring him home now." For whatever reason, his mellow mood did not extend to nurses.

The nurses from the Visiting Nurse Service (VNS) were simply wonderful in their care of William. For years I had been a consultant to the VNS through the NYU AIDS project, running support groups for nurses who worked with AIDS patients. Now I saw them in action and witnessed their skill and compassion. William however, gave them a hard time actually cursing them for their trouble. "Hi, Joan," I would say to the nurse entering our apartment, while William shouted, "Fuck you," as his greeting. It is to their credit that they never wavered in their support.

William rejected the wheel chair until he found that it made him more mobile. I bought a banner on a pole one like one finds for motorcycles and attached it to the back of the wheel chair and taped a large squeeze horn to one side of the chair. "Beep, beep," William called while I squeezed the horn when people were in our way on the street. Each day I wheeled him to Riverside Park and read to him. The last book I read was Golding's "Lord of the Flies," one of his favorites, but I could only read a few pages at a time before he became agitated and we had to return home.

By July 1993, William had virtually stopped eating. Each night he asked for a plate of pasta. Each night I cooked fresh sauce since William refused to eat prepared sauces. I cooked the pasta al dente the way he liked it, put the sauce over it and brought it into the living room. His eyes beamed with delight when he saw the steaming dish, but after one or two mouthfuls he put the fork down and with a dour expression on his face and said that he could not eat anymore. The next night he asked for pasta again, insist that he would finish it this time. I would prepare the sauce and watch while he took one or two bites and push the dish away. This became a stupid ritual that I went through each night like repeatedly watching a bad movie.

"Why am I doing this?" I kept asking myself since I was getting bored eating his plate of pasta. I knew that it was not willful on his part, but the effects of the disease combined with his life-long aversion to food. I tried Megace, a female hormone often prescribed for AIDS patients to stimulate appetite. "I'm gonna' get tits," he laughed with friends when he told them about the drug. He did not get tits or his appetite back. Our doctor then prescribed Marinol, the chemical equivalent of pot. William was enchanted by the idea of doctors prescribing his favorite drug, but he complained that it did not provide a buzz and it did not make him hungry either. "Why am I giving him a chemical equivalent of pot?" I chastised myself, "when I can give him the real thing." William was in heaven puffing on the weed, after which and with a broad smile on his face, asked for his plate of pasta—which I dutifully prepared—and he did not eat.

He switched to pasta fagiole. William particularly liked the way one local restaurant made the dish and begged me to bring home a container for his supper. Dutifully, absurdly, I walked to the restaurant, ordered the soup, returned home and emptied it into a bowl and watched as William did not eat it. After venturing out a few evenings I came to the obvious conclusion that I could make it at home for less trouble and money and cooked up a large pot of the stuff and froze it in small containers. That night I presented William with a plate of homemade pasta fagiole and once again his eyes lit up—and he did not eat it.

The Pasta Period was followed by the Iceberg Lettuce Period. William filled his bowl with iceberg lettuce (all other forms of lettuce were rejected), cucumbers, olives, and whatever items in the refrigerator struck his fancy. Oil and vinegar went on top. At first he ate the salad every day, but in time as with the pasta, he stopped eating them completely.

The Candy Period followed. First there were "Mementos." These I bought by the dozen in a local store where the clerks called me "the candy man." That was followed by the "Mike and Ike" Period (another candy). At the same time William was using Nicorette the gum we both chewed in order to stop smoking. I had stopped smoking after a three pack a day habit, but William did not, so that he ended up smoking cigarettes while chewing Nicorettes, smoking pot while taking Marinol, while munching on Mementos, and Mike and Ike's.

William finally settled down into a routine of eating only Crunchy Cheese Doodles. In this advanced state of his food fetish, he rejected Puffy Cheese Doodles as counterfeit; it was Crunchy Cheese Doodles or nothing. His hands, mouth, the couch, and everything he touched were painted yellow by the Cheese Doodles.

He was just as picky about beverages. Earlier in the year his favorite drink was hot tea mixed with some orange juice. By July he had stopped drinking hot tea perhaps because he could no longer hold a hot drink in his hands without spilling it and burning himself. He switched to Mystic and Snapple Iced Tea. Daniel often accompanied me to a store in order to bring back cases of the tea and we laughed all the way back home at the absurdity of the situation. At one point I brought home the hand truck from the country in order to carry the heavy cases of beverages.

William's world was narrowing. On a good day he could take a short walk outside. What little pleasure he took in food was completely gone and his former propensity to drink alcohol and take drugs were relics of the past. An occasional joint was his only pleasure. Few friends called. Daniel never wavered in his loyalty to William and continued to help even as William continued to insult him. Al Sbordone often helped me get William to an Italian restaurant, wheel chair and all so that he could have an occasional night out and where William ordered all his favorite foods and liquor, none of which he ate or drank. But we all had a good time, especially William who lost no time insulting the waiters. Whenever possible we returned to the Bello Restaurant with our puppets "Cranky" and "Whimpy" where the waiters were solicitous in trying to make William feel comfortable.

Felice Picano and I were scheduled to fly to Tokyo on July 7th for the publication of the Japanese edition of *The New Joy of Gay Sex*. Long before I had accepted the fact that William would become an invalid, but I thought it unwise to make myself an invalid as well. I would often leave the house for a couple of hours at a time and have dinner or see a movie with a friend. Of course I worried about him while I was away and hurried home afterward. I decided to go to Japan and made extensive preparations for his care in my absence.

It is extraordinary how many people volunteered to help. Al Sbordone made a schedule and friends and neighbors volunteered to visit with William for hours at a time, so that there was usually someone with him. My neighbor Miles Parker and Daniel came over every day. I secured the services of a paid aide for the morning hours and someone to sleep in the apartment each night. Al's master schedule was printed and distributed to the volunteers. The schedule also contained the names and addresses of all his doctors and a list of his medications and dosage. At the end of each day reports were phoned into my cousin Marilyn who faxed the news of the day to my hotel in Tokyo. While Daniel took a shift like everyone else, he came over every day. Nurses from VNS visited to check his health and to provide for his medical needs. The whole system worked perfectly.

I called every day from Tokyo. William was in good spirits but complained about all the people who were in the house. He kept asking when I would return because he had lost the capacity to measure time, so I asked Daniel to draw a large calendar of a week and to cross off each day, showing him when I would return. It seemed to help.

One day in Tokyo a guide took Felice and me to one of the most famous Shinto Temples in the country. After performing the symbolic cleansing ritual of washing one's hands, she showed us the place where people wrote their prayers to the Gods on a piece of paper and tucked them into a section of the wall. I instantly knew the prayer I wanted answered. On a ragged slip of paper I asked that William be given a painless death and placed it a crack of the wall alongside the prayers of hundreds of other people.

A week after returning from Japan, I went to Houston for the National Gay and Lesbian Health Conference. I had long before committed myself to running a clinical workshop. More important I wanted to see Ken again. He was on disability and I wanted to spend most of my time with him.

Ken picked me up at the airport and together with my colleague Al Sbordone we had dinner al fresco at a local restaurant. Toward the end of the meal I noticed that Ken had stopped talking. He was looking around as if watching something in the distance but never focusing on one spot. I called to him but he could not hear me even though I was sitting next to him with my hand on his shoulder. I had seen that look once before, an aura before a friend had a grand mal seizure.

Small tremors came from Ken's body, and then he was hit by a full convulsion as if an earthquake was shattering him from within. Every muscle of his body attacked him at once and he fell off his chair and onto the cement pavement. I was terrified. Al and I sat Ken upright so that he would not hurt his head on the cement, but there was nothing more we could do until the tremors stopped and the ambulance arrived.

He was completely back to normal as we waited in an examining room in the hospital. "What am I doing here?" asked Ken. He had no memory of the convulsions or being taken to the hospital. He did not even remember being with us during dinner. "I must have made quite a scene at the restaurant," he jokingly remarked.

"Look Ken," I said, "if you didn't like the food, you could have just made a simple complaint." He roared with laughter glad to have the humor lighten his obvious worries. But a few minutes later he said, "This is not good." A year before Ken had been hospitalized with toxoplasmosis. Medications had reduced the cerebral abscess and to the best of Ken's knowledge, the disease had been cured. He was now worried that the toxo had reappeared.

I returned to the hospital early the next morning. His personal physician was there, a woman whom Ken trusted completely. As I talked with her, Ken cracked jokes about his failing memory. Suddenly his voice changed and I could hear the telltale signs of toxo in his speech. She heard it too. Then Ken started cursing loudly and both she and I recognized that he was about to have another seizure. She ran for help while I watched Ken's body shudder with convulsions of a far greater magnitude than the night before.

How long is a second when you are watching someone you love go through such pain? I stood there alone next to the bed, wanting magic, wanting to hold him, to turn off the electrical charges spiking from his brain to the muscles in his body. But I could only watch and cry as doctors and nurses rushed into the room in an attempt to stem the convulsions. For a long time they could not and even though they kicked me out, I could see them attempting to get an IV into his arm in order to pump in whatever fluids they believed might halt the seizures. It took many minutes for them to succeed, after which Ken, his gown dripping in sweat, relaxed and fell into a deep sleep. His doctor said he would be asleep for hours now and suggested that I return in the afternoon. By then she would have the results of a CT scan.

Ken was awake when I returned. His hands were cuffed to the bed to prevent him from hurting himself should another seizure occur and his bloodstream was filled with Valium. I resented Ken's being restrained like a criminal even if they considered it for his own good. Ken tried to joke about it. "Charlie, if I have to take a leak, will you take my cock out and point it toward the cup?"

"Ken," I replied, "if I take your cock out, I'm going to kiss it." We both stared at the doctor sitting nearby who got the point and said that she would call "security" to remove the restraints. After fifteen minutes "security" had not yet arrived. "Don't you have something to do for a few minutes," I said to the compassionate doctor who caught on immediately and left the room. I unbuckled the cuffs and Ken sat up and gave me a big hug.

"Ken, who's going to take care of you when you leave the hospital?"

"I have friends who'll look after me. If I call, they'll come right over."

Ken was still having difficulty talking so I left intending to return after dinner. His doctor walked over to me as I left the room. She was wonderful and treated me as if I were family. She explained that the CT scan showed a large abscess in the brain in the same location as the year before. She compared the new CT scan to the one from the year before and it showed that the toxo was out of control and expanding its territorial conquest. She said that the medication Ken was taking since his prior hospital stay is usually only effective for about a year. We were right on schedule.

"Are there any other medications to control it?" I asked.

"No," she said. "I'll do the best I can to make him feel comfortable at home."

"Does Ken know yet?"

"Oh! I think he knows, but I'll talk to him about it before I leave for the day."

I did not ask "How long?" I had to return to New York the next morning and knew that I would never see Ken again.

And I felt furious. I wanted to attack someone, get even for Ken's death and for the deaths of so many friends and patients. The rage bubbled up in my body like magma, red hot, circulating underground looking for an open vent leading into the atmosphere, but with no object to attack, to destroy, to scream at and curse. There was no one, no thing I could overcome, no battle I could fight that would make the slightest difference, that could save Ken's life or save William sitting at home wasting away to a skin covered skeleton.

I wished for a bona fide enemy, but everyone in the hospital was so nice, so accommodating and compassionate. Wrapped tightly by my sadness, I walked through the hallway looking straight ahead like a man with tunnel vision, avoiding the potential smiles from staff and down the elevator to the street. There I gazed up at the hospital, I do not know why, mesmerized for minutes, wanting to stay, wanting to go, wanting to implant my feet firmly in the ground like a bronze statue. Wanting to be cold and devoid of feeling, of affect—of helplessness.

Early the next morning, my bags for the flight home at my side, I walked into Ken's room. He was awake, alert and sitting up. I sat next to him on the bed. I touched his hands as he touched my shoulder. We hugged for a moment but he broke it off quickly, dropped his head to my chest, rubbing it back and forth as I ran my fingers through his hair. His eyes were red; so were mine.

"No good-byes," he said. "That's the way I want it."

"I'll call you each day from New York."

"I'll be pissed off if you don't."

I called Ken each day for the next two weeks. There was not a lot to say. There was information about drugs, neurological exams, CT scans and friends helping at home. But the real message was Ken's speech that became more labored as the days progressed, words harder to pronounce as the abscess marched through his brain. I thought how difficult it must be for him to speak and used that as my excuse for calling less often. The reality is that it was too hard for me to listen.

A few weeks later Michael Leonard called from London. I instinctively knew the message he was bringing. There was a special relationship between them, the artist and his model and I was pleased that it was Michael who bought me the news that Ken had died only hours before. I never told William about Ken's death, nor did he ever ask about his former lover again. I learned from one of Ken's friends in Houston that his parents refused to come to his side even when they were told that he would die in the next day or two. Not all the decades of experience as a psychologist then or now explain such cruelty to me. I knew very little about his relationship with them but I cannot conceive of anything that would justify their total abandonment.

From August and into the fall life at home continued its quiet routine. I often thought during these days how fortunate I was to live and work at home. Even while seeing a patient in my office, I felt comforted knowing that William was sitting quietly on the couch in the next room and that should he need me, that I could be at his side in seconds. Between therapy sessions I would sit next to him, open up a Nicorette for him since he could no longer do it for himself, or make his hot tea with orange juice, putting a long bendable straw in it so that he would not have to hold the hot glass. We might talk about the old movie he was watching on TV When the buzzer rang signaling the arrival of my next patient, he would kiss me good-bye, knowing that I was to shortly return to his side. After I finished for the day, I would do those chores he could no longer safely do for himself such as shave him every couple of days next to the kitchen sink or give him a haircut since sitting in a barber's chair was beyond his ability.

Bathing was more of a problem. At first we used to walk together to the bathroom but when his gait became dangerously unsteady, I would sit him in the wheel chair and push him down the hall, backing up the chair into the bathroom. He was terrified of falling while trying to step into the tub, so I attached a handle to the side of it and screwed another one into the wall so that he could hold onto one of the handles with one hand and onto me with the other. If he had still been playful, I would have gotten into the tub with him, but he was so uncomfortable that I had to wash his body quickly while on my knees next to the bathtub.

Getting him out was a chore because of his fear of falling and his tendency to become chilled, so that even as he stood up I wrapped him in bath towels and only then helped him out and dried his body. Afterward we sat on the couch, his new living center of our home while he cuddled next to me for warmth.

I felt wonderful about taking care of him. There is something special about the role of a person who tends to the most basic physical needs of someone he loves. It is about vulnerability and trust. I was his nurse and he accepted me in that role with full confidence. One day, for instance, when one of the VNS nurses arrived, he shouted at her, "I don't need you, I already have the best nurse there is." Manipulative to the end, I thought. My caretaker role led to a never-ending series of intimate moments between us, a shared sense of warmth from William's knowledge that I would never desert him and my awareness that these last weeks or months would be filled with love.

I often thought of Herodotus, the ancient Greek writer who said in his *Histories*, that you could not judge a person's life until he died. The rationalization of his argument aside, I applied his belief to William and me. All our conflicts, the years of alcohol and drugs leading to my resentment of him and his depression over my desertion were history. Now William expressed only loving feelings toward me. All the bitterness of his youth, all the times of anger toward me had evaporated. While sitting on the couch, wrapped in the shabby blanket he preferred, smoking a cigarette or a joint (while chewing a Nicorette), he would glance at me, smile, kiss me or lay his head on my shoulder.

Perhaps this change was another effect of the dementia. He also understood that he was dying and that might have contributed to his desire to make his last days as loving as possible—at least toward me. But he still rejected most verbal expressions of affection. He never talked about his illness or his impending death or the deaths of close friends. Only a few days before he died, I started to reminisce about our foreign travels to which he immediately and angrily said, "Cut it out." With or without dementia, William could not handle sentimentality.

The grand rounds of traveling from doctor to doctor absorbed our time: dermatologist, neurologist, internist, dentists, galium scan, x-rays, blood tests, lung capacity tests, blood infusions (during which I stayed). I would wheel him down the hallway of our apartment, into the elevator to the ground floor and to the front door of the building. Then I had to fold up the wheel chair and tuck it under my arm, while with my other arm open the heavy front door and find yet another to hold William while he walked down the steps to the street. Yes, too many arms were needed but one learns to cope.

In August our landlord replaced the entire elevator mechanism in our building. It would be out of order for five weeks. Since we lived on the seventh floor it meant that William would be trapped in the apartment the entire time and that I would be unable to get him to his medical appointments. I stocked our apartment with cases of Snapple and Mystic Iced Teas, bought up every package of Crunchy Cheese Doodles on the Upper West Side, packed the freezer and stored cases of non-perishable food in the cave. When the repairs began I spoke to the men and explained my dilemma. They immediately came to my rescue. I let them know when a doctor's appointment was scheduled and they manually brought the elevator from the basement to the seventh floor and brought William and me in his wheelchair to the ground floor. They brought us back up the same way. We never missed an appointment and they adamantly refused a tip for their kindness.

"Wigstock" was on September 6th that year. It was still held in Tompkins Square Park on the Lower East Side where it had originated years ago by a group of local drag queens. Traditionally held on Labor Day, it was a quintessential gay event in the city and a favorite holiday for William and me. We rarely dressed up ourselves, but this year William wanted to wear the shaggy black wig he had often worn in Miami and to put on make-up. I invited a dozen friends for brunch. Our friend Virginia Record arrived with her makeup case and spent thirty minutes making up William's face. I marveled at her ability to help William and to keep her own counsel about the extent of his physical deterioration since his face was virtually expressionless, the characteristic facade of advanced dementia.

After arriving at the park I put William in his wheel chair and we meandered our way slowly through the enormous crowds of people on the pathways. Many stopped to take a picture of him, recognizing I believe, the fun and enthusiasm still in his frail and emotionless body. After each of them took a picture, William tried to sell them a copy of his book. Within an hour he had had enough of the crowds, we returned home and I washed the make-up from his face. I felt very proud of him.

On September 18 I attended the memorial service given for Jim Owles, one of the founders and the first president of the Gay Activists Alliance. He was one of the guiding stars of New York's successful radical gay liberation movement in the early 1970s where I learned the tactics of radical gay politics. I last saw him at a celebration at City Hall a year before in honor of Gay Pride Week. "I don't remember who you are," he had said to me, his face more radiant than I had ever seen it before, "but you must be a friend if you came down here today." The speakers at the memorial were dreadfully serious. I wished that they had spent more time talking about the fun times in the Firehouse.

As William's health declined his sister Margaret, the youngest child in the family and the closest to William visited more often. She had been working full time for years in a yoga ranch in the Catskill Mountains not far from our house in Napanoch. Recognizing that her brother was not going to survive much longer, she arrived at our home often and brewed special teas for him and brought her warmth to bear in attempting to influence William's food intake. He loved having her there, drank her tea, but continued to eat only Cheese Doodles.

No new illnesses surfaced. In this respect William and I had an easier time with the disease than so many other gay couples in which there were repeated hospitalizations for opportunistic infections. William was never hospitalized. On the other hand his whole body was deteriorating at once. It was clear that if he persisted in his strange eating habits that he would ultimately die of malnutrition.

In October he lost control of his bowel movements and the angels at VNS quickly ordered a commode. I placed it next to the couch so that when he needed the toilet, I could quickly place him on the commode and clean him afterward. This was not a chore for me as it might have been for someone else—even when there were "accidents." What I thought of most during those times was not about my discomfort, but rather how a diet of Crunchy Cheese Doodles could produce so many feces. One sunny day with Al Sbordone's help we drove to the Brooklyn Aquarium, put William in his wheel chair and looked at fish. Sudden diarrhea overcame him and we wheeled him back to the car many blocks away. William was quiet, humiliated. After arriving home I stripped him in the bathroom, put him in the tub and washed his body. We made sure to kiss and hug a lot.

By early November William, barely communicative stopped eating completely and dangerously reduced his fluid intake. Margaret started spending weekends with us, sleeping in the guest-room, the former cave. Her swami visited often, greeting William warmly and trying to offer words of affection. William responded warmly to his sister but ignored the swami. He slept on the couch in the living room watching old movies on AMC and in the morning he would often tell me that he saw a wonderful film the night before although he could never remember what it was. I was distinctly uncomfortable about the arrangements because he had no way to communicate in case of an emergency, with me sleeping in the bedroom. But he insisted that I not sleep near him in the living room and that I leave him to his own devices at night. As I left each night, I gave him a big hug and a kiss. So did he. "I'll see you in the morning," I would say and on more than one occasion he responded, "Hopefully."

In the morning I rushed into the living room where he would be sitting up talking to himself or gazing off into space. When he saw me he put out his arms toward me as best he could and say, "Hi, Charlie" and sitting next to him we would cuddle. "Good-morning, honey," I would say, feeling so grateful that he was still alive.

Within a couple of weeks William was bare skin and bones and now unable even to smile. I became frightened that I was not caring for him well enough. I questioned whether I should have him hospitalized. With great difficulty I took him to his internist's office. William was lying on an examining table staring blankly at the ceiling while Dr. Young talked to me. "What do you want to accomplish by putting him in a hospital?" he asked. His simple question had the effect of making me realize that I was in a panic, frightened because I knew we were near the end. I was trying to shift the responsibility for taking care of William from myself to the sterile environment of the hospital.

"Where does he want to die?" Dr. Young asked. The answer was obvious. William hated hospitals, most doctors, and all nurses. He wanted to die at home surrounded by people who loved him. These realizations strengthened me and appreciative of the doctor's sobering questions I brought William home, laid him on the couch and made him as comfortable as I could. Margaret came over immediately to be party to the deathwatch. It was November 9th.

Hourly I spoon-fed water into William's mouth because he was seriously dehydrated. He started to have considerable trouble breathing while lying down, so I propped him up using pillows for support in order to help clear his lungs and he felt much better afterward.

The next evening while Margaret was sitting next to her brother, he said "I'm dying." Miles Parker came up to visit that evening as he often did, but this time to draw pictures of William. Miles had many friends who died of AIDS and he painted memorial pictures of each of them. This was the first time he had the opportunity to paint a friend as he lay dying. He intended to produce an exhibit of memorial paintings in the future. He also brought a present for William, a joint. (The finished painting illustrated William sitting on the couch, a cigarette in his hand, and his Buddy cap on his head. It's titled, "The muse doesn't mess around for too long," one of his favorite expressions.)

"William, look what Miles brought you." William smiled as best he could and with what little manual dexterity he had left grabbed it from my hand. "Wait, I'll help you," I said. I put the joint in his mouth and lit it. He drew in the smoke, more animated than I had seen him in weeks, his eyes brightened with pleasure. He took a number of tokes, blew out the smoke and satisfied put the roach into the nearby ashtray.

I called William's family that night telling them that they had better come over quickly to say their good-byes. Most of them arrived the next day, Thursday. My cousin Marilyn, who always felt close to William, joined the deathwatch. Except for Margaret, William's family arrived and went home on Thursday. That evening my friends from New Jersey arrived. William always adored Virginia for her wit and capacity for fun. Understanding that he was close to death she wanted to wash his body. Since moving him to the bathroom was out of the question, we removed the shirt and pants he was wearing and with clean sponges and towels she washed William from his face to his legs, all the while talking gently to him, an act of extraordinary love that is forever etched in my mind. William made no verbal or physical response to her actions and I have no idea whether he understood what was happening.

Then I brought out his favorite shirt. It was a silk Hawaiian Aloha shirt that he had bought in Miami with a black background upon which were a multitude of white orchids. It seemed only right that he should die in it. Virginia and I put the shirt on William and then wrapped him in blankets to keep him warm.

Friday morning, November 12th, William was still alive but barely.

The nurse from VNS examined him briefly and said that she did not think he would survive the weekend. William continued to sip water from a spoon for as long as he could. He was still sitting up, his gaze focused downward. He was totally uncommunicative even as I touched his face or kissed him. Margaret often sat next to him speaking softly, convinced that somewhere in his soul he knew of her love and that it would comfort him.

Al arrived in the afternoon and providing mutual support to each other we waited for the end. By six p.m. William was having considerable trouble breathing so I adjusted his position on the couch. After a few minutes he seemed to breathe more quietly. Al, Margaret, and I sat down at the dinner table and snacked on whatever food we found in the refrigerator, gossiped about this person or that, making inane conversation to take up time.

At 7:15 p.m. I walked into the living room to see how William was doing. I sat on the cocktail table only inches from him. His eyes while gazing downward were lifeless and he was not breathing. Al and Margaret were still sitting and talking in the dining room, so I had these few moments to be alone with him. I leaned over and whispered softly so that only he could hear. "I love you. I'll always miss you."

There was one more thing I wanted to do. I lifted his hand and touched his forefinger to mine. "Buzz." I took William's lifeless body in my arms and kissed his face already cooling to the touch, pressed his face next to mine, held him tighter and cried hysterically.

Al and Margaret were at my side instantly. Margaret sat next to William and kissed him. The three of us stood up and with arms around each other hugged and cried.

William had his wish to die at home and I had mine that he would die without pain written on a slip of paper at the Shinto Temple in Tokyo.

Two men came to remove William's body. Al stood with them giving the required information in order to fill out forms. There was something more I could do for William even after his death. I removed an Italian coin from my desk and bending over him, opened his mouth slightly, just enough to slip the coin in.

"William, for the Ferryman," I whispered.

At the William Bory Memorial Totem Pole
Left to right: Nando Davila, Terrance Flynn, Alvin
Shields, Albert Sbordone, Charles Silverstein

Photo courtesy of the author.

Twenty-two

How the Fuck Did We Know It Was Three Hundred Years Old?

I sat in my apartment after William's memorial trying to take stock of myself and what I wanted to do with my life. William's tall bookcases were virtually bare; the only books left were those he was unable to sell. The totality of his record collection was also sold, or those records rejected by used bookstores thrown away in the trash. I felt as if the bookcases with their deep cavities reflected the emptiness in my life and for that reason, I knew that it would be a long time before I emptied the closets and dresser drawers of his clothes. I could not yet live in the apartment without his presence.

What emerged most from my thoughts were William's claims of sexual abuse in New York and Europe. While still alive I attempted to engage him in discussion about them, only to be met by avoidance or rage. Virtually everyone believed him, the counselors at Pride, all my colleagues and friends who had witnessed his tears and shaking body. Everyone but one person.

Keith McDermott has been a friend for over twenty years. He had studied acting at London's prestigious Academy of Music and Dramatic Arts in the 1970s and starred in two Broadway shows. He is an actor of considerable talent. Keith and I sometimes went dancing together at Greenwich Village's Monster.

At dinner one evening Keith confided his suspicions to me. "Why did you believe William?" he asked. "I knew the whole crowd of upper-class gay Brits William talked about. I know their reputations and I even went to some of their parties. They're not like that. They have lots of money and they pay for what they want, but I never heard of anyone who was sexually abused by them."

Keith was touching a nerve, a question that had been haunting me ever since Pride: what kind of relationship did William and I have if these events could have been hidden from me for all those years? I was also acutely aware of my own doubts about the London period, but ever since Pride had decided that the best course of action was to put it on the back burner of my consciousness. I am a skeptic about the current fad of repressed memories; I do not believe in them. I believe that people forget many things, but remember trauma with great clarity. I am also highly suspicious when "repressed memories" arise as a result of psychotherapy. William and I had often talked about repressed memories and sexual abuse and I knew that he believed the same, making his phone call to me all the more remarkable.

Keith's next question forced me back into reality. "Can't you see how literary the stories were? William was writing a pornographic story in his mind, but instead of putting it on paper, he conveyed it verbally."

Keith's logic was compelling. I instantly thought about some of William's pocket-sized porno books still lying on the floor in his closet at home, stories about power and control, prison rapes—the usual stuff in books of that genre. Keith's words convinced me that for my own peace of mind I had to search for the truth.

I hoped there was a middle ground to the stories. Like my mother William loved to lie and to manipulate people. He had described his "abusers" as if they were monsters. Were they that, or innocent of his charges or something in between? I felt responsible for seeking the truth for William's sake, for the people he had named on both sides of the Atlantic and most important for myself. I wanted my search to be honest and respectful of William's memory, but not to slander innocent people. I certainly had enough names and records in my possession to begin.

I made a list of people to contact. The first was Tom since he still lived only a few blocks away. I had sent him an invitation to the memorial, which he attended and he had sent me a kind note afterward saying how much he would miss William. I had not the slightest doubt that he would speak openly to me.

Tom's life is still highly structured. He rises at five-thirty a.m. and retires at eight p.m. every night. When I called and explained that I wanted to talk to him about William, Tom welcomed the opportunity. He arrived at my apartment a few days later and we began by chatting for a few minutes about the old days of gay liberation politics and the GAA Firehouse. Since I already understood many of William's inconsistencies about his days at Tom's house, I decided to make my questions broad-based. I asked Tom how he and William met.

Tom's eyes lit up as he described their first meeting and I could see that his attraction to William was still alive. GAA had a Speaker's Bureau and Tom was one of those members assigned to talk about homosexuality at institutions that invited us. Tom had spoken at Queens College, and William, then an undergraduate student was in the audience. After Tom's speech William talked to him. Tom was mesmerized by William's charm, his brightness, that tantalizing quality of his personality that acted like a magnet and by his hair, which in those days came down to his waist. It was through Tom's suggestion that William started participating in GAA's activities. Tom also invited William to visit his Upper West Side apartment, mentioning that other gay boys could often be found there. Mick, destined to be William's best friend during that period, was one of the boys. Tom was not exactly sure where Mick and William had met, at the Firehouse, in his apartment or in Central Park where Tom and Mick often walked.

"The boys used to come and go. I never knew who was going to come over or how long he'd stay. Sometimes a bunch of boys came over and we'd smoke some weed, and then they'd leave and go to a bar or dancing. Occasionally one of the boys would sleep over on the couch and then he'd be gone the next day. I liked having them here. I particularly liked William because he was so beautiful and so highly educated. We used to spend hours talking about literature and historical periods. He was astounding."

I asked Tom about drugs. He said that the boys smoked a lot of pot at his house and that he often shared whatever recreational drugs he had at the time. I had the distinct impression that his largesse in handing out free drugs was the mechanism by which Tom alleviated the loneliness in his life, drugs insuring the company of young, attractive gay men. I knew that Tom was too poor to hand out drugs in the quantity William had described.

"How did William and Mick get to Lord Radson in London?" I asked.

"William was still a student at Queens College and he wanted to go somewhere during the summer, but he didn't have much money. Neither did Mick. So I suggested they visit Radson. I knew the kinds of boys he was interested in, and they were perfect. He could put them up. I called Radson and he said okay. And they left."

"William said that Radson had served a jail term for molesting Boy Scouts in his sauna. It is true?"

Tom laughed. "No, Walter rented property to people who violated some laws about sex and because he owned the land, he was held as responsible as the renters. It was a technical thing. He couldn't have molested anyone in his sauna because he didn't have one."

I thought it counterproductive to ask about the sexual scenes William described at Tom's house or whether the boys were locked in at night. The questions were insulting and I was already certain that the stories were fabrications. I wanted one more thing from Tom however, to get confirmation about what happened that summer from the only other person who was there, Mick. I asked if he knew how I might contact him.

"Of course. He still lives in New York. His number's in the phone book."

Mick was in the phone book! Mick and William had been the best of friends, but when William moved in with me he had cut Mick off completely. To the best of my knowledge William never spoke to Mick for the whole of our twenty years together. That was very much like him. I desperately wanted to speak to Mick since he held the key to understanding the London period. But I had not seen Mick in twenty years and had not the slightest idea how he would react to hearing from me.

Twenty years ago, Mick Ortiz was a hot Latin number who had set his heart on becoming a rock star. He had the look for it. His ideal like so many other young men of his generation was Mick Jagger of the Rolling Stones, whose records as DJ he played continually at the Saturday night GAA dances. Whether for lack of talent or bad luck, or the fact that millions of young kids were competing to be stars Mick never made it. But he never gave up his dream and even during the last few years of his life persisted in playing in any Lower East Side club that allowed these dreamers to play *gratis*. For twenty years Mick waited to be "discovered." He never was.

Mick exuding a hostile sexuality immediately attractive to many gay men, and although he and William had sex together and jointly with others, it was a close friendship not a love relationship. Still, they were the best of friends and it seemed to me at the time that Mick was visibly upset at losing William. The few times we had met, we eyed each other suspiciously and conversed not at all. I therefore, decided to be careful not to threaten him by my visit. I called him that evening and to my surprise he welcomed a visit.

He lived in a sparsely furnished, ground floor studio apartment in New York's Hell's Kitchen. The room was dark; some of the walls were painted black, much in fashion decades ago. Posters of rock stars were taped to the walls and former generations of audio equipment were set one upon the other on the floor in a tower.

Mick greeted me very warmly. His physical condition was deteriorating at a rapid pace and although he never mentioned his impending death, it was obvious that he did not have much time left. The AIDS virus was circulating freely in his body and at his last blood test he had only eight T-Cells left.

"You were really uptight," Mick said about our first meeting twenty years ago. "I thought you didn't like me." I told him that I had believed that he was jealous when William moved in with me, but he said that was not so. I had no idea which of us (or both) had been distorting the past.

I met with Mick four times over the next few weeks, either chatting in his apartment or taking him out to lunch. He wanted to reminisce about the past and did not shy away from talking about either Tom or his London experience with William. I understood that it was only the past he had left; there was no future for him. Mick said that he and Aldo met in Central Park one weekend. The attraction must have been magnetic, both with very long hair, tall and slim, both potheads. Mick had often stayed at Tom's house and he took William there that day. That much of William's story was confirmed.

Mick laughed at William's description of the jerk off scenes, the locked door, and the fetid smells. He said none of it was true. "Tom was always a nice guy and we went over there because he had lots of pot and other drugs. We did drugs, spaced out—sometimes Aldo and I had sex there together, or with some of the other guys that showed up. I don't think Aldo ever had sex with Tom. Then we'd come down and leave. Aldo and I also used to take acid there. I remember we used to go to his house on Saturday night a lot before we went to the Firehouse. We'd get smashed there first so we could dance for hours. Then we'd go downtown. We hardly ever stayed over because his apartment was so small and there weren't any beds, only a couch and nothing else."

Spontaneously Mick began talking about London. He had only been there for about a month when he decided to return to New York and take up with a new boyfriend whom he had met at GAA. William remained for another two weeks. The approximate dates tallied with those stamped on William's passport. Mick was both excited and intimidated by the British high society that feted him and they satisfied his every sexual fantasy. Most of the time he and William lived in Radson's London townhouse where a passing parade of young gay boys from around the world crashed anywhere from a night to a week and with whom both of them had sex. Like William, Mick was clothed and presented to wealthy gay British gentlemen with whom they had sex at parties and dinners.

"I had the time of my life," he said. "So did Aldo." That was the opening I was looking for.

"When William went to Pride because of his crack addiction, he claimed that he recovered memories of being sexually abused in London." A quizzical look came on Mick's face. I read from William's Pride diary in which he detailed instances of sexual abuse by Radson and the rich, gay upper-class men who surrounded him; Radson's rape of them both their first day, the dog and scat scenes. I read him the section where William described being taken to Paris and being sexually abused by two Black men during the making of a pornographic film. Also about their stealing the pill case, being kidnapped and sent to Morocco as slaves and how they finally escaped. For at least a couple of minutes afterward he sat quiet, looking confused and trying to form a response. I knew that he would immediately pick up the errors of fact, but I did not know what else he would tell me.

"That's the weirdest shit I ever heard, man. Almost all of it is bullshit. Aldo loved being in London. Listen we slept in the same bed every night in London and in Salisbury too when we went there. He never complained to me about anyone doing anything to him that he didn't want. I know exactly what kind of sex he had with these guys. He always came home with lots of money in his pocket and we'd go out and have a nice dinner. If Aldo didn't have money, maybe I'd have money from some guy I fucked with. But we always had money. When other gay guys crashed with us, we'd take them out, then we'd do drugs and have sex with them back in the apartment.

"Radson never raped us. He was always kind to us. I still keep in touch with him. He's even been sending me money because he heard that I was sick. Some of these British guys were into kinky scenes, so it's possible that Aldo did some S & M stuff, or weird stuff with them, but I don't think that anyone ever forced him into anything. I think I remember one guy who was into a scat scene. I refused to go with him. Maybe Aldo did. I'm not sure. But I know that he could have refused. No one ever burned him with cigarettes. We were naked in the apartment all the time and I would have seen marks like that."

Mick stopped talking for a moment, an expression of annoyance on his face.

"That's really fucked man. Walter wasn't a pimp. He's a rich man and he was always generous to us. And we never went to Paris. That stuff about Morocco is crazy. I don't even know where Morocco is. It never happened."

"Did you guys steal something from the house of a British titled lord?" I asked.

"Yea. Aldo and I stole this small pill case that was on one of his dressers as a souvenir. It was some house! We just wanted something to show friends when we got back to New York. How the fuck did we know it was three hundred years old? Radson asked for it back and we gave it to him. That's all. Nothing happened. I don't know why Aldo was so angry at Walter. He showed us a really good time and he didn't try to control us. We could have left anytime we wanted."

"So what you're telling me, Mick, is that you and William were high paid hustlers in London. Is that right?"

"Yeah, and we also got a free apartment, money for sex, clothes, meals and sometimes we had his car and driver to sightsee around

London. It was great. It was better than eating rice and beans in New York and travelling in the hot subway for the summer."

"Who was Giorgio?" I asked.

"Giorgio was this beautiful dark-haired kid. We met him in London, but he was from New York. He used to go with us to some of the parties and he had sex with the same guys we did. And sometimes he'd come back to the townhouse and fuck with us. I think Aldo was really turned on to him."

I read the section from the Pride diary where William tells about Giorgio being killed—"Shut the fuck up or the same thing will happen to you," Radson shouted, according to William's account. I read him William's touching poem that he dedicated to Giorgio, one of the poems I included in the memorial brochure.

Mick looked as if he was in shock. "Giorgio came back with me to New York on the same plane I did. He's still alive. I think he moved to live somewhere in Texas. I think I still have his phone number here somewhere. Can I have a copy of the poem?"

Mick looked for Giorgio's phone number while I took out a memorial brochure to leave with him. After a few minutes Mick found the number but it was twenty years old. There was no way to know if Giorgio still lived there. I returned home to call it.

A "non-working number," the telephone intercept said. I called telephone information in every city in Texas without success. His name was not listed anywhere in the state.

Within a couple of months of our first meeting, Mick called to tell me that he was singing with a rock group at an East Village club that Saturday night. He invited me to hear them. Ordinarily I would refuse such a request. I can think of nothing more awful than spending hours at those seedy smoke-filled clubs that kids go to, crunched together like happy sardines whose eardrums are being destroyed by extremely loud music with a bass that seems as if it is about to send your body into convulsions. But I could not refuse him. I met Mick and his friends in front of the club where we stood for a couple of hours before their set was on. He was still dreaming of being a rock star. I listened to his set, complimented him endlessly on it—and returned home to recover.

*

On March 16, 1994, Edmund White and his lover, Hubert Sorin (who was in the final stage of HIV disease) were in Marrakech, Morocco, when Hubert became deathly ill. Ed took him to the local hospital, a miserable, filthy place with roaches running on the floors and dirty sheets on the beds. Hubert was admitted and Ed sat with him through the night. At five a.m. Ed talked with Hubert briefly, and then fell asleep. At seven a.m. Ed woke up. Hubert was dead. Because of legal technicalities, Ed was forced to leave Hubert's body in Marrakech while he returned to Paris. It would take two weeks of filling out forms in order to get Hubert's body back to Paris, where Ed had it cremated and placed in a niche in Paris' famous Pere LaChaise Cemetery.

On April 28th, John Preston died in Portland, Maine. I knew for months that he was near death. We had been friends since he arrived in New York City in 1972. I kept telling myself that I did not have the money to fly there, but I knew that the real reason was that I was emotionally unprepared to see John's wasted body. I could not watch him die. Not another friend.

There was a huge "reading" for him in New York City. Friends called it that because John said that he did not want a memorial service. It was held in New York City's Lure, our premier S & M bar. About a dozen people read from their works, much of it pornographic and they talked about John having been an inspiration to them as writers. I was distinctly unfriendly and even though I saw friends, I avoided them. I am sure they never noticed me. I left before the program was over.

Mick died three months later.

I spent an afternoon with William's mother. I turned the conversation to the stories William had told about his father's cruelty. I wondered about the story of his father burning his blocks in the furnace. "That's impossible," she said. "We had an oil furnace. You can't burn things in it. And Mr. Bory never threw Billy into the water either. My husband was afraid of the water and he never went swimming so he wouldn't have taken Billy to swim."

I asked about the account of her taking William for ballet classes, only to have her husband pull him out. "I never took him to a ballet class," she said.

The next person on my list was Dan Kopka, who had been William's best friend at Pride and with whom he took drugs after they returned to New York. The last time I had seen Dan was when I visited him in a closed ward for heroin addiction six months before William died. He was no longer living on the Lower East Side, but I learned that he and his wife had moved to Brooklyn. He was quite pleased to get my call but began to cry when I told him that William had died. He agreed to spend an evening with me talking about Pride and his relationship with William after they had returned to New York.

Dan was one of the few bisexuals I know, maintaining a sexual relationship with his wife as well as a strong sexual desire toward men. Heroin destroyed his career as a master piercer and after his wife became addicted they both entered recovery programs. Afterward she went back to work while Dan, because of his HIV status went on disability, but he continued to use heroin.

We spent the evening around the dining table. Dan's friendliness was palpable. There was still a glow about him that he expressed toward me, a sense of trust based upon his experiences with William and me during his stay at Pride and afterward in New York. Dan started talking immediately.

"I never saw William so happy as in the days you showed up at Pride for the weekend. He was constantly talking about you for a week before you came. He bragged about all the important things you did for the gay movement and the books you wrote. And you wouldn't believe how proud he was seeing you play in the ping-pong tournament that night. It meant so much to him. It was important to me too, to see how much he loved you, even though he used to complain about you so much. All the boys were watching you guys like hawks. I saw what the truth was when you came. William loved you a lot. He was my only real friend there, so I wanted to help you guys as much as I could. And you didn't freak out when you saw all the piercings I had on my body. You treated me like you cared about me."

I pointed out that I had not seen all the piercings on his body, only the ones above the neck. I was well aware that they represented only the iceberg of flesh-protruding metal beneath his clothes and underwear. (I always wondered how people like Dan handled metal detectors at airports.)

"Both of us were just biding our time, waiting to get out. William made my stay more pleasant because he was so entertaining. We knew that we were going back on drugs as soon as we got out and we talked about it a lot. We couldn't wait to get back and start using.

"He could intimidate anyone. He used language in such a way that made you feel like you had to climb over a barbed wire fence to get to him. He scared the shit out of a lot of the guys there because they couldn't compete with him verbally. He'd just cut them to pieces."

"William turned off a lot of people at Pride when we had our groups. He used to tell these really mean stories about wanting to infect people with the virus. I remember one story he told about meeting this guy who wanted William to fuck him, so he bit off the tip of the condom before he put it on and gave him a real hard fuck so the guy would bleed before William came inside him. He told this story at an AA group we went to in Minneapolis one night. Then he got into an argument with one of the other guys and they threw him out of the AA meeting."

I pointed out that William was thrown out of a sexual compulsive group in New York afterward. Dan's information meant that William had been thrown out of two 12-step groups—that we know of. Dan started to laugh, saying, "He was an expert in getting out of any group."

"It was one of the ways he kept people at a distance," I said.

"William refused to come out of his room for two days. By this time, he didn't have a roommate and everyone thought he was in a serious depression. His counselor thought William had suffered a breakdown, so he asked me to go in the room and check on him. I walked over to the bed and I could see that William had the blanket over his head. I was a little afraid because I didn't know if he'd hit me or something. So I reached down and petted his head and called his name very gently. William pulled down the covers when he heard it was me and he had this big grin on his face. He said, 'I'm sick of these people!' He was just getting attention this way. This was already after the sex abuse stuff where he kept monopolizing all the time and not letting anyone else talk.

"'So,' I said, 'it's just about revenge?'

"William sat up and said, 'Yes, revenge!' and he started to laugh.

"Revenge became like a joke between us. Sometimes either he or I would say 'revenge,' and then we'd both start laughing. No one else knew what we were talking about. It was our little joke."

"You were there when William started talking about sexual abuse," I said. "Did you believe the stories?"

"I asked him and he started to laugh. He was very amused at what he got away with. He told me that most of them were bullshit. He told me that he came up with the idea to get out of the groups and get people to leave him alone until it was time for him to go home. He really freaked when he found out that the counselors at Pride believed him, because they wanted to send William to a special hospital somewhere where he'd have to stay thirty more days in a locked ward with people who had been tortured. Political prisoners who had electrodes shoved up their asses like in the movies or who were raped every day—with people like that. He was hysterical about it. He was terrified that you and his counselor would arrange to send him to the torture hospital instead of letting him come home."

"You know, Dan," I said. "I wish I had sent him there. Thirty days in a torture hospital would have served him right!" We both burst out laughing. What a wonderful irony that would have been, I thought.

"William said that the dog story was true. He also talked a lot about his fear of losing his looks and not being able to attract good-looking men. He didn't want to ever look older."

They started using drugs as soon as they returned to New York. Dan liked heroin, while William preferred crack and cocaine. At first William liked the ritual of mainlining and Dan did the injecting for both of them. Within a couple of weeks, Dan was making "Speedballs," a combination of heroin and cocaine. They would use these drugs at William's retreat on the Lower East Side. Shortly thereafter, William returned to crack and used it exclusively. Dan refused to join William in smoking the drug and ultimately this conflict became the source of their separation.

"He became very hateful to me about it. Very abusive. We had spent so much time together. We were such good friends. Then one day when I said that I wanted to cool it on the drugs, William said to me, 'That's all we have in common.' It really hurt me. That's when we stopped seeing each other. He really hurt me."

I felt very sorry for Dan. He already knew that I was his friend and I told him that I wanted to keep in touch with him. We met together a couple of times and then his wife called to tell me that Dan died of an overdose of heroin. It was about six months after he returned from Pride with William.

There were two more names on my list: April Martin and *The Sally Jesse Raphael Show.* April had been William's therapist for about four to six sessions after he returned from Pride. What had he told her about the stories of sexual abuse? We met for lunch and I told April why I wanted to learn what William said to her. She agreed that since he had died, confidentiality was no longer an issue.

"The first time William came in, he told me the stories about being abused. The next week he came back and said that he had been exaggerating. When I asked him what he meant by exaggerating, he said that they were all bullshit. He had made them up so he could get out of participating in the activities at Pride. I also want you to know that he loved you very much, but he was so terrified of seeing his body decline that he didn't have the psychological strength to quit drugs and deal with his death."

The Sally Jesse Raphael Show. One of William's most powerful poems was "A Poem That Threatened Not to Be," the one he read at his book publishing party. It was an account of a young Boy Scout bicycling to a scout meeting who was raped and murdered by two men who plunged a pole up the boy's rectum. He said that he had heard the story on *The Sally Jesse Raphael Show.* Every time he read the poem he cried, much as he did when he repeated his stories of sexual abuse. It was dreadful to contemplate. But did it happen or did William make that up too? I wanted to know.

Here is part of the poem.

I have a bad taste in my mouth,
And I want to put it in yours,
A tongue kiss from Hell,
Tasting of blood and fire.
The demons wore blue jeans and red flannel shirts.

The mother's tears were dripping down her face.
The father was searching for a place to

Drop his grief.
The boy never woke up again,
And I can't sleep.

I wrote to the executive producer of the show telling her about my search and asking if there was a record of a show about a Boy Scout murdered in the manner described in William's verse. She asked if I knew the date of the show and she did not wince when I said that it could have taken place anytime between 1990 and 1992. A few days later, Josie Bonanni the show historian called and asked me to send her a copy of the poem. She said that she would have to check the archives in California. It would take a while.

"I found it," she said when she called back a couple of weeks later. "I'll fax it to you." The program called "Monstrous Murderers" aired on February 25, 1991. The boy whose real name was Raymond was twelve-years-old when he was raped by two teenagers, who attempted to burn his body and when they found him still alive, shoved a broom handle up his rectum. It was Raymond's father who found the body later that evening. The poem was a faithful rendition of the awful crime and of William's sorrow and identification with the boy's dreadful death.

Twenty-three

I Had to Give Up These Anchors

Alone. Not in a physical sense; I had been alone for months. After decades of a relationship one welcomes occasional times alone. But now the quiet was deeper, longer. Whatever resentment I had felt toward William had long since vanished. I put the photos of William from his summer in England in a file together with letters and mementos, the transcript from *The Sally Jesse Raphael Show* and the notes from my interviews.

It was about a year after William died that I decided to write this book. The first chapters I wrote were about Steve, Pete, and Mark. I realized that I was not merely writing an account of unrequited young gay love; rather I was reliving the pain and deep sense of loss they represented. William's death had reactivated parallel feelings from my pre-coming out youth.

I spent a week in Paris visiting Ed White. I arrived with Terrance, a young Bostonian I had met some months before. At the time Terrance was a devotee of late night dance clubs where he swallowed the requisite ecstasy, after which he danced until the sun came up. I often started the night with him (*sans* the ecstasy), danced a bit and after kissing him good-bye, returned to Ed's apartment. There we two widowers talked for hours into the night about our recent losses—and our divided feelings, both before and after the deaths of our lovers. There was a healing quality to it.

When I awoke one morning, Terrance was asleep beside me. I knew from experience he would not arise for hours. Ed was out doing errands. I left the bedroom and closed the door behind me and sitting at the dining-room table began to write about my relationship with Mark. I became overwhelmed with sadness. It was only then that I realized the full extent of his loss—and that of the others I had pined over in my youth. Images from the past forced me to feel again the pain I had felt then: sitting outside Steve's door when I wanted to hold him; Pete's walking over the Catskill bridge and resting his head on my shoulders; Mark's walking out of my apartment the night I came out to him.

For months afterward I was saddened to read those chapters, sometimes more than I did about William's loss. I came to realize that I could never fully grieve over William's death until I ended my long, irrational attachment to Steve, Pete and Mark, the three boys from my youth who had preceded him. I had not yet put the past to rest so that I could get on with the rest of my life. But how I wondered could I cut my attachment toward men I had not seen for up to forty years? The answer was obvious; contact them now. I pondered both the wisdom and the absurdity of this idea. These men were memories, holograms of a sort, distorted over time and mixed with the fantasies of a lonely youth at once attracted to them.

I wondered what they looked like now, what kind of families they had fathered—how they would react to my contacting them. I admit to feeling sexually excited by the idea of contacting Steve, my first love. More than any of the others, he still lived in me. Yet I instinctively knew that I took the chance that all three of them might reject me again.

How many times have I heard this same story from my clients? For decades I have listened to the pain of unrequited love and rejection, particularly in gay clients fearful that coming out (or coming on) to someone would end in disaster. "What do you want?" I always asked them. I listened carefully to their answers in order to learn whether they wanted to live in the past and relive its hurts, or to give up being a victim and live in the present. The victim never heals his wounds and every disappointment adds to the list of indignities and resentments that ultimately rules his life. These resentments only serve to justify our failures in love, but they keep us anchored to the past and hinder our search for intimacy. I had to give up these anchors.

I knew how to contact Pete. For years he had been a mogul on Wall Street and his picture often appeared in the business section of *The New York Times*. I copied a photograph from Boy Scout camp and mailed it to him with a short note. He called immediately after receiving it, pleased to hear from me. We chatted over the phone for a while, answering some of his questions ambiguously, because I did not yet want to tell him about my gay life. I did not know how he would react to it. I tried to arrange getting together for lunch or dinner and he always responded that he would call back to book it. He never did.

After a couple of weeks I decided to write him. I told him a bit about my past life and about William's illness and death. I was impulsively trying to push him and it backfired. A few days later he left a message on my answering machine expressing sympathy at William's death, but annoyance at my letter, saying that it had been forty years since we had last met and that "maybe we should wait another forty years for us to meet." I obviously muffed that one.

I searched the Internet and found phone numbers for Steve and Mark. Steve now lived in Miami. Mark was a psychologist and head of the department of psychology at a State of Washington hospital. Although terrified, I forced myself to call them.

A woman answered the Miami phone number. I asked for Steve and she told me that he had died two years ago. "Who are you?" she asked. I told her that Steve and I had been friends when we were teenagers and about our days in scout camp. She said that she didn't know much about that period in her husband's life and she queried me about our friendship. I told her about our hiking trips together, our Saturdays at the movies and the times we slept over each other's houses. She told me that she and Steve had three children, all grown up and with children of their own. "If you come this way," she said, "please visit me. I'd like to hear more about you and Steve when you were kids." I said I would and thanked her for her kindness in talking to me.

I knew that Mark would talk to me. He was not the kind of person to turn his back upon the past, but I hadn't the faintest idea what to say to a man I had not seen or talked to since 1973. "Hello, Mark," I said when he answered the phone. "This is a voice from the past, Charles Silverstein." Mark responded with recognition and friendliness. We talked for the next ten minutes, first finding the common denominator of our professional careers, then about more personal matters. I asked if he remembered the last time we had met, the night that I came out to him. He clearly did not at first, but then said that he did. I thought Mark's first reaction right, but I did not want to embarrass him by discussing the details. We were both different people now.

Mark talked about raising his two children and his enjoyment in watching them grow. He also remembered my work with kids from years ago—typical of Mark's drive to find a bond between himself and another person.

"You've been a bit of a revolutionary," he said after I discussed my role in gay liberation. "And that's a compliment," he added.

I felt wonderful about our conversation, although in all honesty I think Mark was far more relaxed. I remembered all the things I liked about him, his enthusiasm, his ability to connect on an emotional level and his sensitivity. He had lost none of it over time.

There were no more people to talk to, no more events from the past to relive. It was over and I felt all the better for it.

Twenty-four

Way to Go, Henry

April 2011. It has been four decades since I walked through the doors of the Gay Activist Alliance and began my journey coming out. I remember the energy of those days, the sense that right was on our side, that society should and could be changed so that gay people might stand in the sunshine beside the heterosexual majority. So much has happened in America since those days including foreign wars and the changing of presidents who did nothing to help us. There have been, however, many changes for LGBT people since the days of radical gay politics in the 1970s. There are no more demonstrations in the streets or breaking up of professional meetings. The mimeograph machines we used to make flyers advertising our protests have long since been replaced by e-blasts and Web sites devoted toward gay causes. Few people worry these days about the cost of long-distance phone calls when one can simply text on the ubiquitous cell phone to another person anywhere in the world.

Until 1973, the year I came out on the floor of the American Psychological Association, there were no openly gay groups within the organization. We now have an official division with over nine hundred members, sponsor programs at the annual convention and a few of our openly gay or lesbian members have run for president of the organization. Every professional association in the country has an LGBT subgroup within its membership. There are even openly gay pastoral counselors. All these groups have made public statements opposing sexual reorientation, and they publicly advocate for gay civil rights. While I hid my homosexuality during my graduate school years, many masters and doctoral level programs in social work, counseling, psychology and psychiatry invite LGBT people to apply for admission.

It is only in some religiously oriented groups such as fundamentalist

Christians, Mormons, Catholics and Orthodox Jews that homosexuality is judged to be a sin and therefore, to be cured. They have devised a treatment for homosexuality called, "Reparative Therapy," in which guilt-ridden LGBT people are told that through prayer they will be cured of their sexual affliction and become heterosexual. They often hold weekend retreats designed to inflict this propaganda on their victims.

I chaff at the denouncement by fundamentalist religious groups of our lives; at the hypocrisy of their clergy; at the straight jacket they would force the rest of us to wear in order to control us. While we live in a multi-cultural society, religious bigots fight to convert us to be a bunch of ticky-tacky houses—look the same, act the same—and tell lies about our lives in order to feel morally superior.

Why are these fundamentalist groups still in operation? In earlier years there was an implicit coalition between orthodox religion and the psychiatric establishment. Religious forces called us sinners and accused us of "recruiting" children to our ranks, while the medical establishment added the pejorative label of mental illness. Together they justified the harsh legal penalties against us in the name of sodomy laws even used against consenting adults. The 1973 decision by the American Psychiatric Association to remove homosexuality as a mental disorder broke the coalition and the foundation for legal penalties collapsed. The fundamentalists now stand alone as a decadent moral force, isolated against the background of a country coming to terms with sexual variations. The fundamentalists fear our spreading the truth about civil rights.

We gay people however, continue to meet their "cures" in backrooms and bathhouses just as we did with the cures of the 1970s psychoanalysts. Hypocrisy is spread evenly in every religion.

The *Journal of Homosexuality* was founded in 1974 because unbiased research on our life-style could not be published in any of the other professional journals. They now all publish well-written academic papers on gay people and rarely print anything similar to the old "cause and cure" theories of the past.

The legal status of homosexuality has also been revolutionized. Sodomy is no longer a criminal offense and that has led to local and national LGBT law groups keeping a watchful eye upon any attempt to curtail our civil rights. While "moral turpitude" clauses were used to deny licensing of attorneys in previous generations, LGBT law is now a recognized legal specialty.

Perhaps the greatest change can be seen in young LGBT people today. "I always knew that I was gay, so that's that" is what they say. No drama like we had in the past. While my generation was sneaking around dark corners for quick sex in public parks, they come out to their families while in their teen years and begin to search for romantic partners almost at once. I feel proud of them. But I do want them to know that we gay people have had a history and that it goes back hundreds, perhaps thousands of years. I would like them to know that there was a time when conviction for sodomy could mean death, and that as late as the last century gay men could be castrated and/or sent to jail for no greater offense than loving another man.

There was a change in society's attitude toward gay people when the medical profession in the last century convinced legal authorities that the offense of homosexuality should be treated medically, rather than by imprisonment. While the medical profession thought they were doing good, we still ended up being considered pariahs. Instead of jail we were subjected to aversion therapy, cerebral ablation and years of psychoanalysis—none of which changed anything, only served to make us feel guiltier. The proponents of these treatments thought they were doing good by removing us from the hands of legal authorities and into the world of medicine. I am reminded of a statement by Henry David Thoreau—"If I knew for a certainty that a man were coming to my house with the conscious design to do me good, I should run for my life." Way to go, Henry! The only reason we have succeeded in gaining some civil rights is because we have fought for them. I want young people to learn about our culture—the artists, writers and composers who have contributed to society. I want them to know about military leaders including kings who were gay. I also want them to know why some gay people in previous generations committed suicide because they feared exposure. Most of all, I want them all to find someone to love and someone they can marry, if that is their decision.

But young gay men do have one liability coming out sexually that an older generation did not —HIV. The words "Safe Sex" were unknown in the 1970s because our health concerns were about STDs that could easily be cured with antibiotics. No one died of syphilis or gonorrhea in the days when a gay man was considered rude if he did not let a sex partner come in his mouth, and therefore receive pleasure from the ejaculation. Of course we swallowed. Rude again, if we did not. I remember an evening just over the wall in Central Park near the bridle path when I was first coming out and learning about gay life. There were about a dozen men standing about, and even in the dim light they all looked attractive to me. I was still too shy to make a move. Suddenly another man appeared and boldly placed every one of us with our backs to the wall. One by one, he unzipped each of us, pulled out our cocks and gave head until all dozen of us had come in his mouth. Then without saying a word, he turned around and walked away. He got the mouthful he came for, and maybe a bit more in the name of some pesky STD—but he did not have to worry about an illness like AIDS. He would not die from his incorrigible appetite (forgive the pun).

I am profoundly grateful that I do not have to watch more gay men die of AIDS. I do not want to make any more hospital and homes visits, or attend their memorial services and hear friends talk about how bravely they faced their slow deterioration and death. I would rather hear how good they had become giving head like that man in Central Park—but safely. The death and dying of the 1980s and 1990s is over, thanks to the medical advances in treating HIV. That is another positive change in the twenty-first century.

These political advances are all part of the assimilationist agenda, not the radical gay movement of the 1970s. While political change may be initiated by radical politics, cultural change always moves toward the center. LGBT people like the Black and Women's Movements before them are banging on the door of society to be let in. They are not revolutionaries; they are conformists who want no more than to be governed by the same laws as everyone else. The recent battles over the right of LGBT people to marry prove the point. (*Stop preaching, Silverstein.*)

*

May 2005. It took a heart attack for me to realize that it was time to revise my will. I looked at the old one when I returned from the hospital after bypass surgery and noticed that it had started to yellow with age. "Just like me," I thought. A revision was obviously long overdue, since it left the whole of my meager estate to William already dead for thirteen years. Loyal friends took care of me after the hospitalization as lovingly as they had cared for William toward the end of his life. They even made a daily schedule so that someone would always be with me during the day and others to sleep over so that I was never alone or wanted for anything. I wanted to thank them in my revised will for their support. Unfortunately my savings were not great so that I devised the following plan. I stipulated that about a dozen people were to be treated to an all-expense paid vacation to any place in the world. Whatever money was left over together with my art collection would be left to the LGBT Community Center in New York City. I admit to feeling self-satisfied by this solution, perhaps smug since it was a unique idea, sounded like fun, and expected that at dinner one night, they would order bottles of champagne (at my expense) and drink a toast to me—wherever I might be. I may even have so stipulated in the will.

Peggy Brady, a classmate of William's from Rutgers Law School, called to tell me that the will was ready to be signed and asked that I come to her office to do so. "Read the will," she said when I arrived, "and I'll come back in fifteen minutes for the signing." I started reading. The only new feature in it was the provision for providing funds for the two-week vacation for my friends. I read it and became furious! I was jealous! "They are going to drink *my* champagne and have fun while I'm coming out of the other side of a crematorium? No—I won't do it. If they're going on a fabulous trip to celebrate my life and death—I'm going with them!"

"No, Peggy," I said when she returned to the room. She was obviously shocked when I told her to redo the will without the two-week vacation for friends. I had already hatched a new idea. "I'm going with them," I said to Peggy who must have thought that I was going bonkers.

The Charles Silverstein Memorial Vacation was born and it became my new project. I was going to take these friends on a vacation while I am still alive, and if there is one thing that I know how to plan, it is a vacation.

Charlie Seton, my fifth grade student, now a professional photographer, came to my apartment a week later, and we spent most of the day photographing me as an angel—halo and wings included. We did it so that it would look like I was floating on a cloud. The humor of what I was about to spring on my guests appealed to both of us. "I want to go with you," pleaded Charlie. "And so you shall," I replied.

"That's nice," said Charlie, "but how are you going to decide where to go?"

"We're going to Thailand," I said. It was an easy decision. I had already been there twice before and knew exactly what my friends would enjoy on the tour. Thailand was my favorite Asian country and besides sightseeing, it would give me another opportunity to add to my extensive folk art collection. The photograph was to be the cover for a detailed itinerary to be mailed out that included our hotels, restaurants, tours, and special activities like the puppet theater in Bangkok, riding elephants near Chiang Mai and visiting the bridge on the River Kwai. Charlie was assigned to be the official trip photographer and between us we would provide enough video and still photographs to make a souvenir DVD of the memorial vacation.

On Saturday January 21st, 2006 we left JFK at 11:05 a.m. onboard a non-stop Thai Air plane bound for Bangkok, and arrived at 4:05 p.m. the next day. We returned to New York on February 4th. It was inevitable that I would think about William during our days in Thailand. How he would have relished spending hours among the archeological sites throughout the country, and he would have been far more interesting as a tour guide than the ones I hired.

Like Sherman's March to the Sea, our group cut a swath of shopping from Bangkok to Chiang Mai. Within days my guests had swallowed up any number of statues, masks, ceramics, jewelry and clothes to the grateful smiles of our guides who probably received a commission from the shop owners. I never travel without a large supply of bubble-wrap that I use to wrap delicate pieces of folk art. I brought a huge roll of two-hundred fifty square feet of it with me to Thailand together with a roll of duct tape, and ended up wrapping these souvenirs for my guests. (On a future trip to Indonesia with my close friend Terrance Flynn, I brought the same sized roll of bubble-wrap and we used the whole of it between us before we returned to New York.)

Back in New York, Charlie and I combed the hundreds of photographs and hours of video until we culled out the best of the lot. I wrote a script and invited Bill Bartelt and Alvin Shields to join me in adding a narration to the recording. The whole gang was invited to view it and everyone was given a DVD and a few photographs of themselves in Thailand. *The Charles Silverstein Memorial Vacation* was a huge success. If I were a rich man, I would have a memorial vacation every year. But when I returned to New York I had to go on with my life.

I think about William every day. My home is filled with pictures of him: sitting on a hill overlooking the pyramids, in his faun costume, of the two of us in the apple tree, and less appealing the photograph of him at Wigstock before he died. Over the years the pains of our relationship have receded into the background, only to be replaced by the fun times. I remember, for instance, when so many married men called at the Institute for Human Identity after we advertised for a married men's therapy group. They all interpreted our announcement as an opportunity to have sex. We had no money in those days and lived from paycheck to paycheck, so we wondered if we could cash in on the army of horny but closeted married gay men in New York City. We decided to form a private membership club for them. We knew that virtually everyone would use an alias, but we didn't care since it would be a cash only place of business. The men would be enticed with a stable of hustlers, a bar would provide additional income, but no sex would take place at our club. We did not want to be accused of prostitution. We even consulted an attorney who would defend us in case of arrest.

"I'm going to be the madam," said William. His charm and magnetic personality was perfect for advising the men about the services of the club. Finally I got cold feet, terrified that if arrested that I would lose my license to practice. Although disappointed, he understood.

Unfortunately although a master at understanding the structure of language, he had a writing block. He majored in Chinese and Russian, taught himself Egyptian hieroglyphics, ancient and modern Greek, picked up Portuguese in our travels, but could not put the English language to paper. He would occasionally outline a book but never get to actually write it. Since his literary ideas were brilliant, but unwritten, I suggested that we write some pornography together. William was thrilled at the idea and immediately went to work outlining one dirty plot after another. Our favorite was a story about teen-aged gay twins who spent every night fucking each other while their parents thought that they were doing their homework. But like other projects, he just could not finish writing them. At least his book of poetry gave him some solace during his last year of life.

I also remember my years as a volunteer fireman in Napanoch, our home bought with the advance from *The Joy of Gay Sex*. William was not pleased that I had joined the company, afraid that I would come to harm while fighting a fire. Each year we had an annual fireman's dinner and dance and I always brought a female friend or relative. Everyone in town knew that we were gay because they had seen me on television or one of my books in a bookstore. They didn't care. "As long as you don't try to be gay with us," said the fire chief, meaning not to hit on one of them. He did not have to worry on that score. But one year a few of the fireman said, "Why don't you bring whoever you really want to the dinner?" They meant that I should not hide my lover and that the fire company would welcome him. I was very touched by their affirmation and insisted that William come to the dinner that year. He agreed but only if we left the party early, to which I agreed. During the dinner many of the fireman and their wives came over to meet and talk with him. I found it astounding that people would be so gracious in an upstate New York conservative town. I had vastly underrated them.

The fun of *The Charles Silverstein Memorial Vacation* made me think about my relationship with William. If I had it to do over again—would I choose him as my lover for life? Isn't that the question that all long-term relationships must answer? When he was not hounded by the HIV and his fear of dying, or not depressed because of his writing block when surrounded by successful gay writers, he was a man of extraordinary talents. At dinner parties we were an awesome duo, complimenting each other's arguments. Only Ed White could match his knowledge and strategy in argument and it was an amazing show to listen to them both in discussion.

Even our sex life began (and continued) with talk about the Gods of ancient Greece and with Gregorian chants in the background. The intellectual affinity between us and our mutual passion for fighting for gay civil rights lasted far beyond our sexual needs for one another.

It is clear to me that the years suppressing my homosexuality made me emotionally needy, and I believe that this trait bred insecurity in our relationship. What William needed was a strong lover, one who could create well-defined boundaries in our relationship, not the namby-pamby man I was at the time. My forgiveness of his occasional inappropriate behavior only made him feel less secure. He even once said to me, "Stop being so nice!" He was right, but I could hardly understand in those days.

William has never been replaced. There has been no other man that I can call "husband." Instead, I have populated my life with a number of friends toward whom I feel as loyal as they do toward me. A couple of them stand out.

October 2007. I do not remember fainting that Sunday morning. While at one moment I was waiting for Terrance to return from taking a picture across the grass, the next I was on the ground and hearing him call my name. I was flat on my back and had no idea why. Terrance had already rushed into a nearby building and called an ambulance that arrived quickly. We were in Newport, Rhode Island for the weekend to see the homes of the wealthy patrons who lived there years ago.

The afternoon was taken up with a variety of tests all of which turned out negative, but I was admitted to the hospital because of my previous bypass surgery. Terrance drove to his Braintree home for the night and took off work on Monday so that he could return to Newport to take care of me. He adamantly refused to allow me to return to New York by myself, drove me home, then turned around to drive back to Braintree so that he could return to work on Tuesday. The reason for my "syncope" as doctors call it, was being over-medicated.

We met in 1993 in a New York bar and have been intimate friends ever since. We are very tuned into one another and can accurately judge the other's mood simply by hearing the word "hello" when answering the phone. While fashion conscious he is not overly so, in contrast to me who puts on whatever shirt and pants are nearby. When we go out together, he will often insist that I comb my hair or just do it for me. I might consider him fastidious as to dress, if I had the slightest idea of what that meant when choosing one's clothes and care of the body. He has shown me for instance, how spray and solid deodorants differ, a subject I have about as much interest as whether my shirt and pants match (or whether I am wearing different color socks, for that matter). If going out to a show in New York he will put on a facial mask, wait for it to dry, and then peel it off while I tease him about the wasted money. He made me aware of how profitable the vanity business must be.

While he arrives at my apartment carrying a hair dryer, he does not use make-up. When getting a haircut, he observes all the barbers in a shop for a while before choosing just the right one and he gives careful instructions about how he wants his hair styled. I am always amused by this procedure since he always gets his hair cut in exactly the same style anyway. In contrast I go to whatever barber motions toward me, refuse discussion with this murderer with scissors and hope that the nasty procedure will end in five minutes and become petulant when it doesn't.

He was a great help to me in Napanoch. Every year he came down from Boston to clean out the Lilly pond I built near the house. It is a particularly filthy process, but he volunteered to do it and never complained. He also helped cut down the tree on my property that I would carve and paint together with friends that I called the "William Bory Memorial Totem Pole." My friend Nando Davila was particularly skilled at painting the figures on the pole after we had carved them. At first I placed it in front of the house, but after I sold the property I moved the pole into my New York apartment where it now stands.

Terrance was also an excellent swimmer in his youth, and at the age of sixteen saw a man drowning at Castle Island in Boston, jumped in and saved the man's life. For this act of bravery, he received a commendation from the City of Boston and appeared on their *Good Day* TV show.

Terrance has had a few problems in his life. He comes from a South Boston Irish-Catholic background where family discord is the norm. I will cite only a couple of brief examples. His father was an art thief, breaking into people's homes and stealing whatever he found of value. He was caught and served time in prison for it. On more than one occasion as a child, he would hear his father attack his mother, and ran with a baseball bat in order to defend her.

A more serious problem began in adulthood. A few years ago while Terrance was sleeping in bed, a thief threatening with a gun robbed a 7-11 in Boston. Terrance was accused of the crime, a ridiculous accusation, but do to false testimony he was indicted by the Grand Jury. That began a three-year odyssey to prove himself innocent that cost thirty thousand dollars, his mother to mortgage their house, and for Terrance to fear becoming a felon and serve prison time.

Since there was no evidence against him, the district attorney dragged out the case, offering a reduced sentence if Terrance would plead to a lesser charge, to which he refused. He was finally offered a deal to plead guilty to a misdemeanor that carried no jail time at all—but he had to plead guilty to it—or go to trial for armed robbery. His lawyer told me that if convicted at trial, he could be sentenced to nine years! Terrance had to decide whether to accept the guilty plea or go to trial and borrow more money to pay for his defense with the knowledge that if proven guilty he would serve hard time.

What fork does a person take in the road? What would you have done, taken the easy way out and plead guilty, or fight the charge going further in debt and maybe still go to jail? This is what I believe integrity is about, a trait that I value in a person's character. He and I discussed it for a long time over the phone. I knew what I would do, but I had no right to impose it on him because he was the only one who had to suffer the consequences of his actions. By the end of the phone call he said, "I'm innocent. I'm not going to say I'm guilty when I was sleeping in bed. I'll take the chance of going to jail. I didn't do it." I loved him for his decision.

The district attorney was informed that Terrance refused the deal and would appear at the trial. And what happened? The district attorney dropped the charges! They would obviously lose because they had no evidence against him. But Terrance is still paying off the thousands of dollars he borrowed to pay for his defense.

We travel together almost every year to exotic places in the world. At Wadi Rumm in Jordan we rode camels that he nick named Mabel and Matilda and rode his side-saddle to the amusement of the locals. In Jakarta we stayed with my friend Ted, Deputy Chief of Mission at our embassy and dined with local diplomats. In Bali a monkey bit him while

**Travels
with
Charles**

Top left: Terrance Flynn riding side-saddle in Wadi Rumm, Jordan, 1995; Top right: The author with Bill Bartlelt at the Atrium of the Vestal Virgins, The Forum, Rome, 2011. Middle left: The author as angel on the 2006 Invitation. Bottom photo: The Charles Silverstein Memorial Vacation group in Chiang Mai, Thailand, 2006.

I was off shopping for local art and we shared a bed in our cave hotel in Cappadocia, Turkey. Although he might yell at me for not combing my hair or matching my clothes correctly, he watches over me as we travel the streets, silently waiting at stairs I find difficult. He has been as reliable as a good Swiss watch.

Although he graduated from Northeastern University with a solid academic background, he has not William's extraordinary intellectual and cultural brilliance, nor his Darth Vader's meanness and manipulation. He is a loving friend and I cherish the time we spend together. There is trust between us and I expect that our friendship will last a lifetime. I would feel very lonely without him. His main liability has been indulgence in alcohol that made a trip to Thailand very difficult, but embarrassed over his own behavior, he has successfully radically reduced his consumption and is all the more fun to be with. I am amazed at how successfully he has turned his life around. One of Terrance's favorite stories about our travels was the day in Jordan when our driver drove up a sand dune only to get stuck there for five hours. "Allah is angry at you for doing this," said the man from the tour office sent to rescue us.

My travels continue even as I have arrived at the cusp of old age. Arthritis, spinal stenosis and my other medical conditions have not kept me from foreign lands, most recently to South Eastern Asia. Bill Bartelt is one of my most frequent travel companions, sometimes together with Terrance, sometimes only with me. While Terrance will never make a list of places he wants to see in some foreign city, leaving it completely up to me, Bill will make out a list of more places to see in a day that a reasonable person could visit in a week. And my list? They are places to buy folk art, but I compromise by allowing a visit to any museum or archeological site in a direct line between folk art galleries! But Bill also likes to shop and it is not unusual for us to spend many hours on a trip bargaining with shop owners about a piece of art that one or the other of us covet. While Terrance invariably shies away from advising me on what to buy or how much to pay, Bill tells me what I should buy and how much to pay for it—whether I want his advice or not.

Bill, however, does have one peculiar trait that has occasionally been a source of conflict between us. Coming from the mid-west, he has this peculiar idea that all traffic laws must be obeyed as if they were the tablets brought down by Moses himself. If, for instance, there is a stop sign, one must come to a complete (and I mean complete) stop before the sign, then look around for traffic (meaning that there is not another car in sight for at least a half mile) and proceed only if safe to do so. (Of course I exaggerate, but that is the privilege of being the author.)

Born and bred in New York City, I believe that traffic laws are matters of interpretation, not obedience to the Gospels. I look at the Gestalt of the situation and stop only if that makes the most sense. This difference between us occurred one day when we were driving a country road in the Yucatan Peninsula when it came to an end in a T. The Yucatan is absolutely flat, and we could see for miles around in every direction and there were no other cars in sight. The largest feature we could spot was a small anthill. Bill came to a complete stop at the sign, looked around and slowly made the turn. "What the hell are you stopping for?" I bellowed. The conversation deteriorated from there. He has been a good and loyal friend and I cherish his company and his reliable support when I need it—even with his liability of obeying authority.

*

While the times have changed from the 1970s to now, I think that my values and passions have not been compromised. Older, hopefully wiser, certainly walking with a slower gait, I still remember the day when I was ten years old that my family drove by the road gangs on our drive from Brooklyn to Miami. I also remember my father being fired from his job in Los Angeles the next year because he was Jewish and our having to drive cross-country in order to return home. I remember with pristine clarity how in the 1970s we fought against oppressive psychiatry to remove homosexuality as a mental disorder from their classification of diseases. There were so many people, men and women in New York and in many other cities of the country, who joined in the struggle to provide mental health services for LGBT people. Most of all I remember the people who died of AIDS; William, Ken, Chris, Jason, and John—writers, painters, composers, and many others who died only because they knew nothing about a new virus that had infected their bodies.

The removal of homosexuality was only a step in our march toward

LGBT civil rights. There are many other fields of battle being waged now and our community should join the fight for social change. The *Diagnostic and Statistical Manual (DSM)* of the American Psychiatric Association is currently being revised for publication in 2014. For the first time they want to include a new category of mental disorder for people who have too much sex, with their deciding how much is enough! They would also continue to include gender identity disorder in children and adults (although they propose to give it a different name) when there is no evidence that it is a mental pathology. Kinky sex, called "paraphilias" have been in *DSM* since the first printing in 1952 and they are scheduled to be included in their entirety in the new edition for no other reason than their being considered socially wrong. Fortunately there are many clinicians and sex researchers arguing for a more liberal *DSM* that would respect sexual variations. The LGBT population should join them in arguing for a liberal, not moralistic view of human sexuality.

I will be there—even if I have to show up in a wheel chair.

William Bory and Charles Silverstein

Photo courtesy of the author.

Twenty-five

We Were Like Gilgamesh and Enkidu

Last night William shook me awake. "Come with me, Charlie," he said. He led me out of the bedroom and into the hallway. We walked out of the apartment and found ourselves in a wide stairway with metal banisters as one finds on the steps of large institutions, the walls and banisters painted hospital gray. We descended at least two flights of stairs and entered a cavernous room in which small groups of people sat on the floor talking quietly to one another. There was no furniture in sight.

"Let's sit here," he said. William took out a bunch of maps, some old, their edges tattered with use, others brand new. He spread them around us. The old maps were those from foreign trips we had taken, the new ones the destinations we had planned for the future.

"Is Whimpy still home? he asked.

"No. I gave Whimpy to Margaret's son, Satya, one day when they visited. I also gave him some of your old seashells. I thought it was appropriate to give him these things since he'll never grow up playing with his uncle. I hope you don't mind."

"I like that. And what about Cranky? Where's he?"

"Cranky's sitting on the bookcase. I don't take him out very much, but I took him to Vietnam. Judy and I traveled there last May and we stayed with Ted in Hanoi. We took Cranky everywhere in the country and he made quite a hit with the children. He still has lots of attitude. Sometimes I put him on the shelf with your ashes and the hat that you wore at your poetry book party."

"What are you going to do with my ashes?"

"I'll be cremated when I die and Virginia and Bill will go to Palermo, combine our ashes and spread them in the city."

He looked lovingly at me—raised my hand to his lips, kissed it and

*held it against his cheek. "You and I, we were like Gilgamesh and Enkidu,"
he said. "We fought many battles together, but now I have to leave and
you have to return home. Charlie, I want you to find another man to love.
I'll always love you, but I can't travel with you anymore. I have to go now.
The Ferryman is waiting."*

*William looked deeply into my eyes, kissed my hand again, then
my lips. He touched my index finger with his, held it there as he started
to move backwards so that within seconds our arms were stretched to
their full length. After a few more seconds he stood up sharply, turned
and walked away. I watched as he reached the far end of the room that
started to elongate as he walked. With each step the room opened more
deeply until he appeared as no more than a spot on the horizon, finally
disappearing completely. I gathered and folded the maps, tucked them
under my arm and walked back to my bedroom, where I fell asleep.*

Acknowledgments

A number of people have helped me complete this book. Most of all I am indebted to Patrick Merla who worked against odds to translate my writing into English. A later version was critiqued by Dorothy Hoobler who chastised me for the sin of flash-forwards, by my friend and neighbor Manette Berlinger who was required to constantly sharpen her pencil, and by Virginia Record who may have felt as if she were tilting at windmills when correcting my idiosyncratic use of the preposition. Edmund White and Felice Picano were early and enthusiastic supporters of this work and consistently encouraged me even after yet another mainstream publisher rejected the manuscript. I have always been touched by the support and kindness of all of them.

Dr. Charles Silverstein at his office in Manhattan.

Photo courtesy of the author.

About the Author

Dr. Charles Silverstein is well known in the gay community for his activism in the struggle for gay rights, his professional contributions toward providing counseling for gay people, and for his publications.

Silverstein's 1973 historic presentation before the "Nomenclature Committee" of the American Psychiatric Association led to the removal of homosexuality as a mental illness from the diagnostic manual. He was in the vanguard in the fight to stop the use of aversion therapy on gay people, and founded two gay and lesbian counseling centers in New York, Identity House and the Institute for Human Identity. He was also the founding editor of the *Journal of Homosexuality*, now in its fifty-seventh volume.

In publishing, he is best known for the groundbreaking 1977 (Crown) *The Joy of Gay Sex* (with Edmund White), subsequently translated into five other languages. In 1992 (HarperCollins), he published *The New Joy of Gay Sex* (with Felice Picano), bringing the original book up-to-date with regard to the AIDS crisis and other changes in the gay community. HarperCollins has published *The Joy of Gay Sex: Third Edition*, May 2003, once again with Felice Picano as co-author.

His *A Family Matter: A Parents' Guide to Homosexuality* (McGraw-Hill, 1977) was the first book to assist parents who learn that a son or daughter is gay. *Man to Man: Gay Couples in America* (William Morrow, 1981) was the first book to examine the nature of gay male love relationships. *Gays, Lesbians and Their Therapists: Studies in Psychotherapy* (W.W. Norton, 1991) is a professional book clarifying how feelings by a therapist toward his/her patient influence the course of therapy.

Silverstein's last book was *The Initial Psychotherapy Interview: A Gay Man Seeks Treatment*, published by Elsevier Insight in January 2011. The book is meant as a training guide for graduate students preparing for the profession of psychotherapy.

He was a Clinical Instructor in the Department of Psychiatry at New York University Medical College, a consultant to the New York University AIDS Project, and now a Supervisor of therapists at the Institute for Human Identity. He is a member of the Ethics Committee of the New York State Psychological Association, a Fellow of the American Psychological Association, and a Diplomate of the American Board of Sexology.

In August 2011, Silverstein was awarded a Gold Medal for Lifetime Achievement in the Practice of Psychology from the American Psychological Foundation, and a Distinguished Book Award from Division 44 of the American Psychological Association. He was awarded Distinguished Professional Contribution by the APA in 2005 and a Presidential Citation from the American Psychological Association in 2009. He was also honored by Gay and Lesbian Psychiatrists of New York in 2002.

Silverstein can be found on the Web at www.drcsilverstein.com.

CPSIA information can be obtained at www.ICGtesting.com
Printed in the USA
BVOW010156200911

271602BV00001B/4/P

9 780983 285120